Minimum income schemes in Europe

Edited by Guy Standing

INTERNATIONAL LABOUR OFFICE • GENEVA

Edited by Guy Standing
Minimum income schemes in Europe
Geneva, International Labour Office, 2003.

Guaranteed income, low income, poverty alleviation, social policy, Belgium, Finland, France, Greece, Ireland, Italy, Portugal.   02.15.1

ISBN: 92–2–114839–4 (printed)
92–2–114840–8 (pdf)

ILO Cataloguing in Publication Data

Printed by the International Labour Office, Geneva, Switzerland

Minimum income schemes in Europe

Edited by Guy Standing

TABLE OF CONTENTS

Tables

Figures

INTRODUCTION

1

Guy Standing [1]

The history of anti-poverty schemes is an indictment of the human capacity to overcomplicate and to condemn. In the early years of the 21st century, even the richest countries in the world have levels of poverty that few social thinkers would have anticipated a century ago if told what their countries' per capita incomes would be today. The saying that "the poor are always with us" is only true because politicians and policymakers choose that this should be the case. And yet the political rhetoric is constant that the eradication of poverty is the primary goal of social and economic policy.

One would think, if one came fresh to the subject, perhaps from another planet, that the easiest way to deal with the poverty associated with lack of money would be to provide everybody with enough money to buy the food, clothes, housing and other basic needs to ensure survival. The planetary observer would see that in rich societies, there are obviously enough resources to permit that. However, he or she would be quickly disabused of the naiveté. Giving people money would encourage them to be idle, it would divert resources from other priorities, it would be unfair on those working hard, it would mean taxing those who have been working responsibly, it would be administratively hard and costly. The familiar arguments would leave our observer wiser but sadder.

He or she would be further befuddled when told of the sophisticated reasoning of mainstream welfare reformers of the late 20th century. According to the modernizes — and those political wordsmiths who coined the famous phrase "end welfare as we know it" — the poor in rich societies are in that state because of cruel combination of lack of capability and induced dependency, from which they need to be rescued. Therefore, they reason, if we want to help the poor, policy must increase their capabilities and induce the unfortunate to overcome their social exclusion, by guidance, direction and coercion if necessary.

---

[1] Director, Socio-Economic Security Programme, International Labour Office, Geneva.

The desire to be compassionate must be blended with the need to make the poor socially and economically functional. The difficulty, for these thinkers, is that the systems of income transfers that developed in the 20th century welfare states — most notably contingency risk transfers such as family benefits, unemployment insurance benefits, disability benefits and healthcare insurance benefits — are prone to "poverty traps" and "unemployment traps" and various moral hazards. In other words, they create circumstances in which it is financially better to remain in the state that is justifying the compensation. Such transfers compensate for adverse events that put people in risk of poverty or for the extra costs of living. If the person tries to work to gain more income, they are likely to lose more than (or almost as much as) they would gain from the work.

This quandary was intensified in the latter part of the 20th century by changes in the labour markets of industrialised countries and by powerful pressures, partly ideologically driven, to cut social spending and to shift it away from social protection to "human capital". As unemployment rose, as poverty rates rose and as the incidence of people being in jobs with inadequate incomes rose ("the working poor"), governments initially tried to target shrinking resources on the poor by increasing selectivity. In doing so, the extent of poverty traps increased. These and the lower benefits meant that the socially vulnerable were more impoverished.

Governments started to deal with the perceived moral hazards by tightening conditions for entitlement to benefits, and gradually the rhetoric switched to the requirement that benefit applicants should be required to show "socially responsible behaviour". The 1980s and 1990s became the decades in which the language of social policy became full of colourful euphemisms, notably with notions of active and pro-active policy being desirable to overcome the deficiencies of the passive policies that supposedly went before them.

The public policy debates have been fascinating, in part because there has been a strange consensus across a wide range of politically disparate types, just about covering the underlying ideological struggle. Many of those who have favoured "active" policy have done so because they believe their fellow citizens are in need of help, and that their poverty (and the overall incidence of poverty) is due to the fact that many of the poor are disadvantaged. Others who have favoured "active" policy have done so because they believe many of the poor and unemployed are merely "lazy", if not "cheats", "living off welfare". The consensus between these two rationales is that active policy is desired.

The reforms over the past decade or more have varied in many respects in Europe and North America. The notion of workfare has been pushed most strongly in the USA, and the 1996 welfare reform there was a major step in that direction.[2] In Europe, many governments have tightened behavioural conditions for access to various income transfers, and some have moved perceptively towards something close to workfare, most notably in the United Kingdom. But in continental Europe, social reformers have been drawn more to the gentler notion of the French RMI — the idea that a minimum income should be provided to the unemployed in return for their agreeing on a "contract" that they would be assisted in (re-) integrating into the mainstream labour force.

This book is about recent developments in minimum income schemes in western Europe. The picture that emerges is one of unfinished business. This introduction will raise some of the questions thrown up by the new policies.

The underlying facts are that higher levels of public spending on social protection is associated with lower poverty rates, as is shown by Bea Cantillon, Ive Marx and Karel van den Bosch in chapter 2. But what is more interesting is that countries with relatively large numbers of working poor are also countries with low social protection spending, a finding described by some observers as "the puzzle of egalitarianism". And so-called "targeting" of social spending is not positively with "effort". A key point is that societies that have a tradition of "wage egalitarianism" have a tendency to practise solidaristic social protection policies, whereas targeting is most likely in societies that have considerable income inequality. The paradoxical nature of current trends is that, according to the simulation conducted by the authors, raising social spending on existing policies would not reduce the inequality. Selectivity is not a promising route to poverty reduction.

What the targeting trend and the minimum income schemes has in common is a fundamental reliance on means-testing. For several decades in the 20th century, mainstream opinion in social policy regarded means-tests and the notion of social assistance as residual and rather unacceptable form of social protection. But throughout the industrialised world, more people have been put in situations of dependency on means-tested forms of income support. Have the old and familiar objections been resolved? Scarcely.

The primary objection is that means-tested minimum income schemes do not reach many of the poor. The main reason is that there is a low take-up, due to a wide variety of behavioural and administrative factors. A dispute usually arises at this point, threatening the consensus. Some attribute the low take up to failings of policy design, plus the stigma associated with applying for means-

---

[2] For a critique of workfare, see Standing (2002).

tested benefits and the fear of bureaucracy among potential applicants. Others claim that what it really reflects is that many of the poor or unemployed are not really in need, and that the process is sorting out the "deserving poor" and unmasking "the benefit cheats".

No doubt there are some people who do not apply because they know that they would not qualify. However, the overwhelming evidence is that low take up reflects a real inability of such schemes to reach all or even the majority of the poor. It would be too cynical to suggest that this is what policymakers want, even though it can be convenient – allowing them to claim that they have a policy for providing minimum incomes to all the poor while keeping down expenditure. However, defenders of means-tested minimum income schemes have not been put under enough pressure in recent years.

Even if the take up were raised, there would still be ample scope for criticising means-testing. The mere application of the tests is demeaning for "the clients" and is extremely costly. It is also likely to be inegalitarian in the way it operates. The really poor and the frail are less likely to face the bureaucracy than the young and relatively educated. As noted in the case of Finland in chapter 7, receipt of means-tested benefits is only weakly correlated with poverty — the near-poor are at least as likely to receive the benefit as the really poor.

In any case, the social engineers who have steered social policy reform in recent years have faced the other major drawback of means-tested income transfers by resorting to behavioural testing. That other drawback, of course, is their tendency to put recipients in poverty traps and unemployment traps. Because these are endemic to such schemes, social reformers have tended to move in two directions. They have tried to reduce the traps by trying to "taper" the effective marginal tax rate. In other words, with old-style means tested benefits, a person going from receipt of benefits to an earned income would face a very high "tax" rate, in some cases exceeding 100%. A way of reducing that tax rate is to allow greater "income disregards" or to introduce "in-work benefits" for the working poor. The development of earned-income tax credits has been the other great social policy reform of the past quarter of a century. Suffice to state at this stage that, while being a major advance on fiscal policy, these do raise other problems.

The other direction taken by reformers has been to tighten behavioural conditions for receipt of means-tested benefits. This is where the various groups have found consensus. If the poor are trapped, and are in a situation where moving into available jobs would actually impoverish them, then local social workers must oblige them to take those available jobs. This can be and often is rationalised by claiming that this is for their own good and for society's good, and that it helps to legitimise social spending that would otherwise not be supported by "the middle class" voters.

This is where the "insertion" school of thinking meets the "anti-dependency" school. Those who want to see the socially excluded assisted to be included find partnership with those who want to force the dependent to take jobs. The former typically feel uneasy about the latter tendency, and thus favour giving those deemed socially excluded more "options" and a loose "contract" that imposes obligations on both the social service and the individual client.

Where does the policy go at this stage? The well-known documentary film *Bowling for Columbine* has almost become a metaphor for the potentially worst failing of activating minimum income schemes. The mother of a child who went on a killing spree had been forced to take a very low paying job involving her in long daily commuting that resulted in child neglect. Defenders of the schemes may find answers to the implied criticism, but they should feel uneasy.

1.   Evaluations of national RMI schemes

The idea of having a single policy to tackle poverty and perceived social exclusion took shape in France, and as Serge Paugam argues in chapter 3, the policy of combining income transfers to combat poverty with state guidance to achieve individual "inclusion" in society stemmed very much from the republican state tradition established in 1790. The terms "insertion" and "inclusion" have been used inter-changeably, and in English both seem to have appeal as ways of explaining what has been intended.

For French social thinkers, and for much of the public, poverty is fundamentally a matter of a threat to social cohesion. This has meant that, ever since 1790, central government as the State has had an obligation, a duty, to provide assistance to the poor. The RMI was a means of strengthening that obligation, in part because it responded to the growing perception in the 1980s that French society was being jeopardised by growing inequalities and social fragmentation. It was a way of imposing a centralised social policy, even if operated at local decentralised levels.

A difficulty was that the right to assistance for the poor is quite different from a "right to insertion". And social workers have also, to their credit, found it hard to justify saying that the right to assistance justifies an obligation to be "inserted". This is why the notion of insertion "contract" has been applied only patchily. Paugam argues that the contract is a policy to regulate social relations, through social control mechanisms and norms. But social workers have tended to interpret the contracts loosely.

Among the features of the French RMI is that it has excluded youths. Other countries have extended their equivalent schemes to teenagers. However, in Portugal the new right-of-centre Government on its election promptly announced that it would be restricted to those over the age of 25, rather than 18, which had been the case. The rationale for excluding the young has been flawed by what might be called the logic of categorical generalisation. Somewhat surprisingly, social policy has been severely afflicted by this logic in recent years.

Basing social policy on a mix of contingency risks and probabilities is fraught with potential failures, which might be called Type I and Type II errors — including people as beneficiaries when they are not in need, and excluding many of those in need because they do not fit the beneficiary categories.

In France, according to Paugam, the right to assistance has been based on the primacy of social status, in that those provided with assistance should be left below those who do not in terms of net income. When the RMI was being developed, the view was prevalent that those under the age of 25 would be enabled to be dependent and in effect be given an advantage over those over that age. This perspective was surely based on an unproven generalisation, and has resulted in intensification of inter-generational inequalities.

In the light of Paugam's rather sceptical assessment of the RMI, it is perhaps no surprise that Nicolas Farvaque and Robert Salais note in chapter 4 that it has tended to replace any prior pattern of dependency on social assistance with a new form, that of dependency on being in an insertion policy scheme!

Complementing Paugam's analysis, Farvaque and Salais focus on the impact of the sections of the 1998 Law to Combat Exclusion that relate to those people under the age of 25 excluded from the RMI. They see the changes as moving towards a rights-based approach in French social policy. The big questions are, first, whether the right to assistance can be preserved against the typical pressure to conform to behavioural norms, and second, whether the paternalistic instincts of social engineers can be held in check.

It is notable that the Access to Employment Grant (BAE), introduced as part of the new programme, has not been regarded by the French government as a minimum income scheme for youth. At this point, it is difficult to escape the view that the grant is being used as an attempt to induce behaviour on the part of individual recipients that is desired by social policymakers.

Farvaque and Salais argue that the new policies are enhancing people's capabilities, which they believe reflects the type of State that characterises France. One suspects that there would be many analysts who would take issue with this perspective, in that it is hard to reconcile the promotion of individual autonomy through the application of conditions and State direction.

Other countries have tried to emulate the French RMI in their own way. The Portuguese experience, as presented in chapter 5, has led to the familiar range of opinions. Initially, it was a means-tested income scheme involving the individual obligation to sign and adhere to a social insertion contract, and was applied to anybody over the age of 17. It is surely not correct to call the resultant income grant a "right". It has been more like a means of directing poor people to behave in certain ways desired by policymakers.

As in France, it seems the RMI has had a modest effect on the incidence of poverty, but may have reduced the intensity of poverty among the poor, particularly for women. A beneficial effect has been that it has given recipients a sense of greater regularity of income, an important aspect of income security. But there seems to be extensive non-take-up of the RMI.

The drift back to categorical generalisation was epitomised by the raising of age of entitlement to 25 on the grounds that the young were endangered by "subsidy dependency", although there does not seem to be strong evidence of that.

What is interesting is that the social workers required to operate the Portuguese RMI have very mixed feelings about it, and testify to the positive side effects. This may reflect the fact that employment services were relatively undeveloped in Portugal before 1997 when the RMI was introduced. As a result of the scheme, the service workers believe the unemployed or poor in general have access to more information and can develop occupational skills. But this may not be a positive testament to the RMI per se, merely to the desirability of comprehensive employment and labour market services.

Indeed, one issue that comes up in the Portuguese case and elsewhere is the view that because poverty and social exclusion are "multi-dimensional", the policy directed at resolving them should also be "multi-dimensional". It brings to mind the famous economic rule formulated by the Nobel Prize winner Jan Tinbergen that there should be distinctive policies for distinct problems. Trying to do too much with a single policy usually results in it being ineffectual in all respects.

Characteristically, in Italy moves towards a minimum income scheme have been piecemeal and hesitant, only being introduced on a small experimental scale by the Prodi Government. David Benassi and Enzo Mingione argue in chapter 6 that the RMI was seen as desirable as a means of replacing the myriad local schemes with their numerous differences that has resulted in inefficiencies and inequalities across the country. As the authors argue, it is difficult to form definitive judgments on the Italian experiment. Part of the reason is that it has been regarded very much as a "last resort" measure. It may have reduced poverty modestly but does not appear to have much impact on the "insertion" part of its function.

2.   Minimum income and basic income

In Ireland, as Sean Healy and Brigid Reynolds show in chapter 7, minimum income schemes have had a long and convoluted history. What the authors show is that the system of social transfers is enormously complex, with numerous categories receiving differentiated amounts of support, even though the share of social spending in national income is the lowest in the European Union. The arbitrary nature of this patchwork should be evident to anyone examining their tables. One does not doubt the commitment of successive governments to poverty relief, but the inefficiencies and inequities must be considerable.

The Irish case is a puzzle. Widely called "the Celtic Tiger" because of the country's remarkably robust economic growth, the incidence of poverty has remained high and has probably worsened, while income inequality has increased. It is in that context that the authors examine the evolution of the national debates on the desirability and feasibility of a basic income, as distinct from a means-tested minimum income. This led to the Government issuing a "Green Paper" in mid-2002, a means of taking public stock of the debate on a particular policy or area of public concern.

While the debate on a basic income has ebbed and flowed in Ireland, earned income tax credits have become central to social protection policy. The authors see these as creating the basis of a basic income. But the existing tax credits are highly differentiated by category of person — by age, various types of disability, marital status, household status and so on. Making tax credits "refundable", as they suggest, would help, but unless reformed excessive categorisation will remain the enemy of equity and efficiency.

In Finland, as in other parts of Scandinavia and elsewhere, the drift of minimum income policy has generated ironies and paradoxes. Simo Aho and Ilkka Virjo, in chapter 8, trace the evolution of Finnish labour market policy from a "right to work" approach to "activation policy", in the context of high unemployment. They focus on the major reform of 1994, which should be examined by all those wishing to go in the direction of increased selectivity and activation.

The 1994 reform increased use of categorical rules in social policy, tightened conditions for entitlement to income support and introduced means-testing. The reforms were aimed at young labour force entrants. What the authors show, drawing on sophisticated data, is that the activation policy had precisely the opposite effect of what the policymakers and advocates intended and claimed. Instead of boosting "autonomy" and reducing "dependency", the combination of means-testing and activation led to a new — or at least newly appreciated — form of dependency, on the scheme.

In Belgium, there has been a steady and considerable drift away from the Bismarckian social insurance system, as Ive Marx documents in chapter 9. While benefit level differences have narrowed, levels have tended to fall, entitlement conditions have been tightened, and the problems of poverty trap and unemployment trap have become much more severe. The result is a bit of a mess.

The following chapter pursues one of these issues in more detail, the extent of the unemployment trap in Belgium. Among the main findings is that many women who move from unemployment to employment actually experience a decline in their income due to the design of the benefit scheme. Particularly ironic is that the poverty-unemployment trap is greatest for those who have been pushed into long-term unemployment. The difficulty is to draw the appropriate policy conclusion from these findings. The authors refer to the need for incentive schemes. But an alternative would be to reduce the unemployment trap in the design of benefit policy.

The final chapter shows how a country that is trying to move into the mainstream of European policy by introducing comparable welfare policies is likely to plunge into a series of partial measures that are ineffectual and inequitable. What comes across is a picture of Greek policymakers and advisers ill-at-ease with the nuances of social protection policies, in part because of their unfamiliarity with the issues that had been at the forefront of policy debate for generations in other parts of Europe.

The result has been the emergence of a patchwork of selective measures that is essentially arbitrary. The base of the nascent Greek welfare state may be Bismarckian social insurance, but it has been something of a façade. A fundamental problem has been the fragmentation of the system by designated groups, requiring a major exercise in consolidation to create the basis of a more universalistic system.

3. Concluding reflections

There is one outstanding conclusion of recent analysis of social protection policies. If you want to achieve low levels of poverty, and a low incidence of poverty, a country needs mechanisms to reduce wage inequality and needs universal benefits, not a system of selective benefits targeted on the poor. Regrettably, it is precisely the latter combination that has characterised recent trends.

There have been great decisive moments in the evolution of social policy, not all of which have been progressive in character, although many have been subsequently seen in that way. What is very clear indeed is that policies that have been regarded as unrealistic, unfeasible and out-of-the-question have a habit of suddenly becoming reality.

The RMI was one of those. In the period just before the French Presidential election that saw Francois Mitterand re-elected, the consensus among social policy experts was that a minimum income scheme was out of the question and impractical. Then, weeks to go before the election, Mitterand wanted a big new idea for his second term, and the RMI was born in 1988. What had been out-of-the-question became policy almost overnight.

Now, as some of the authors of the following chapters mention, the same sceptical arguments are being voiced against a genuine basic income scheme, providing a minimum income as a right, rather than as a complicated entitlement hedged with conditions and linked to means-testing. Soon, we predict, a new round of experiments will start. Economic rights will come.

Reference

Standing, G. 2002. *Beyond the new paternalism: Basic security as equality* (London, Verso).

WELFARE STATE PROTECTION, LABOUR MARKETS AND POVERTY: LESSONS FROM CROSS-COUNTRY COMPARISONS

2

Bea Cantillon, Ive Marx and Karel Van den Bosch [1]

1. Introduction

Welfare states in OECD countries appear to be deadlocked. Despite generally falling unemployment, and stable social expenditure, poverty and income inequality did not fall during the 1990s, but rather increased in a number of OECD countries (Förster, 2000; Atkinson, 1999). Most figures for the United Kingdom and the USA indicate at best a stabilisation during the mid to late 1990s. The overwhelming impression is that progress in the field of poverty reduction stalled.

Views on how to resolve this apparent deadlock remain wide-ranging. There are widely different assumptions about the linkages between such key variables as employment, low pay, social transfers and poverty. Take, for example, the link between work and poverty. An important section of opinion assumes that more people in work equal fewer people in poverty and, by implication, that a high level of social spending is not a prerequisite for a low level of poverty. This view was epitomized by Dutch social policy during the 1990s, summarized by the Dutch government as: "work, work and work". Others, by contrast, assume that there is an effective trade-off between employment (that is, non-subsidized employment) and poverty. The idea is that high levels of non-subsidized employment can only be achieved at the expense of a large low-paid service sector and increased — though perhaps temporary — "poverty in work".

[1] University of Antwerp, Centre for Social Policy, Belgium.

This chapter to presents evidence on the validity of such assumptions. We look at cross-country correlations between key variables such as employment, low-wage incidence, social expenditure and poverty. We show that striking cross-country correlations prevail, but not, as is often assumed, between low pay (wage compression) and employment performance, or between employment performance and poverty. Instead, we find a strong positive cross-country correlation between the incidence of low pay and the incidence of relative poverty, an equally strong negative cross-country correlation between level of social spending and the incidence of poverty and a strong positive cross-country correlation between low pay and social spending. The causal mechanisms behind these remarkably consistent relationships remain obscure. For example, the cross-country correlation between low pay and poverty is, contrary to belief, not due to a strong link between low pay and poverty at the individual level. The explanation must be more complex and probably runs through the correlation between the incidence of low pay and the level of social spending, which affects the level of protection offered to the non-employed.

This paper continues with a more detailed look at the link between social spending and poverty. Since there is such a strong negative link between social expenditure and poverty, it is tempting to think that more social spending offers a route out of the impasse of persistent poverty. However, a simulation exercise using the 1997 wave of the European Community Household Panel suggests that expanding welfare state expenditure within existing social transfer systems would have a surprisingly small effect on poverty.

The principal variable is poverty. Throughout the chapter we use a relative poverty threshold and do so because we are interested in how well countries succeed in protecting those who are, relative to the average standard of living, least well off in income terms. Perhaps it would be more accurate to use the term "low income" instead of poverty, but in line with common practice and to avoid awkward formulations, we will continue to use the word "poverty". The definition of other concepts will be clarified in the text.

2. Cross-country correlations

Within any country, poverty among those with paid work is far lower than among those without such work. However, between countries there is no such link between employment and poverty, as shown in figure 2.1, which plots poverty rates for the working-age population (aged 16–64) against employment rates for the late 1990s. Actually, the relationship is positive, implying that more employment is linked with more, not less poverty. It is striking that the relative poverty rate for the working-age population in the USA is almost twice as high as in Germany or France, and almost four times as high as in Belgium, although a far higher proportion of the working-age population is employed in the USA.

Within the sample of countries presented in figure 2.1, only Austria and Sweden combine a high employment rate (over 70%) with a low poverty level. Sweden (as well as other Scandinavian countries) has in the past pursued active employment policies, and has a large subsidized employment sector, unlike the United States and Canada. At the other extreme is Italy, where employment is low and poverty high. However, many continental European states, including France and Belgium, have relatively low poverty rates despite a relatively high level of non-employment.

Similarly, countries that performed well in terms of employment growth have not necessarily performed well in terms of poverty. Figure 2.2 show that the top five performers in terms of employment growth from the mid-1980s to mid-1990s experienced a rise in their relative poverty rates. Most striking is the Netherlands, where a dramatic rise in employment was accompanied by a substantial rise in relative poverty.

Figure 2.1   Employment performance and poverty

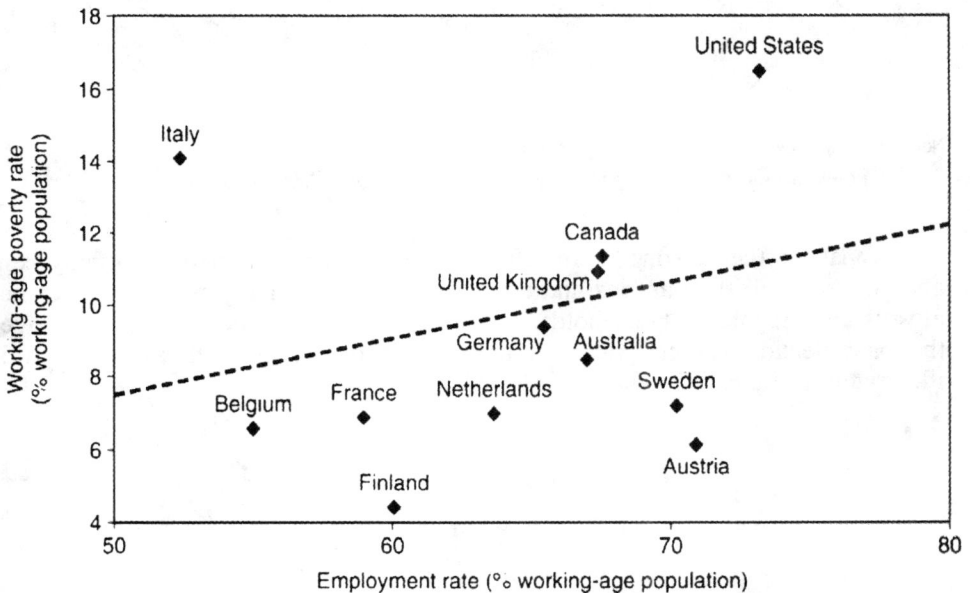

Sources. Employment rates OECD (1998), *Employment Outlook*, Poverty rates Förster (2000).

Figure 2.2   Changes in employment and poverty rates, mid-1980s to mid-1990s (percentage points)

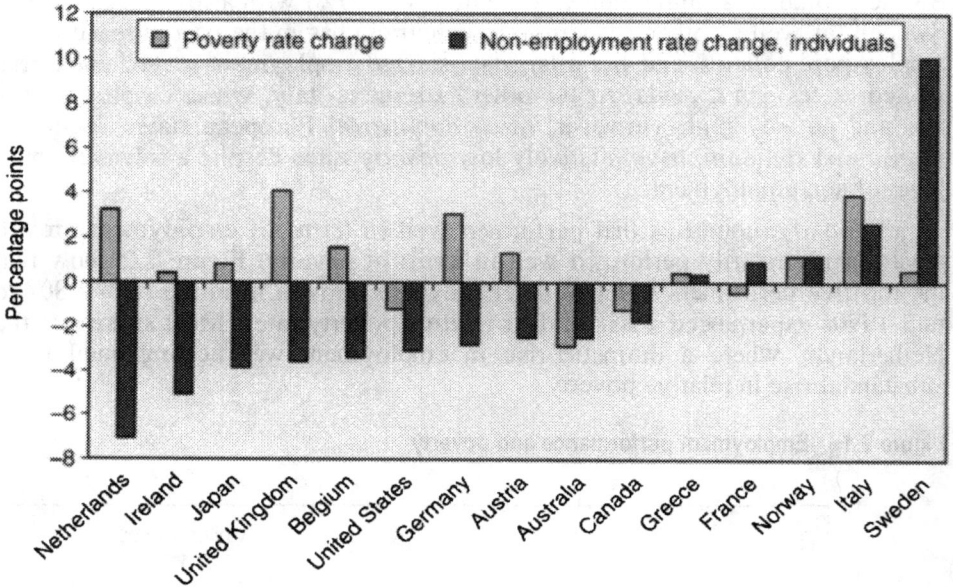

Note.   Poverty is relative poverty rates for working-age individuals

Sources: Poverty rates: Förster (2000), Employment rates· OECD *Employment Outlook* (1998)

What are the reasons behind the lack of relationship between employment and poverty, across countries and across time? One is that job growth does not always benefit jobless households. In some countries, employment growth over the past decade has not been to the benefit of workless households, as is illustrated in figure 2.3.

Figure 2.3   Changes in non-employment rates at the individual and household level, mid-
1980s to mid-1990s (percentage points)

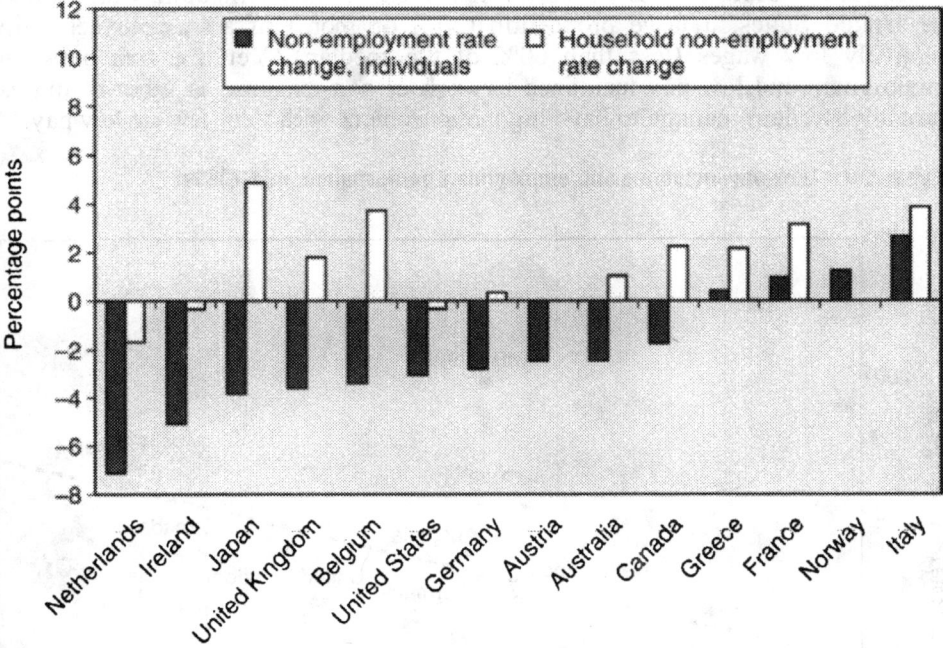

Sources. Poverty rates· Forster (2000), Employment rates. OECD *Employment Outlook* (1998)

Most remarkably, in the "job miracle" countries, the Netherlands and Ireland, massive employment growth at the individual level has not led to comparable employment growth at household level. Even more striking, perhaps, is the example of the UK. As pointed out by Paul Gregg and Jonathan Wadsworth (1996), the much-vaunted rise in the UK employment rate during the 1980s and 1990s masked a polarization between so-called work-rich and workless households. The proportion of working-age individuals in work had risen in the UK, but so had the proportion of households with nobody in work. Job growth mainly benefited households that already had one person in work. De Beer (2001) has documented a similar dynamic in more detail for the Netherlands. He shows that job growth there has mainly benefited new labour-market entrants and previously single earner households.

A second possible reason for employment and poverty not being closely related is that additional jobs are gained at the price of more wage inequality. Indeed, a familiar argument is that countries like the United States achieve high employment at the cost of large-scale poverty in work. Similarly, there exists a perception that some countries, like the UK or even the Netherlands, owe their progress largely to an expansion of "bad" jobs — insecure, low-paid service sector jobs. Indeed, figure 2.4 shows that in the United Kingdom, Canada and the United States, a large proportion (20% or more) of all employees earn relatively low wages (less than 60% of the median). Yet, the link between employment and low-pay incidence is weak or non-existent, as other countries (notably Sweden) manage to have high employment with very few on low pay.

Figure 2.4   Low-pay incidence and employment performance, mid-1990s

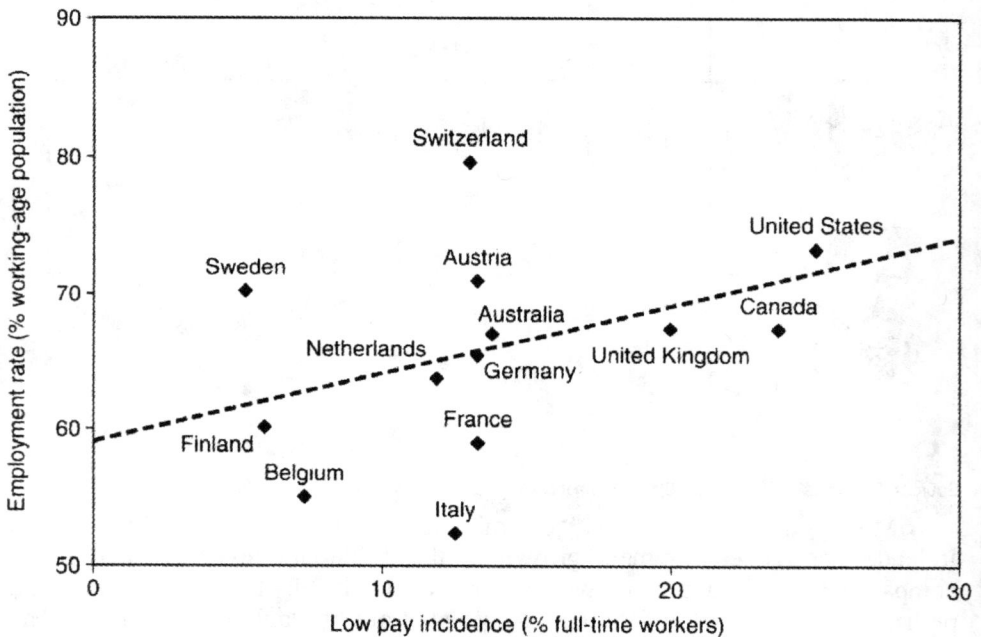

Sources: Poverty rates: Forster (2000); Employment rates: OECD *Employment Outlook* (1998).

Figure 2.5 show there is a fairly strong relationship between the incidence of low pay and poverty among the working-age population. The seemingly obvious interpretation would be that a low-wage earner also tends to be in poverty. However, this is only part of the explanation. While poverty rates are usually higher in countries with a comparatively high incidence of low pay, the incidence of poverty *among* low-paid workers themselves tends to be lower than generally believed, even in countries where low-paid work is widespread.

Figure 2.5   Incidence of low pay and poverty, mid-1990s

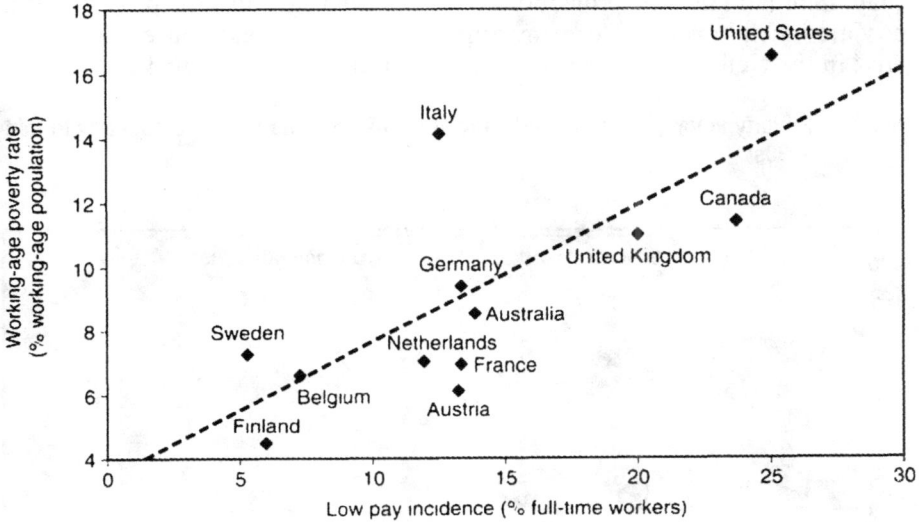

Sources: Low pay OECD (1996), *Employment Outlook*, Poverty. Forster (2000)

As figure 2.6 shows, in most European countries less than 10% of low-paid workers (by a definition of 66% of gross median earnings) live in relative poverty (Marx and Verbist, 1998). The USA is an exception because poverty in work is a substantial problem. The principal explanation for the weak overlap between low pay and poverty is that most low-paid workers live in multi-earner households. This is certainly the case for low-paid women and youngsters, who make up the majority of low-paid workers. It is possible, however, that low-paid workers are "forced" to live in multi-earner households and that latent poverty among the low-paid is consequently much higher than observed poverty. But the income from a low-paid job sometimes provides a second household income needed for single-earner households to attain a reasonable standard of living. If a better-paid job is not a feasible alternative, low-paid work can actually reduce poverty.

The working-aged non-employed are by far the most vulnerable group in every country, particularly those living in households with nobody in work. Poverty rates for workless households are high in most countries (figure 2.6). The average poverty rate for workless households with a working-age head in the 16 OECD countries surveyed by Förster (2000) is 36%, against 13% for households with one worker and 3% for households with two workers. However, there are important variations between countries in the incidence of poverty among workless households. In North America the poverty rates (as measured in the mid-1990s) for these households are extraordinarily high: 75% in the USA or 61% in Canada. Although European countries also fare badly in providing adequate minimum income protection to workless households, the proportions in poverty are much lower: in Germany almost 45% of workless households live in poverty; in the Netherlands, France and Sweden the figure is around 25%.

Figure 2.6   Poverty among low-paid and individuals in workless households, early to mid-1990s

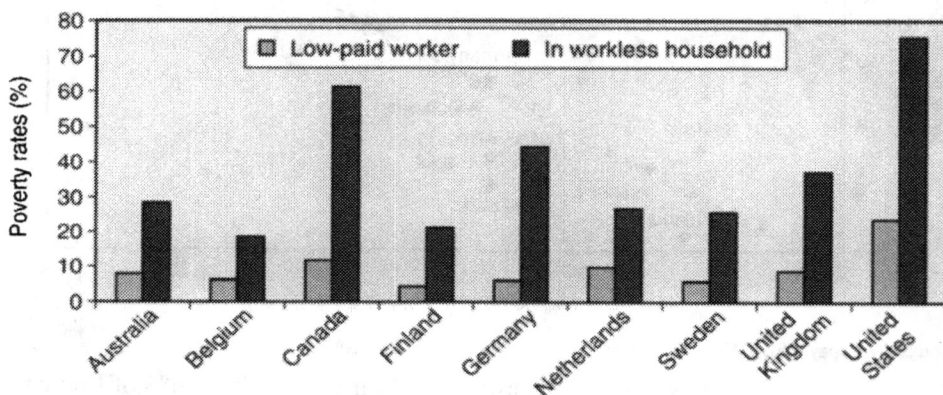

Sources: Poverty rates for low-paid workers (full-year, full-time workers earning less than 66% of the median gross wage) from Luxembourg Income Study: Marx and Verbist (1998); poverty rates for workless households: Forster (2000)

These relationships suggest the high poverty level in some countries with high non-subsidised employment is connected to inadequate minimum protection for those out of work (e.g. unemployment benefits and social assistance). Figure 2.7 shows that, across OECD countries, social expenditure and the incidence of low pay are strongly negatively related, which may come as something of a surprise. Alvarez (2001) calls the finding (which he documents extensively) that wage-egalitarian societies have the highest levels of welfare effort and redistribution "the puzzle of egalitarianism".

There are three possible interpretations of this puzzle. First, the direction of causality may go from an extensive welfare state to a condensed wage distribution. This is the line followed by Alvarez (2001), who argues that second-order effects of social expenditure are a large part of the explanation: the higher taxes and transfers of large welfare states influence labour supply in such a way that a more condensed wage distribution results. High-wage earners substitute leisure for income in response to taxes, while generous benefits reduce the labour supply in the low-wage sector through high reservation wages.

Second, a low level of wage inequality may somehow give rise to a well-developed welfare state. This may seem less plausible, as one might expect that high wage inequality and a large number of low-wage earners would create a demand for income redistribution (Alvarez, 2001). But a highly unequal distribution of market wages may make it politically and technically difficult to pool risks, and to develop social insurance systems, especially replacement income schemes involving a floor (Cantillon, 2002).

Third, an extensive welfare state and a limited degree of wage inequality may both be the result of a third variable. As Atkinson (1999, pp. 67-68) suggests, countries may have notions of equity that are widely shared within any society, but that differ across societies. A society with a common value of solidarity may at the same time support pay norms, collective agreements and adequate minimum wages, quasi-universal and generous benefits.

Figure 2.7   Incidence of low pay and social expenditure, mid-1990s

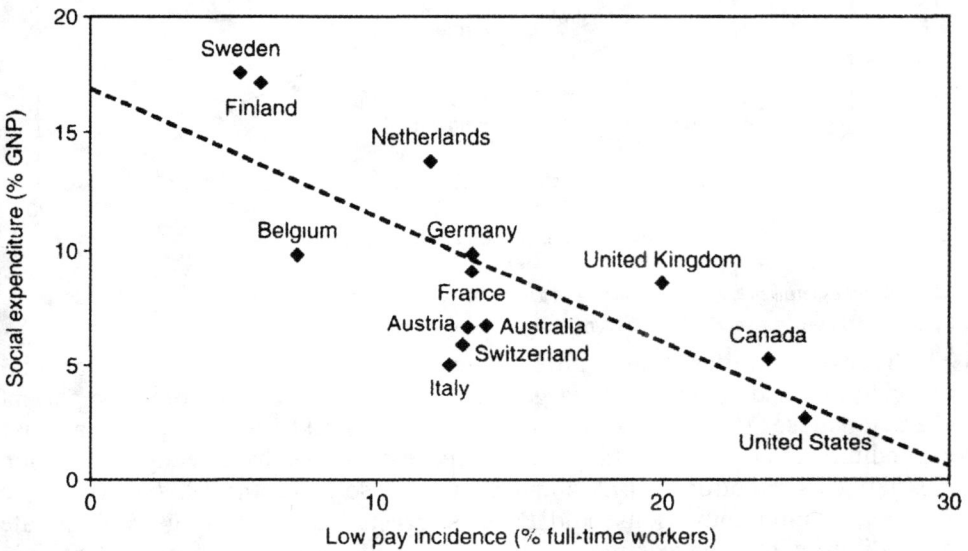

Note.   Social expenditure is non-education expenditure for the working-age population only.
Sources Low pay: OECD (1996), *Employment Outlook*, Social expenditure: Bradbury and Jäntti (1999).

This leads us to the link between social expenditure and poverty, shown in figure 2.8. The strong negative relationship between social expenditure and income poverty (as well as income inequality) has been well established (Cantillon et al., 1997; Bradbury and Jäntti, 2001; Atkinson, 2000; Beblo and Knaus, 2001; Oxley et al., 2001). As Oxley et al. (2001, pp. 392-396) show, some countries achieve better "efficiency" in terms of child poverty reduction (i.e., poverty is reduced more for each euro or franc spent) through targeting low-income groups. However, "effort" and "targeting" are negatively related, and thus "countries with higher 'efficiency' due to targeting have traded a good part of this away by reducing 'effort'".

Figure 2.8   Social expenditure and poverty, mid-1990s

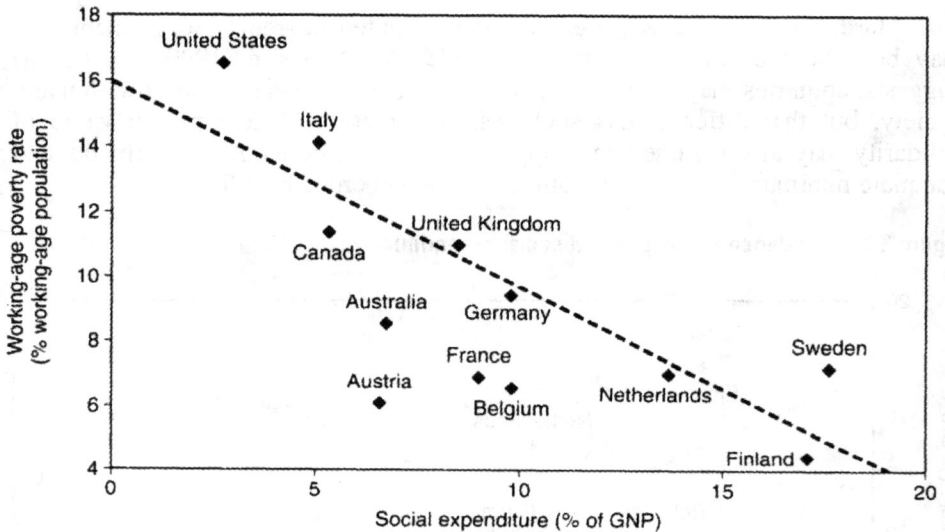

Note: Social expenditure is non-education expenditure for the working-age population only.
Sources: Social expenditure: Bradbury and Jantti (1999); Poverty Forster (2000).

However, welfare states differ in more respects than in the size of total expenditure and degree of targeting. If they were the only important characteristics, the policy recommendation would be simple: increase expenditure and/or improve targeting for those countries that already spend a lot. It is not so straightforward. A simulation exercise using the 1997 wave of the European Community Household Panel suggests that expanding welfare state expenditure within the existing social transfer systems would have a surprisingly small effect on poverty rates.

The simulation was done in the following way. In each country, the transfers received by working-age households were increased by the same proportion, so that they constituted 18% of aggregate income of all working-age households. This is slightly more than the actual percentage of the best-performing EU member state — Denmark. At the same time, all income other than transfers was also adjusted proportionally in the opposite direction, so that average and aggregate total household income remained constant. Next, poverty rates were recalculated from the micro-data [2]. This simulation is equivalent to an across-the-board and proportional increase in all social transfers, paid for by a proportional tax or contribution (bonus) on all other income sources.

Table 2.1 shows the results. The most eye-catching, and perhaps surprising, result is that the simulated convergence in transfer expenditure does *not* produce a convergence in poverty outcomes. Indeed it contributes little or nothing to such a convergence. The difference between the highest and lowest poverty rate increases slightly from 16.1% to 16.4%, and the standard deviation in the poverty rate across countries also goes up from 4.6% to 5.5%. There are some countries where poverty would be greatly reduced by an increase in social transfers, notably Ireland, France and Germany. But for most countries, poverty does not decrease much, if at all. It even increases for some high-poverty countries such as Italy and Greece [3].

Table 2.1   Simulated poverty outcomes when the share of transfers in aggregate income of working-age households is 18%

	% share of social transfers	Poverty rate		Gain in poverty rate/ increase in share of social transfers
		Actual %	Simulated %	
Denmark	16.0	6.2	5.40	- 0.40
Netherlands	12.4	11.5	8.00	- 0.63
Belgium	13.6	12.3	10.70	- 0.38
Austria	11.2	12.4	8.60	- 0.56
Sweden	15.9	12.5	11.40	- 0.50
Germany	7.9	14.6	5.70	- 0.88
France	9.9	17.4	7.40	-1.24
Greece	4.4	18.4	20.20	+0.13
Ireland	12.3	19.9	8.90	-1.93
Spain	7.5	20.2	17.10	- 0.30
Portugal	7.8	20.3	17.70	- 0.26
Italy	7.9	20.6	21.90	+0.13
United Kingdom	10.7	22.3	16.80	- 0.75

[2] Using a poverty line defined as 60% of median equivalent household income in each country, with the modified OECD equivalence scale, which has weights of 1.0, 0.5 and 0.3 for the first adult, other adults and children below 16, respectively.

[3] In Van den Bosch (2002) the effects of the simulated increase in social transfers on the *poverty gap* are also shown and discussed. While there are some significant and interesting differences with results based on the poverty rate (headcount), the important results are the same.

For some countries, notably Sweden, the limited effect is due partly to the fact that social spending was already close to the 18% benchmark. The main reason, though, for the smaller than expected response is that, in most countries, poverty outcomes are far less sensitive to increases in social transfers than the cross-country graphs would suggest. For the data presented here (columns two and three of table 2.1), we find a regression coefficient of −0.94 (r^2=0.46) for the cross-country relationship between the share of social transfers and the poverty rate. The fifth column of Table 2.1 shows the gain in the poverty rate divided by the simulated change in the share of social transfers, both expressed in terms of percentage-points. These coefficients can be regarded as sensitivity estimates, and are comparable to the regression slope coefficient of −0.94. Only for Ireland and France do the sensitivity coefficients exceed the cross-country slope estimates. In the other countries, the sensitivity estimates are below, or far below, the latter. In Italy and Greece, they are even positive, indicating that an increase in the share of social transfers implies that, on balance, income is redistributed away from the poor and towards the non-poor.

In order to gain a broader perspective on the results, the exercise was repeated in each country for a number of percentages, ranging from 0% to 20%, in steps of 2 percentage-points. For each percentage, poverty rates were recalculated from the micro-data (though the poverty thresholds were not adjusted), as charted in figure 2.9. The curves indicate that in the southern European countries, poverty among working-age individuals and children is remarkably insensitive to social transfer spending. More detailed analyses in Van den Bosch (2002) suggest that this is due to two mechanisms that cancel each other out. As expenditure is increased, most social transfer beneficiaries escape poverty, but at the same time a relatively large proportion of households, for whom earnings are the most important source of income, are pulled into poverty by the increase in taxes and contributions. In other countries, social transfers apparently cease to have an effect on poverty above a certain level of spending. However, the poverty "plateau" thus reached differs between countries, being surprisingly high in the UK. This suggests that in EU member states a relatively large but differing proportion of the poor are not reached by the social transfer systems.

Figure 2.9 Simulated poverty rates for persons below 60, by share of social transfers in household income

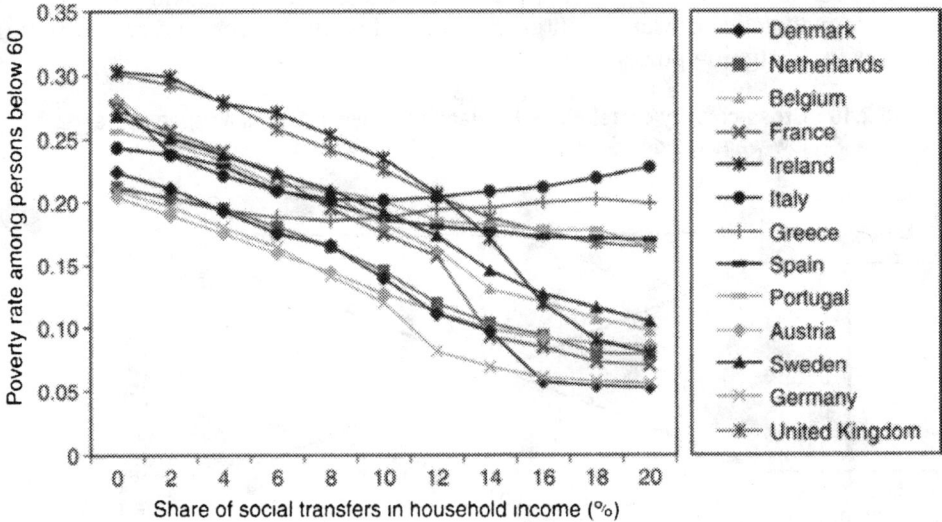

Source European Community Household Panel, Wave 7

3. Conclusion

In the social policy debate, fundamentally different ideas prevail about the linkages between employment, the number of low-wage earners, social transfers and poverty. These diverging ideas and assumptions give rise to very different policy recommendations. This chapter has presented evidence regarding these assumptions, primarily through cross-country correlations. These are summarised in figure 2.10.

Looking at cross-country correlations, we do not find the expected relationship between employment and poverty, nor between low wages and employment. We do find fairly strong relationships between low wages and poverty, between social expenditure and poverty, and between low wages and social expenditure. On closer inspection, none of these relationships turns out to be as simple as one might think, and the causal mechanisms remain obscure. Even in countries with a high number of low-wage earners, poverty among this group remains limited, and is concentrated among workless households. The strong cross-country association between high welfare state effort and low poverty would suggest that increasing spending in currently low-effort countries would lead to a downward convergence in poverty outcomes. However, the simulation of an increase in social expenditure for EU member states within existing systems produces the surprising result that this would contribute little or nothing to such a convergence in poverty rates. The conclusion that wage-egalitarian societies present the highest levels of welfare effort and redistribution remains an intriguing puzzle.

Figure 2.10   Cross-country correlations between employment, social expenditure, low-wage incidence and poverty

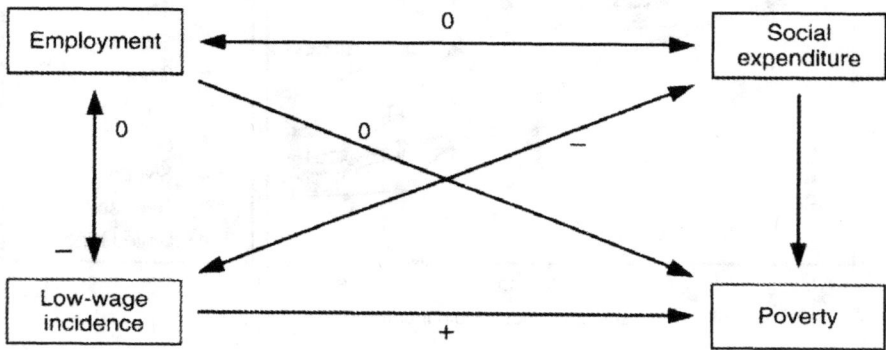

Note: 0: no relationship; + positive relationship; -: negative relationship

Looking at cross-country correlations, we do not find the expected relationship between employment and poverty, nor between low wages and employment. We do find fairly strong relationships between low wages and poverty, between social expenditure and poverty, and between low wages and social expenditure. On closer inspection, none of these relationships turns out to be as simple as one might think, and the causal mechanisms remain obscure. Even in countries with a high number of low-wage earners, poverty among this group remains limited, and is concentrated among workless households. The strong cross-country association between high welfare state effort and low poverty would suggest that increasing spending in currently low-effort countries would lead to a downward convergence in poverty outcomes. However, the simulation of an increase in social expenditure for EU member states within existing systems produces the surprising result that this would contribute little or nothing to such a convergence in poverty rates. The conclusion that wage-egalitarian societies present the highest levels of welfare effort and redistribution remains an intriguing puzzle.

As this paper represents work in progress, it is too early to draw conclusions. What we can do is to suggest a research agenda, or rather the general direction of research into the relationship between welfare state effort (input) and poverty and income distribution outcomes. First of all, descriptions of welfare states should go beyond the level of expenditure. This was already suggested by Esping-Andersen (1990, p.19), who wrote: "Expenditures are epiphenomenalism to the theoretical substance of welfare states".

However, the welfare state typologies introduced by him and others (e.g., Korpi and Palme, 1998) are also unsatisfactory, for two reasons. First, they present pictures of welfare states that are too homogeneous. Different programmes within the same welfare state may well have quite different characteristics. What we need is quantitative and differentiated indicators for separate social protection arrangements. They should reveal the level and composition of the income packages that people can realize, given options for family formation and labour supply. In-work and out-of-work replacement rates are examples of such indicators. Such indicators could be developed on the basis both of model family type simulations (e.g., Bradshaw et al., 1993; OECD, 1999), and as a few promising papers show, micro-simulation tax-benefit models (e.g. Berger et al., 2001; Immervoll and O'Donoghue, 2002).

Second, we should avoid the kind of analysis that regards the welfare state as an institution that belatedly corrects market outcomes. The common comparisons between pre- and post-transfer incomes are an important example of such analysis. The study of market outcomes should be an intrinsic part of welfare state research. Wage inequalities are probably to a large extent not determined by exogenous factors, but by welfare state arrangements. Alternatively, both a high level of social expenditure and a compressed wage distribution perhaps emanate from widely shared value systems emphasizing solidarity and equality. Such values might support pay norms and collective agreements (Atkinson, 1999, p. 68), as well as universal and generous benefits. If the relation between low wages and welfare state effort is upheld in other research, this may point to a solution of Iversen and Wren's (1998) trilemma of the service economy.

References

Adema, W. et al. 1996. *Net public social expenditure,* Labour Market and Social Policy Occasional Papers No.19 (Paris, OECD).

Alvarez, P. 2001. *The politics of income inequality in the OECD: The role of second order effects*, Luxembourg Income Study Working Paper No. 284, (Syracuse, Syracuse University).

Atkinson, A. 1999. "The distribution of income in the UK and OECD countries in the twentieth century", *Oxford Review of Economic Policy*, Vol. 15, No. 4, pp. 56–75.

————. 2000. *A European social agenda: Poverty benchmarking and social transfers*, Euromod Working Paper No. EM3/00 (Cambridge, University of Cambridge).

————. et al. 2001. *Indicators for social inclusion in the European Union* (Oxford, Oxford University Press).

Beblo, M. and Knaus, T. 2001. "Measuring income inequality in Euroland", in *The Review of Income and Wealth*, pp. 301-320.

Berger, F. et al. 2001. *The impact of tax-benefit systems on low-income households in Benelux countries. A simulation approach using synthetic datasets.* Euromod Working Paper (Cambridge, University of Cambridge).

Bradbury, B. and Jäntti, M. 2001. "Child poverty across twenty-five countries", in B. Bradbury, S. Jenkins and J. Micklewright (eds.) *The dynamics of child poverty in industrialised countries* (Cambridge, Cambridge University Press), pp. 62–91.

Bradshaw, J. et al. 1993. *Support for children: A comparison of arrangements in fifteen countries,* Research Report 21 (London, UK Department of Social Security).

Cantillon, B. 2002. *The failures of Bismarck and Beveridge: The case of old-age pensions for the self-employed in Belgium*, Paper for the 9th FISS (Foundation for International Studies of Social Security) seminar on "Pension reform", June 2002, Sigtuna, Sweden.

Cantillon, B., Marx, I. And Van den Bosch, K. 1997. "The challenge of poverty and social exclusion", in OECD *Towards 2000: The New Social Policy Agenda* (Paris, OECD).

Cantillon, B. et al. 2001. "Female employment differences, poverty and care provisions", in *European Societies*, jrg. 3, 4, pp. 447–469.

De Beer, P. 2001. *Over werken in de postindustriële samenleving* (Den Haag, Sociaal en Cultureel Planbureau).

Esping-Andersen, G. 1990. *The three worlds of welfare capitalism* (Cambridge, Polity Press).

Förster, M. 2000. "Trends and driving factors in income distribution in the OECD area", in *Labour Market and Social Policy,* Occasional Papers No.42 (Paris, OECD).

Gregg, P. and Wadsworth, J. 1996. "More work in fewer households?", in J. Hills (ed.) *New inequalities: The changing distribution of income and wealth in the UK* (Cambridge, Cambridge University Press).

Heady, C., Th. Mitrakos and Tsakloglou, P. 2001. *The distributional impact of social transfers in the European Union: Evidence from the ECHP*, IZA Discussion Paper No 356 (Bonn, Institute for the Study of Labour (IZA).

Immervoll, H. and O'Donoghue, C. 2002. *Welfare benefits and work incentives an analysis of the distribution of net replacement rates in Europe using EUROMOD, A multi-country microsimulation model*, Euromod Working Paper No. EM4/01 (Cambridge, University of Cambridge).

Iversen, T. and Wren, A. 1998. "Equality, employment and budgetary restraint. The trilemma of the service economy", in *World Politics*, Vol. 50, pp. 507–546.

Jäntti, M. and Danziger, S. 2000. "Income poverty in advanced countries", in A. Atkinson and F. Bourguignon (eds.) *Handbook of income distribution* Handbooks in Economics 16, (Amsterdam, Elsevier).

Korpi, W. and Palme, J. 1998. "The paradox of redistribution and strategies of equality: Welfare state institutions, inequality, and poverty in the western countries", in *American Sociological Review*, p.661–687.

Marlier, E. and Cohen-Solal, M. 2000. "Social benefits and their redistributive effect in the EU", in *Statistics in Focus, Population and Social Conditions*, Theme 3 — 09/2000 (Luxembourg, Eurostat).

Marx, I. and Verbist, G. 1998. "Low-paid work and poverty: a cross-country perspective", in S. Bazen, M. Gregory and W. Salverda (eds.) *Low-wage employment in Europe* (Cheltenham, Edward Elgar).

Mitchell, D. 1991. *Income transfers in ten welfare states* (Aldershot, Avebury).

OECD. 1998. *Employment outlook* (Paris, OECD).

———. 1999. *Benefit systems and work incentives* (Paris, OECD).

Oxley, H. et al. 2001. "Income inequalities and poverty among children and households with children in selected OECD countries", in K. Vleminckx and T. Smeeding (eds.) *Child well-being, child poverty and child policy in modern nations: What do we know* (Bristol, Policy Press), pp. 371–405.

Sutherland, H. 2001. *Reducing child poverty in Europe: What can static microsimulation tell us?* Euromod Working Paper No. EM5/01 (Cambridge, University of Cambridge).

Van den Bosch, K. 2001. *Identifying the poor. Using subjective and consensual methods* (Aldershot, Ashgate).

———. 2002. Convergence in poverty outcomes and social income transfers in member States of the EU, Paper for the XV World Congress of Sociology in Brisbane, Australia, July 2002.

Van den Broucke, F. 2002. "The EU and social protection: what should the European Convention propose?" Paper presented at the Max Planck Institute for the Study of Societies, Cologne, 17 June 2002. (<www.vandenbroucke.com>).

THE *REVENU MINIMUM D'INSERTION (RMI)* IN FRANCE: THE LIMITS OF A PROGRESSIVE SOCIAL POLICY

3

Serge Paugam [1]

1. Introduction

Differences in the ways that countries intervene to assist disadvantaged people can be seen as the expression of their methods for regulating poverty. These have been shaped by the socio-historic traditions of the networks of interdependence in each country that exist between the poor and the rest of society. Such networks are not static. Although characterized by inertia due to the weight of the institutions involved, they can evolve with the economic and social situation, or under pressure from the players concerned. They also differ in size, ranging from an entire nation to a local council whose means of intervening to help the poor may be, to a greater or lesser degree, autonomous. In other words, a study of the regulation of poverty in a society such as France, entails taking into account what some call "the stamp of history", that is to say, the socio-historic foundations of national systems of intervention to help the needy, and then tracing the way they have changed with reference to recent experience.

The sociology of the forms poverty takes in a given society at a given point in its history is, in fact, the sociology of social ties. The theoretical framework sketched by Georg Simmel in the early part of the 20th century (Simmel, 1998) demonstrates that, in the social relationship with poverty, the principle of assistance reveals not only the tensions, potential imbalances and even ruptures that affect and threaten the social system, but also a method of regulation that

---

[1] Director, National Scientific Research Centre — Laboratory of Second Analyse and Applied Methodology in Sociology — Longitudinal Institute (CNRS-LAHMAS-IdL) and Director of Studies, Institute of Higher Learning in Social Sciences (EHESS).

attenuates its effects and encourages interdependence between individuals and groups, even if these are based on unequal and sometimes confrontational relationships. The social status of the poor is dependent on this method of regulation (Paugam, 1999).

The way in which an issue is debated and solutions are sought is often significant. In France, the debate on poverty and exclusion was an opportunity for thinking on how to maintain social cohesion, particularly during discussions on the law on the RMI *(Revenu Minimum d'Insertion)*, voted on December 1, 1988 [2].

In this chapter, we attempt to show that the RMI is in line with the French tradition for interventions in favour of the poor, particularly in terms of its definition and the administrative management of the benefit, and is also innovative, particularly with respect to inclusion. We assess the limits of this policy on the basis of its traditional and innovative aspects and look at the possibilities for reform after 13 years experience.

2.   The stamp of history

We can use four differentiating factors to help us understand the national particularities of the assistance relationship in France compared with other European countries: the sharing of responsibilities between the State and other players; the administrative definition of the population to be taken care of; the principle governing the definition of the help to be given; and finally, the means of social intervention.

These factors relate to four simple questions to which France, like other European countries, has given specific answers: Who should help? Who should be helped? What principles should govern the giving of help? What resources should be used? We will not enter into details of social legislation, but will try to identify the specific French socio-historic characteristics for each of the four factors.

---

[2] Translator's note: The concept of the *Revenu Minimum d'Insertion* is two-fold: a guaranteed minimum income, plus assistance with social/occupational "insertion". A distinction is made in French between "insertion", used in political and social contexts, and "integration", with its strict sociological definition. The French word "insertion" has therefore been translated in this text by "inclusion", to convey the underlying spirit of the RMI.

2.1 Centralist tradition at the service of the poor

Where welfare is concerned, the sharing of responsibilities between the State and other players, in particular local councils and associations depends on the historical tradition of State intervention in each country. Although each welfare state represents a nationalised social protection system in the sense of a set of nationwide social rights applicable in the place of residence, welfare has remained the responsibility of local councils in many countries as far as administration of benefits and sometimes even their definition are concerned. Often, the extension of the system of social protection founded on the insurance principle has rendered traditional forms of assistance obsolete and residual, to the extent that States prefer to delegate some responsibility to local authorities, especially in countries where the necessary capability exists. For historical reasons, the administrative organization of welfare varies from country to country in Europe. In certain cases the State is the principal player upon which all initiatives converge, in others the principal player remains the local council.

In line with the French State's centralist and supposedly universal principle, initiatives to help the most needy are the responsibility of the nation. When parliamentarians discussed the RMI law, they began by reiterating principles adopted in 1790 by the revolutionaries who set up the *Comité de Mendicité*, the basis of the first national, republican welfare system (Paugam, 1993). Even though this organization was a failure, the spirit behind it did not disappear. One century later, the reformers instituted the right to assistance and encouraged the State to take charge of a sector left largely to private benevolence. Several laws on assistance were passed: free medical assistance (1893), for the destitute (1893), and assistance for the old, infirm and incurables (1905). Although France lagged behind Germany with regard to insurance and the organization of a comprehensive system of social protection, this was far from being the case in the field of assistance, where State regulation appeared very early (Merrien, 1994; Renard, 1995).

Even today, it would be unthinkable to risk inequality within the country by allowing local authorities to define the categories of eligible persons, the means of intervention, and the benefits. Although the decentralization laws passed at the beginning of the 1980s transferred social policies to the *Départements*, in line with demands to involve local players in responsibility for social problems, the State kept firm control by defining and giving the impetus to national policies such as the RMI and ensuring their overall management. The French case, termed "revolutionary centralism" by Max Weber, is an ideal-typical illustration of the rationale of successive state monopolization of collective areas of competence, from the monopoly of legitimate violence to that of provident societies and insurance. The question of exclusion is formulated in France in terms of this restorative principle from which the State cannot escape without provoking fierce criticism from its citizens. It is striking that the principle of State intervention is not often criticized, even by supporters of economic liberalism who view it as a necessity of the Republican pact, on condition, however, that it does not unduly upset budgetary equilibrium.

The sharing of responsibilities between the State and civil society in the fight against poverty and exclusion is also significant. Whereas several European countries give priority to the social services offered by non-State institutions, under the principle of subsidiarity, French charitable associations define themselves in relation to the State. They regard the State as an inevitable partner because it is omnipresent. They put pressure on it to obtain subsidies and hence be recognized as official players in social policy. They also encourage the public authorities to take direct responsibility. Charitable associations played a significant role in furthering the idea of the RMI before the presidential election of 1988. As a group, they are also behind proposals for new laws against exclusion. In other words, they do not contest State intervention and would even like to see it increased. This amounts to a kind of inverse subsidiarity: they will only act on condition that the State and public authorities have exhausted all possible solutions. And where the fight against exclusion is concerned, people have high expectations of what the State should do.

2.2 A categorial approach

Defining the right to assistance means defining, in the administrative sense, the population eligible to claim it. Two opposing ideas emerge. The first is based on a unitary definition; that is to say, the poor are defined in an overall fashion using criteria deemed legitimate by institutions and society as a whole. Monetary criteria are the most generally used, with household poverty defined on the basis of a given income threshold. The first European countries that recognized the right to a minimum guaranteed income for the most needy adopted this unitary principle and therefore defined a single set of rules for the poor. The second idea is based on an assessment of the risks facing certain elements of the population. Poverty is no longer seen as a homogeneous whole, but as a set of impoverished social categories to which it seems legitimate to grant assistance in the form of a minimum income. This second approach leaves open the possibility of creating a hierarchy in the categories defined, on the basis of an evaluation of the seriousness of the problems experienced. The categorial approach has the disadvantage of excluding certain groups from the right to assistance since they are required to fit into one of the categories in order be eligible. If none of these categories corresponds to the situation of the individual in difficulty, he or she cannot be helped unless it is through optional, or extra-legal, assistance. The unitary idea avoids this problem, but has often proved ill adapted to individual cases. This is why countries that have adopted this principle have often left a large degree of latitude to the institutions responsible for its application to allow for solutions to fit the particular needs of individuals and households receiving assistance. Unitary and categorial ideas of the poor are linked to two different philosophies of the definition of benefits.

In France, categorial intervention to help the most needy is a legacy of our social protection system. Legislation on the guaranteed minimum income for the most needy, for example, is founded not on a unitary principle (i.e. a piece of legislation to cover all those judged to be poor), but on a series of minimum benefits established for successive groups of people from the minimum invalidity pension created in 1930 to the RMI in 1988 (see appendix). Today, no fewer than eight such benefits exist to help people who have been excluded either permanently or temporarily from the labour market. The principle of this system is to cover different populations with specific handicaps or exposed to particular risks. The RMI serves as a final safety net and, cannot be defined as a categorial benefit. But since it is a last resort for people who cannot obtain the seven other minimum benefits, it corresponds in reality to an additional category in the social welfare system. The "poor" category is therefore split into several administrative sub-categories and the categorial principle prevails as the legitimate framework for thought and action. In such a system, social work largely consists of finding the appropriate category for the person in difficulty. When their situation does not correspond to any established administrative category, they cannot be helped, except by one-off extra-legal benefits. This type of intervention has repercussions on access to benefits. In a categorial system, despite the variety of benefits available, there are always those who are excluded from aid, all the more so since it's bureaucratic formalities exacerbate its failings still further.

2.3 A principle of status

In order to define the right to assistance, we must also define the benefits to which the poor population may lay claim. Two approaches may also be observed in this area. The first is based on the principle of need, in the sense that the aim is to guarantee the survival of the most needy by giving them the means to satisfy basic needs, in particular food and housing. This ambition is at least partially at the origin of research into the living conditions of impoverished populations. A wealth of literature exists on the subject. Economists and statisticians of poverty, in particular, have always sought to provide a substantialist definition of this social phenomenon with the more or less avowed intention of answering the questions posed by social policymakers.

The second approach relates to the principle of status, in the sense that the aim is to help the most needy in the name of social justice and the community's duty towards the poor, whilst avoiding a substantial change in the existing social structure. In other words, assistance gives social status to beneficiaries, but it must be defined with reference to the other levels in the hierarchy and, must remain markedly lower than that of the lowest-paid workers. There is an underlying notion of need, but it is not the basic criterion for deciding the amount of benefit to be granted. This is mainly defined in accordance with classification of individuals into as many hierarchical levels as socially necessary. The highly legitimate idea of social order justifies these inequalities in status. In this sense, assistance, as Simmel (1998) observed, is not so much a means of helping the poor as a roundabout way of maintaining the social *status quo*. Those European countries that have implemented a minimum guaranteed income, all drew inspiration from one or other of these two principles so that even today, they are still an essential dimension of national differences in the social relationship with poverty.

In France, the principle of status has always prevailed over the principle of need. In 1790, the *Comité de Mendicité* already considered the amount of assistance that should be given to the poor. Whilst ardently defending the right to assistance, La Rochefoucault-Liancourt stressed that it should not give the poor the same status as those in work, and consequently underlined the need to keep people receiving assistance in a far less advantageous situation so as to deter them from living on it. Thus, he was in fact strongly encouraging the Committee's members to adopt the principle of "less eligibility", long before it became the explicit reference in defining assistance in a large number of countries. Two centuries later, when the RMI was under discussion in the National Assembly, members of parliament followed the recommendations of the report by Jean-Michel Bélorgey, President of the Social Affairs Committee. This stipulated that, for want of a precise way of evaluating the needs of the poor, another principle should be used as a reference to set the rate of the RMI. The amount was tied to the SMIC (*Salaire Minimum Interprofessionnel de Croissance,* or minimum growth wage). As the RMI can be cumulated with family allowances, and allows for variable supplements depending on the structure of the household, calculations were made to ensure that beneficiaries could under no circumstances receive payments close to those received by workers on the minimum wage.

This principle was not challenged in parliament. The Communist members wanted the amount to be increased, but on condition that the SMIC was increased simultaneously, hence standing up for workers' living standards in keeping with party traditions.

2.4 Bureaucratic intervention

The fourth factor of differentiation concerns ways of intervening to allow people access to the benefit set aside for them. The assistance relationship may differ radically depending on whether institutions and social workers are able to make autonomous decisions within the standard framework designed to let them respond to those who need help. Two forms of response can be identified in this area of social work [3]. The first is bureaucratic intervention in that the agent of social intervention, be it an institution or an individual, pays scrupulous attention to applying the law without taking individual circumstances into account. The response is always formal and immediate. The individual may either be helped because he or she corresponds to a situation defined in social law, or not helped, and in this case must approach a more informal organization – in the charity sector, for example. The second response is based on the interpretation of individual cases and the search for the most appropriate solution depending on whether the demand is deemed legitimate. This may be termed individualistic intervention. In this case, the social agent is fully involved in the evaluation of a situation. It also calls upon greater professional competence than with strictly bureaucratic intervention. This type of intervention is easier when the prevailing social legislation has defined a wide variety of responses to particular cases. The agent then has to select, from a wide range of possibilities, the solution that seems to suit the individual best.

One might ask which type of intervention best respects the dignity of the individual. Bureaucratic intervention would, at first sight, seem to avoid stigmatising individuals excessively because their situation is treated in an impersonal manner. The social intervener does not judge, but simply checks whether conditions for obtaining benefit have been met, usually on the basis of an administrative file completed by the claimant. By contrast, individualistic intervention almost inevitably entails intrusion into the individual's personal life by social workers, and may result in moralising on behaviour judged irresponsible or deviant.

As we have seen, the French system is based on the notion that poverty is first and foremost a matter for the State. Ancient debates have structured current views of poverty and intervention methods to assist the disadvantaged. The RMI was approved after it became apparent that more and more people were slipping

---

[3] We do not claim to define all aspects of social work here, but limit our discussion to social intervention procedures in the field of access to rights.

through the welfare system's safety nets and that social structures decentralized at the beginning of the 1980s were unable to put this right with the means available at that time. When people did not fall into one of the existing categories of minimum social benefits, social workers could only propose optional or extra-legal assistance given on a discretionary basis. With the RMI, the French State strengthened the foundations of social rights and returned to a more administrative form of intervention. Access to the RMI, as to other minimum social benefits, is granted automatically on the basis of an administrative file completed by potential claimants according to a set of nationally defined criteria. Except in a few cases, the French system does not individualize aid to suit particular circumstances. For the greater part, the system is managed in a bureaucratic way, with no real assessment of the individual legitimacy of the claims.

3. The innovative aspects of the RMI

Interest in the RMI and the consequent mobilization of the public authorities was also the result of its aim to link a guaranteed income system with a series of additional aids designed to favour social or occupational inclusion. This approach to social policy was not completely new — it had been tested in a few towns and *départements* — but implementing it on a national scale was a challenge for government, the social aid institutions and, more generally, for all public and private bodies involved in the fight against poverty.

The change was due to a transformation in the notion of assistance (Lafore and Borgetto, 1996). In particular, the reference to the principle of inclusion made it possible to carry out large-scale experiments to search for solutions at departmental and local levels through coordinating different players. It also helped improve methods of social intervention. The reference was no longer limited to an individual's material needs defined in terms of poverty criteria, but also involved occupational training, health, housing, family relations, children's education, psychological well-being, etc. These aspects complement the financial assistance given in the form of a minimum income.

This reference to inclusion also led to innovations in the search for personalized solutions. The idea was not to find the best possible way of adapting the assistance to different categories of the population defined according to their specific problems but of adapting to individuals by building a project to change the course of their lives on the premise that they are capable of finding their place in society. People were no longer to be put in fixed, unchanging categories, but were to be helped to evolve, whatever their initial situation. At least in theory, these involved drastic changes in the ways social workers were to intervene.

3.1 Decentralizing social inclusion

As we have seen, the fight against poverty is a matter of national solidarity in France. However, there may be cause to wonder, given the example of the law on the RMI, whether this tradition of State intervention is, at least partially, being called into question. The law applies to the whole country, but obliges local players to take responsibility for its main component, namely the inclusion of the most needy. The aim is to encourage the *départements* to face their responsibilities and to oblige them to develop their own programmes by earmarking an annual credit, as a separate budget item, to finance actions for RMI recipients [4].

The parliamentary debates illustrated a concern that poverty reduction should not be a matter for the State alone. Michel Rocard, the Prime Minister who inspired the law at that time, said himself that "it is the commitment of all the parties – associations, local councils, *départements*, administrative authorities – to the Departmental insertion programme that will bring success". Concerned to make the public authorities more efficient, in the spirit of decentralization, he advocated a moral stance of renewed, deeper solidarity (Rocard, 1989). This philosophy of political action probably has its roots in the human rights struggles of the 1970s and the radical criticism of "everything is political". The aim, perhaps also the utopia, was to devise a new form of social contract, no longer based exclusively on State policies but above all on a return to ethics in social relationships. Pierre Rosanvallon, a supporter of this thinking, pointed out at the beginning of the 1980s that the crisis in the welfare state showed there was no alternative to "bringing society closer to itself", that is "making it more dense, by multiplying the intermediate layers of the social structure and reintegrating the individuals in direct networks of solidarity" (Rosanvallon, 1981). In practice, the rediscovery of poverty in the 1980s gave more weight to this view of social malfunctioning and the powerlessness of the welfare state.

This is why the RMI was not designed simply as an additional allowance in the social welfare system, but also as a means of strengthening social cohesion by encouraging everyone to participate. Parliamentary declarations took the form of calls for public-spiritedness. The problem of social relations was often raised, by the Left and Right alike, as in the following two examples:

---

[4] This credit must equal 17% of the sums paid by the State in the *département* in the previous financial year for the RMI.

Are we capable of giving new meaning to, and obtaining public support for demands for solidarity? Can we invent new ways of organizing it and find the mechanisms for rebuilding social links in our fast-changing society, constantly threatened by new rifts and further marginalization? (Jean-Pierre Worms, MP, Socialist Party (PS), October 4, 1988).

If we wish to succeed in reintegrating as many as possible of those who have fallen by the wayside, every mayor, and departmental councillor, but also every association president, social worker, head of a public service, and even every company manager, must feel personally concerned. (Jean-Yves Chamard, MP, Rally for the Republic (RPR), October 5, 1988).

However, it would be untrue to say that the idea of forging solidarity through active partnerships on a local level was unanimously approved. Some people, particularly the Communists, saw a risk of weakening the State, based on the argument that local authorities already played a key role in the field of social aid since the decentralization laws and that it was important not to weaken it further by transferring additional responsibilities. Others also underlined that the obligation for *départments* to finance inclusion policies was contrary to the spirit of decentralization. Behind the universally accepted principle of the need to strengthen social cohesion, there were different options concerning the degree to which the State should intervene. However, the adopted text confirms the desire to find a balance between national solidarity, financed by the State, and local solidarity in implementing more limited action. It set up consultative bodies at the local and regional levels to find solutions suited to the recipients' needs (*commission local d'insertion* and *programme départemental d'insertion*).

3.2 Inventing the right to "inclusion"

The principle of inclusion gave rise to an excellent debate in parliament on recipients' commitments under a contract with a so-called "local inclusion committee". The discussion also dealt with the obligations of local authorities, in particular the actions designed to give renewed confidence and hope to the most needy, by enabling them to participate more in economic and social life. The law also stipulated that each *département* was to draft and implement a "departmental inclusion programme".

For the interdepartmental official responsible for implementing the policy, the aim was to "take the allowance as a stepping stone to help beneficiaries gain, to the greatest possible extent, their social and economic independence. The allowance is only the basis of a more global right: the right to inclusion, with its corollary of an obligation for the national community" (Fragonard, 1989). In this spirit, the contract of inclusion cannot be considered as a return for the payment of an allowance. In her comparative research, Sylvie Morel showed that the French RMI could not be regarded as similar to workfare programmes in the USA (Morel, 1999). As we shall see, social workers responsible for offering support to RMI claimants rarely see the inclusion contract as a strict question of return.

Lawyers have also asked questions about the contractual side of the RMI. Some queried whether it was a right or a contract, underlining that the vagueness of the law on this point gave its main original feature a demagogic connotation (Mathieu-Cabouat, 1989). Others argued that the parties' obligations remain hazy and suggested that it was more of a two-way commitment to "good conduct" than a contract. Robert Lafore (1989), for example, considers that the usual features that define a contract in legal terms are not to be found in the RMI law. His view is based on three factors:

- the inclusion contract is not concluded by two parties at free will, as should be the case when drawing up a legally binding contractual relationship, as its aim is to "motivate the beneficiary of the RMI to become included in society". The contract is a form of incentive to participate in economic and social life and is a means of encouraging acceptance in exchange, thus of strengthening the social relationship;

- the beneficiaries' commitments are not legal obligations, but rather declarations of intent, which can change over time and cannot be seen in terms of rigid principles;

- if the contract referred to real rights and obligations, there should be a stricter system of sanctions, both for local authorities, who propose insufficient or inappropriate actions, and for beneficiaries who do not honour their commitments.

The vagueness of the law from a legal standpoint can be seen as an illustration of the weakening of the traditional norms imposed on individuals by constraint or manipulation, and the search for a compromise through the processes involved in negotiating rules that have not been fixed in advance. At the time of the French Revolution, it was proclaimed that able poor people were obliged to work. Although the means for reaching this objective were limited, the normative reference system was clear and firmly imposed. In the case of the RMI, the law does not say exactly what "inclusion" should be, but paradoxically, it does state that it is a national imperative. In other words, it defines the general framework, states the collective will, but leaves it up to the players in the field to come to agreement and to adapt to the different and complex situations of poverty. In fact it is a policy to regulate social relations, and an example of modern current tendency to develop control mechanisms and norms to guide societies' relationships.

We could almost define the inclusion contract as an instrument serving to negotiate the different forms of participation within society. It is indeed a means of reviving social relations. The legal form of the contract is not only aimed at determining the precise obligations and rights of the different parties, in this case the beneficiary and the local inclusion committee; it is more of a general framework that helps find solutions.

3.3 A new approach to social work

Social workers have a limited amount of influence on the possibilities of inclusion, but they play a key role in drawing up the contracts. Generally speaking, they consider that the inclusion contract, linked to the payment of an allowance, is the primary advantage of the RMI compared with the other benefit systems. Before the RMI, they were faced with a number of problems stemming from the fact that they could only deal with poor families' budgetary difficulties at an administrative level. The distribution of financial aid according to their own view of the situation placed them in complex assistance-based relationships, where they often felt unable to carry out fully their mission of education and social support. Caught in a process that encouraged people to stay on benefits, but nonetheless obliged them to respond to urgent situations, they were not always able to draw up a real "project" with the people who came to them for assistance. It was all the more difficult to follow up with specific action because the institutional means available in the *départements* were often very limited.

It is clear, at least in principle, that most social workers think the combination of contract plus allowances introduced new dynamism. Its implementation is designed to make the beneficiary more responsible. The procedure intensifies practices already at the heart of social work, but on a more informal basis.

The inter-personal relationships built up between social workers and RMI recipients have advantages for both parties: the former are offered more, probably also more legitimate, means to provide the latter with the confidence and assistance required to motivate them to draw up a plan for the future.

The contract is usually implemented according to an educational approach, which is in line with social workers' professional culture: respect for persons, concern for adherence and response to demands. In this general framework that encourages inter-personal relationships, there can be no question of productivity, although the statistics on the number of contracts signed in each *département* are used to measure the performance of the institutions concerned with the RMI.

However, there are great variations in the way the RMI law is interpreted. Some refer to the principle of law, others to the principle of return. For the former, the contract must correspond to beneficiaries' demands and cannot be imposed. A large number of social workers refer to this liberal principle. For the latter, the contract is an effective means of persuasion. The possibility of suspending the allowance is used to make beneficiaries adhere to a "realistic" project as quickly as possible, so there can be no question of leaving them without a contract. On the contrary, they must be encouraged to take the steps leading up to signature.

It is clear from all the observations made in the *départements* when the law was assessed ((*Mission de recherche expérimentation* — MIRE, 1991), that the first approach is to be more widespread. In the context of an employment crisis, the notion of return obviously has its limits, and social workers increasingly accept that individuals must be able to find their place in society even if they do not have a job. Consequently, they believe that the search for other forms of social integration should be encouraged, leaving the beneficiaries free to define their own project for participating in collective life in the wider sense of the term.

We could say that the inclusion contract is an educational contract, because it is based in practice on an inter-personal relationship and the principle of mutual consent, but it is also a public partnership contract as it mobilizes the means provided by the community as a whole. Thus, supported by an educational approach that is vital if the project is to be respected, the inclusion contract also encourages the public authorities, through social partners, to come closer to the real problems faced by RMI recipients and to find appropriate solutions. Social workers play an essential role in this process by building bridges between supply and demand for social inclusion.

4.   Limits and resistance to change

In the light of over 13 years experience, the RMI can be seen as a means of regulating social relations for two reasons. The first concerns changes in social action: the RMI has reinforced the ways of taking care of poverty on a local level and encouraged partnerships between institutions. It has provided an answer to the limits of the welfare state by extending the scope of solidarity to other players, in particular local authorities and associations. The second reason concerns the solutions proposed to beneficiaries to try to avoid the pitfalls of assistance and encourage them to take part in economic and social exchanges.

In its final report, the national committee responsible for assessing the RMI (*Commission d'évaluation du Revenu Minimum d'Insertion*, 1992) did not hesitate to speak of "unquestionable social progress". The new benefit has offered the most disadvantaged people greater material security against the risks of extreme poverty and access to basic social rights. The guaranteed income has helped beneficiaries satisfy their basic needs and eased their financial difficulties.

Nonetheless, the RMI has its limits. There is also a great deal of resistance to change, leading us to wonder whether this policy can be improved.

4.1 Inequalities from one département to another

The law's limits have already been examined on a number of occasions. Although an agreement was reached when the law was passed concerning the diversity of forms of inclusion, special attention is always paid to the results for occupational inclusion and the evaluations are rarely considered satisfactory in this field. In the survey carried out by the *Centre d'étude des Institut et des coûts* (CERC) in 1990 and 1991, only approximately 8% of beneficiaries had found a "real" job and no longer claimed the RMI at the last interview (Euvrard, Paugam and Lion, 1991). Another survey of people no longer claiming the RMI found that in January 1998, 26% of those claiming the RMI in December 1996 had a job, but that 17% were inactive and 57% were unemployed (Rioux, 2001a). If the RMI is judged by its impact on returning people to work — which, according to declarations made by certain members of parliament, was one of the main aims of the law – the results are admittedly modest. However, it is important to note that, although the population of recipients is extremely heterogeneous, it appears that a high proportion are distanced from the labour market and characterized by a breakdown in social relations. The results in terms of occupational inclusion must be assessed in the light of the difficulties encountered.

The number of recipients grew steadily until 1999 when the trend was reversed in metropolitan France [5]. However, the number of recipients continued to grow in the overseas *départements* (*Cour des Comptes* [French Court of Auditors], 2001). The big increase during the first 10 years of the RMI can be explained first and foremost by the deteriorating economic situation. *Départements* with high unemployment rates have a high percentage of RMI recipients. When the job market deteriorates, the number of people claiming the

[5] From 1999 to 2000, the number of recipients in metropolitan France fell from over 1 million to 965'000 (DREES {Ministry of Employment and Solidarity}, 2001).

RMI increases and few people are able to leave the system. Designed as a temporary aid on a "path to inclusion", the benefit is in fact a durable solution for a large proportion of the recipients who are distanced from the job market.

Is there a case for blaming inertia or unwillingness on the part of the local authorities for the mediocre results on inclusion? Although we cannot give a categorical answer, the data communicated by the interdepartmental delegation for the RMI (DIRMI) does underline differences from one *département* to another.

According to the results for 1993 (when the rate of unemployment in France was about 12%), the growth in the number of recipients was less than 10% in certain *départements*, but as high as 40% in others. Spending on inclusion per recipient varied from 5'000 F to 2'000 F. The rate of signature of inclusion contracts was only about 15% in some *départements*, compared to a national average of 47%.[6] Finally the "employment solidarity" contracts, which are an indicator of local mobilization — as the employers are local authorities, public establishments and associations — involve nearly 30% of recipients in the best *départements* and less than 5% in Seine-Saint-Denis (Paris region) and the Bouches-du-Rhône (Marseille region).

Five years later, there were still striking contrasts between *départements*. The DIRMI estimated an average rate of "contractualization" of around 50% in metropolitan France [7]: 72% in the 20 smallest *départements*, only 36% in the 20 largest. There was still a considerable difference between urban and rural zones: the Paris *départements* did not exceed 10% and Seine-Saint-Denis stagnated at 8% (*Cour des Comptes*, 2001).

Of course, these differences cannot only be explained by the motivation of local players, and we must also take into account demographic, economic and social differences between *départements*. When a *département* has a low rate of long-term unemployment, RMI recipients, particularly the youngest, have more chance of finding a job, almost regardless of the dynamism of the social aid institutions. The differences observed also reflect the density of the associative fabric: it is easier to build partnerships for inclusion projects in *départements* with many different associations. It is also true that the large size of certain

---

[6]According to the DIRMI, the average rate of signature of inclusion contracts was still about 50% in 1997. For a study of inclusion contracts and recipients leaving the RMI system, see Zoyem (2001).

[7] The department in charge of social action at the Ministry for Social Affairs estimated the rate of contractualization at 49% in 2000.

départements at least partly explains their difficulties. All the same, it is clear that there is not the same determination everywhere to find solutions. Quite often, there is an almost total failure to follow the methods proposed in the law and this is a constant concern for those responsible at national level. In a recent survey of 19 *départements,* the *Cour des Comptes* found that only two of them had used the total amount of the departmental credits that they are legally bound to allocate to inclusion (*Cour des Comptes*, 2001). Finally, implementation of the RMI was hampered in a number of places by institutional rivalries, conflicts between the State and *départements* and between *départements* and *communes.*

Inequalities in the amount of assistance given result in inequalities in the recipients' chances of inclusion that is contrary to the spirit of the law. Admittedly, as with the poor results in terms of access to employment, this was to be expected. By making local authorities responsible for the inclusion projects, the State took the risk that certain *départments* would actively look for new, appropriate solutions, and that others would be content with simple administrative management or even refuse to apply the law. The process of decentralization is still incomplete, and the balance between the different forms of solidarity has not yet been found. The deadlock is part of a vicious circle: as long as local authorities continue to show a lack of dynamism, the State is obliged to take corrective action, together with various sanctions, which can only take it further away from its role of organizing social policy. Butas long as the State exercises pressure and threatens the decentralized local authorities, this can only deter them from taking their responsibilities and lead to counter-productive administrative problems.

4.2 A never-changing categorial approach

In 1998, France adopted a new programme to fight against exclusion and passed a law establishing the new guidelines in July 1998. However, the law did not take into account certain important claims and avoided a number of issues although they are at the heart of thinking and research on the mechanisms of exclusion. Of particular note was the refusal to grant the RMI to people less than 25 years old despite demands from the unemployed movement.

Apart from countries in Southern Europe which do not yet have a unified national minimum guaranteed income, France is the only European nation to have excluded young people from this right. And yet the young in France have one of the highest risks of unemployment. Young people are particularly exposed to poverty in France, as nearly 20% of households in which the reference person in is 25 years can be considered poor on the basis of a threshold of 50% of the median income. By contrast, the poverty rate for 65 to 74 year-olds is lower than 5% and fall significantly over the long term (*Observatoire national de la Pauvreté et de l'Exclusion sociale* {National Observatory of Poverty and Social Exclusion}, 2000).

The difficulty with granting the RMI to people under 25 is mainly due to the widespread belief that the benefit would make them dependent on assistance and be prejudicial to their inclusion. A report by the *Commissariat général du Plan* (State Planning Commission) on the future of young people explicitly underlined their need to become independent and assume their responsibilities "by investing in their own future — training and work — rather than being financially dependent on the family and State charity" (*Commissariat général du Plan*, 2001). It is striking that, although the RMI was passed in a spirit of national solidarity to widen the base of social rights, there is still no question in France of it being considered a right for young people. And yet the argument put forward by several politicians, including Lionel Jospin when he was Prime Minister, that the RMI would confine young people to assistance, has not been proved. The argument is based on the idea that there are inactivity or unemployment "traps", and that young people would in some way be satisfied with the benefit and so not look for a job.

Studies have not found any major disincentives stemming from allowances such as minimum social benefits or unemployment benefits in terms of their impact on behaviour concerning employment (*Connaissance de l'emploi, des revenu et des coûts* (CERC)-Association, 2000). According to recent research, the reservation wage, i.e. the minimum wage below which work is refused, is lower for unemployed people receiving the RMI than for other unemployed people, because two out of three demand the SMIC (minimum growth wage) hourly rate at most, whereas two-thirds of other unemployed people demand at least the SMIC hourly rate. Similarly, RMI recipients accept much lower wages than other unemployed people (Rioux, 2001b). Finally, research in Europe shows that the relative generosity of unemployment benefit systems does not lead to a decrease in the unemployed persons' commitment to finding employment, even taking into account the effect of age (Gallie and Paugam, 2000). It is also well known that young people generally do more to find a job than older people, even when they receive satisfactory social benefits. In fact, the better protected they are, the more able they are to confront the labour market.

Similarly, the argument that the RMI would replace family solidarity has not been proved either. Studies have shown that the RMI has brought relief to many low-income families, which bore the brunt of difficulties with the social and occupational integration of young adults often living with their parents — but that it has not led to a complete breakdown in family solidarity. As the RMI represents a very modest sum, and the chances of occupational inclusion are fairly limited in certain cases, family support is still important. Private and public solidarity can be said to be cumulative. The results do not confirm the hypothesis that the RMI has become a direct, large-scale substitute for financial support from families (Paugam and Zoyem, 1997).

Extending the RMI to cover this age group would help reduce the inequalities between young people in terms of their assets and chances of inclusion, but the French political community is not in favour of this for the moment. The main candidates in the 2002 Presidential election excluded the idea from the outset, but some, including the elected President, made reference to the idea of a categorial independence allowance for young adults less than 25 years. The amount varied depending on the proposals and was usually justified by the need for training and inclusion. This thinking is in line with the traditional categorial approach: rather than adopting a global system targeting the population as a whole, it is always considered preferable to differentiate actions depending on the status of the individuals concerned.

The categorial approach is still visible in the field of inclusion. Despite the sums allocated and a few sensible changes, the programme introduced in 1998 to fight exclusion remains close to the traditional methods, particularly as far as employment is concerned. In partnership with the National Employment Agency (ANPE), the programme developed new measures for occupational inclusion for RMI recipients, but without changing the categorial approach despite its well-known limitations. It is impossible to avoid putting the groups concerned into administrative categories when the proposed measures allow for quotas and upper limits on financing. Actions of this sort always seem more coherent on paper than when they are being implemented in practice. The reinforcement of these complex systems, combining targets for inclusion and economic interests, has been responsible for creating a vast area of precarious employment on the edge of the labour market (Paugam, 2000). In fact, this political stance gives priority to the quantitative objective of reducing unemployment and does not directly take into account the quality of jobs. Nor does it include far-reaching reform of vocational training, which is required.

4.3 The RMI amount remains a problem

The RMI's low level is one of its main limitations. Since the law was passed, successive governments have refused to raise the level of the RMI, other than for price indexation adjustments. Yet the unemployed urge this increase, who voiced their demands during demonstrations in 1997 and after the Government presented its programme in 1998. The left-wing Government of the time justified its refusal by referring to the belief that it is preferable to favour employment and inclusion rather than assistance. Although this may be a strong argument, it distorts the aim of the minimum social benefits, which are not designed to represent public charity but the right to decent living conditions, a right that is just as essential in terms of preventing exclusion as the right to health or housing.

The monthly amount of the RMI seems relatively low today compared with the other minimum social benefits. It is 150 euros less than the minimum old-age pension, the minimum disability allowance and the handicapped adults' allowance. It is difficult to defend the idea that the recipients of these minimum benefits have greater needs than those receiving the RMI. The only way to understand this legal distinction is to refer back to the principle of status. RMI recipients are not old, or sick, or handicapped. They are just "poor and nothing but poor", which is the lowest status in the social hierarchy established by the welfare state. We must also point out that the rate of the RMI is still far below the normal poverty thresholds (50 or 60% of the median income) as it represents between half and two-thirds of these levels. If the aim were truly to deal with the real needs of the people who are excluded either temporarily or permanently from the labour market, increasing the rate of the RMI would be an obvious solution. But this is not the objective. On the contrary, recipients must be confined to a lower status than people who do not receive assistance, so the Government takes the risk of seeing the most needy sink even further into misery.

Is it necessary to point out that too low a level of minimum income obliges poor people to apply for additional aid and to waste a lot of energy just to survive, while being even more dependent on social services? At the very least, following the demonstrations of the unemployed and Marie-Thérèse Join-Lambert's report [8], it would have been normal to discuss the matter. Indeed, the enhanced mechanism for labour participation contained in Martine Aubry's programme, when she was Minister for Social Affairs, could have been reconciled with an increase in the level of the RMI and the solidarity allowance for the long-term unemployed.

4.4 Social action remains bureaucratic

Finally, there is the fundamental question of the inevitable limits of an individualized support system, in a context where increasingly numerous fringes of the population are driven out of the labour market and swell the ranks of the

---

[8] Report on the problems posed by the unemployed movements in France, submitted to the Prime Minister on February 25, 1998.

assisted when there were 350,000 RMI recipients in the first year, it was still possible to think in terms of a personalized inclusion project, but this is no longer realistic at today's figure of around one million, unless there are far-reaching structural reforms and a reappraisal of what is expected of social workers. In what is considered too heavy an administrative environment, there are often gaps in the support and follow-up offered. Many recipients have been in the system for several years without having met a social referral agent or signing an inclusion contract. A report on the Paris *département* indicates two-year waiting lists (*Cour des comptes*, 2001).

Social workers are often responsible for too many RMI recipients and feel they do not have the necessary means to do their work. They sometimes feel that they are "churning out contracts one after another" (Paugam, 1993), which they do not find satisfactory. Their training is another ongoing problem. Many do not feel competent in fields such as occupational inclusion, although one of the main objectives set by the institutions is to improve the recipients' access to employment.

5. Conclusion

As with other public policies implemented in the past few years, the experience of the RMI reflects transformations in the French welfare state. As we have seen in this chapter, although the RMI follows traditional French methods of intervening to help the poor, it also presents several innovations. This applies in particular to the field of inclusion, defined as a decentralized process in the form of a partnership between several players, in the spirit of a new right for beneficiaries, requiring an involvement on their part, but also firm commitments from the local community to respond to their needs and a more dynamic approach to social work.

The RMI law has been seen as offering social progress and has indeed enriched the social welfare system in the sense of creating greater national solidarity for the most disadvantaged. However, an empirical study points to malfunctions, obstacles and inertia in the institutions responsible for drawing up and implementing the reforms, to such an extent that we find the stamp of history of French intervention. These are at least four fundamental limitations:

- social inclusion has not been fully decentralized; in the face of difficulties in implementing inclusion projects on a local basis, the State is often tempted to intervene more directly to correct inequalities between *departments,* at the risk of provoking misunderstandings or even conflicts between players who are nonetheless obliged to work together on good terms;

- despite being based on a more universal concept than the other minimum social benefits, the legal framework of the RMI remains categorical, particularly due to the refusal to grant the allowance to young adults under 25 years of age, even though we know they are the worst hit by poverty;

- the refusal to increase the RMI to bring it closer to the other minimum social benefits and to the poverty threshold also confirms the reference to a principle of status, whose impact is often to maintain beneficiaries in a difficult financial situation, or which in any event hinders their inclusion;

- due to the administrative constraints in drawing up inclusion contracts for what was a growing number of recipients, it has often been difficult to reach the objectives laid down in the law in terms of inclusion and to enhance social work in the way the professionals in the sector hoped when the law was passed.

These are important limitations, but paradoxically they do not necessarily call for different solutions than those envisaged at the start. In a context of economic recovery and a reduction in unemployment, Governments are tempted to step up demands on recipients in terms of their return to employment rather than to increase the amount of benefit to offer better social cover, particularly as the French apparently feel less solidarity with the disadvantaged (Damon and Hatchuel, 2002). This explains why it seems highly unlikely, at least in the short and medium term that the RMI will be redefined as a citizen's income.

References

Afsa, C. 1992. «Le revenu minimum d'insertion: une prestation d'accompagnement?», in *Économie et Statistique*, No. 252, mars, pp. 43–50.

Astier, I. 1997. *Revenu minimum et souci d'insertion* (Paris, Desclée de Brouwer, Collection. «Sociologie économique»).

Castel, R. and Laé, J.-F. 1992. *Le RMI, une dette sociale* (Paris, L'Harmattan).

Connaissance de l'emploi, des revenu et des coûts (CERC)-Association. 1997. *Les minima sociaux, 25 ans de transformations* (Les Dossiers de CERC-Association), No. 2.

———. 2000. *Les minima sociaux: tendances longues et mesures récentes* (Les Dossiers de CERC-Association), No. 9.

Commissariat Général du Plan. 2001. *Jeunesse, le devoir d'avenir*, Rapport de la Commission présidée par Dominique Charvet (Paris, La Documentation française).

Commission d'évaluation du Revenu Minimum d'Insertion. 1992. *RMI, Le pari de l'insertion*, Rapport de la Commission présidée par Pierre Vanlerenberghe, Paris, La Documentation Française, (2 tomes).

Cour des Comptes. 2001. «L'insertion des bénéficiaires du RMI», in *Rapport au Président de la République*, pp. 9–70.

Damon, J. and Hatchuel, G. 2002. «Fatigue de la compassion et contestation suspicieuse», in *Informations sociales*, No. 98, pp. 32–39.

DREES (Ministry of Employment and Solidarity). 2001. «Les allocataires des minima sociaux», in *Etudes et Résultats*, No. 148, décembre.

Euvrard, F., Paugam, S. and Lion, J. 1991. *Atouts et difficultés des allocataires du RMI* (Paris, La Documentation Française, Collection. "Documents du CERC"), No. 102.

Fragonard, B. 1989. «Le revenu minimum d'insertion: une grande ambition», in *Droit social*, No. 7/8, pp. 573–588.

Gallie, D. and Paugam, S. (eds.). 2000. *Welfare regimes and the experience of unemployment in Europe* (Oxford, Oxford University Press).

Guibentif, P. and Bouget, D. 1997. *Les politiques de revenu minimum dans l'Union européenne* (Lisbonne, Unià das Mutualidades Portuguesas).

Kouchner, B. (ed.). 1989. *Les nouvelles solidarités*. Actes des Assises internationales de janvier (Paris, Presses Universitaires de France, collection «Recherches politiques»).

Lafore, R. 1989. «Les trois défis du RMI. A propos de la loi du 1er décembre 1988», in *L'Actualité juridique*, No. 20, pp. 563–585.

_____. and Borgetto, M. 1996. *Droit de l'aide et de l'action sociale* (Paris, Montchrétien).

Mathieu-Cabouat, S. 1989. «Le revenu minimum d'insertion: allocation ou contrat? Un choix nécessaire», in *Droit social*, No. 7/8, pp. 611–619.

Mission de recherche expérimentation (MIRE). 1991. *Le RMI à l'épreuve des faits, Territoires, insertion et société* (Paris, Syros-Alternatives).

Merrien, F.X. 1994. «Divergences franco-britanniques», in F.X. Merrien (éd.), *Face à la pauvreté. L'Occident et les pauvres hier et aujourd'hui* (Paris, Les Éditions de l'Atelier).

Morel, S. 1999. *Les logiques de la réciprocité. Les transformations de la relation d'assistance aux France et en France* (Paris, Presses Universitaires de France, collection «Le lien social»).

Observatoire national de la pauvreté et de l'exclusion sociale. 2000. *Rapport 2000* (Paris, La Documentation française).

Paugam, S. 1993. *La société française et ses pauvres. L'expérience du revenu minimum d'insertion*, 2e édition (1995), (Paris, Presses Universitaires de France).

————. 1996a. «Pauvreté et exclusion: la force des contrastes nationaux», in S. Paugam (ed.) *L'exclusion, l'état des savoirs* (Paris, Ed. La Découverte).

————. 1996b. "Poverty and social disqualification: a comparative analysis of cumulative social disadvantage in Europe", in *Journal of European Social Policy*, Vol. 6 (4), pp. 287–303.

————. (ed.). 1999. *L'Europe face à la pauvreté. Les expériences nationales de revenu minimum* (Paris, La Documention française).

————. 2000. *Le salarié de la précarité. Les nouvelles formes de l'intégration professionnelle* (Paris, Presses Universitaires de France, collection «Le lien social»).

———— and Zoyem, J.-P. 1997. «Le soutien financier de la famille: une forme essentielle de la solidarité», in *Economie et Statistique*, No. 308, 309, 310, 8/9/10, pp. 187–210.

————, Zoyem, J.-P. and Charbonnel, J.-M. 1993. *Précarité et risque d'exclusion en France* (Paris, La Documentation Française, Collection «Documents du CERC», n°109).

Renard, D. 1995. «Assistance et assurance dans la constitution du système de protection sociale française», in *Genèses*, No. 18, pp. 30–46.

Rioux, L. 2001a. «Recherche d'emploi et insertion des allocataires du RMI», in *Economie et Statistique*, No. 346–347, pp. 13–32.

————. 2001b. «Salaire de réserve, allocation chômage dégressive et revenu minimum d'insertion», in *Economie et Statistique*, No. 346–347, pp. 137–160.

Rocard, M. 1989. "Pour une solidarité renouvelée, pour un partenariat actif", *in* B. Kouchner (ed.) *Les nouvelles solidarités* (Paris, Presses Universitaires de France, collection «Recherches politiques»), pp. 367–372.

Rosanvallon, P. 1981. *La crise de l'État-providence* (Paris, Le Seuil).

Simmel, G. 1998. *Les Pauvres*, Paris, PUF, collection «Quadrige» (1e édition en allemand 1908). Précédé de «Naissance d'une sociologie de la pauvreté» par Serge Paugam et Franz Schultheis.

Villac, M. 1992. "Le RMI, dernier maillon dans la lutte contre la pauvreté", in*Economie et Statistique*, No. 252, mars, pp. 21–35.

Zoyem, J.-P. 2001. "Contrats d'insertion et sortie du RMI. Evaluation des effets d'une politique sociale", in *Economie et Statistique*, No. 346–347, pp. 75–102.

APPENDIX

Minimum social benefits in France

The French social security system is categorical in nature. There are no less than eight minimum social benefits: the minimum old-age pension; the minimum disability allowance; the handicapped adults allowance; the lone parent allowance; the widowhood allowance; the specific solidarity allowance; and the inclusion allowance.

The minimum old-age pension has its origin in the pension law of March 14, 1941, which set up the elderly employees' allowance (AVTS). The current form dates back to the creation of a supplementary allowance from the National Solidarity Fund (law of June 30, 1956).

The minimum disability allowance also dates back to the creation of the supplementary allowance in 1956, although its origin goes back to the invalidity insurance system drawn up in 1930.

The handicapped adults' allowance was created by the law of June 20, 1975. It applies to all people who are recognized to be handicapped and who are not covered by the other systems.

The lone parent allowance was created by the law of July 9, 1976 to bring temporary assistance to single parent families.

The widowhood allowance, created by the law of July 17, 1980, is aimed at giving temporary assistance to under 55-year-old surviving spouses of persons who paid social security contributions, and who has or had dependent children.

The rise in unemployment at the end of the 1970s gave birth to categories of job seekers who had not worked, or not worked enough to be entitled to unemployment benefits. A fixed allowance was created in 1979 to meet this need. It targeted first-time job seekers and lone women with dependent children. It was replaced by the inclusion allowance in 1984.

Restrictions on the conditions attached to unemployment benefits, particularly the limited payment periods, led to the emergence in the 1980s of long-term unemployed no longer covered by unemployment benefits. An emergency aid system was introduced at the beginning of the 1980s, replaced by the specific solidarity allowance in 1984.

The RMI, created by the law of December 1, 1988, was the last minimum guaranteed income system to be introduced. It serves, as it were, as the ultimate safety net.

Table 3.A1 Rates, recipients and population covered by the minimum social benefits

	Monthly rates (1)	Numbers as at 31 December 2000		% distribution of recipients 31 December 2000	
		Recipients	Population covered (2)	Recipients	Population covered (2)
Inclusion allowance	280.75	32 100	48 000	1.0	0.9
Widowhood allowance	492.41	19 000	28 500	0.6	0.5
Disability allowance	557.12	99 000	148 500	3.2	2 7
Lone parent allowance	669.76(3)	156 800	426 400	5 1	7.6
Specific solidarity allowance	572 44	429 700	1 032 800	13.9	18.5
Handicapped adults' allowance	557.12	689 000	1 075 000	22.3	19.3
Old-age pension	557.12	700 000	929 500	22.6	16.7
RMI	397.66	965 200	1 891 800	31.2	33 9
Total minimum social benefits in Metropolitan France		3 090 800	5 580 500	100.0	100.0
Overseas Départements		270 800	498 000		
Total France		3 361 600	6 078 500		

Notes: (1) At July 1, 2001 (in euros)
(2) Estimate (recipient, spouse and dependent children)
(3) Rate for a single person with 1 child (159 euros per additional child.

Source: Ministry of Employment and Solidarity — DREES

IMPLEMENTING ALLOWANCES FOR YOUNG PEOPLE IN DIFFICULTY IN FRANCE: ENHANCING CAPABILITIES OR INCREASING SELECTIVITY

4

Nicolas Farvaque and Robert Salais [1]

1. Implementing French public action for young people: Between social assistance and employment policies

French public action to assist young people has been affected by the new and original *Missions Locales* (MLs) for young people. In considering their effect, we must first take note of two main features of traditional French national programme.

First, no social assistance is available for young people under 25: they are dependent on employment programmes, which act as substitutes for social assistance, but which do not have an overtly positive impact on employment. Second, there is a benchmark against which to compare inclusion policies in France, the RMI *(Revenu Minimum d'Insertion)*. We begin with the RMI.

French social protection has operated through successive additions to coverage, pragmatically recognized, progressively implemented. Post-war France thus continually introduced rights for new categories of people. The elderly, the handicapped, etc., received *solidarité* monetary benefits to compensate for social disadvantages. They were allowed to benefit from social assistance without having to demonstrate past paid activity. The latest and most important extension was the creation of the minimum income.

[1] Institutions et Dynamiques Historiques de l'Économie CNRS — Ecole Normale Supérieure de Cachan, France.

The RMI was established in 1988. Young people under 25 were not entitled to it, except as a household head or in specific cases such as single mothers. French public authorities have been reluctant to institutionalise a possible culture of dependency among people who may have never experienced working life (Enjolras et al., 2000, p. 53). The RMI scheme allows a person, under means-tested conditions, to benefit from a minimum income even if he or she has never worked before. But recipients have to reciprocate by making efforts to integrate into the labour market, hence the "I" of RMI. Local commissions evaluate individual efforts on the basis of files and personal knowledge acquired by case-workers (Astier, 1997). The role of commission members is decisive, as they collectively wield discretionary power over benefit awards. The legal option to refuse resources to a needy person on the pretext that s/he has not made sufficient effort seems to be a severe penalty, whether due to conditionality or enforcement of a contract. Both sets of obligations have been criticised. The contract that the beneficiary has to sign with the State often binds two legal persons with asymmetrical powers. The obligation to be involved in an "insertion project" appears unjustifiable for claimants whose need has been already recognized. And the minimum income has been strongly criticised for deliberately leaving one part of the population, especially young people, in precarious situations and at risk of social exclusion.

These criticisms never modified the political choices. Young people are considered as being dependent on their family; otherwise they need to find independent income through work or paid activities. Employment policies that have flourished since the late 1970s have been largely established to help young people under 25-gain access, directly or indirectly, to paid activities. Various programmes have been created, from training measures to subsidized job schemes, from low-qualified public employment to labour cost-reduction schemes, and so on. They all aim to offer work experience, even if the quality is questionable and their impact on people's lives is minimal, especially for the least qualified. But their principal characteristic is that they provide recipients with income [2]. As Enjolras et al. say:

> One could reasonably ask why, in spite of the above evidence [of their limited efficiency], labour market policies have continued to develop over the last decade. The explanation is probably that some labour market policies, and particularly activation policies, act as a *substitute* for missing social policies. This is particularly true for younger people, since social assistance is

---

[2] This is the recipient's interest. The State's interest is obvious, because people registered in these schemes leave the unemployment statistics.

not made available for young people and social activation policies prevent them from falling into poverty and facilitate the extended transition phase between family dependency and personal autonomy. (2000, p. 66).

Hence, the dependency on social assistance that legislators wanted to avoid with the RMI has been replaced by another form of dependency, on employment schemes and massive use of "insertion" policies. Today, 75% of 16–25 years-olds depend, in one way or another, on public assistance and measures, be they students or potentially in employment. In 1975, it was 25% (*Commissariat Général au Plan*, 2001, ch. 2). Moreover, one in two young people depends on one of the multiple employment measures during a period of five years after he or she has left school (ibid). This impressive state-controlled integration from school to the productive system is increasingly debated, given its limited impact on employment. It is one reason behind the creation within the TRACE programme of the "Access to Employment Grant" (BAE, *Bourse d'Accès à l'Emploi*) to address the issue of lack of resources for young people. It was part of a more general hope to restore employment to the centre of employment policy.

Two structures, the *Missions Locales* (ML) and the Advisory, Information and Guidance Centres (PAIO) were created in 1982. These structures have been focused on youngsters out of the school system aged between 16 and 18, and up to 25, since 1984. Their essential mission is, first, to provide information about training and employment opportunities, and the public help available in these fields; and second, to help each young person to build up, with these tools, a personal development plan that solves at least some of their multidimensional problems of inclusion. From a microeconomic viewpoint, these agencies can be considered as "informational agencies" (White, 1990). They also have some latitude to devise their own instruments, for instance, by using local networks and resources, to complement the national ones. They are complementary to public employment agencies, but have no connection with unemployment benefit schemes. Striking features of this system are that these agencies are free of charge for users; their operation is predicted on the voluntary involvement of the young to be helped (everybody is free to enter and leave); if a young person is going to stay, this involvement develops into a personal project, with an advisor attached to him or her; help is multidimensional (finding a job is important, but not the sole aim); agencies operate at a local level at the centre of a network of various specialised agencies.

These agencies thus have a wide field of intervention with considerable discretion in their actions. The scale and nature of their intervention are decided individually for each young person. Furthermore, the intervention can be adjusted by analysing progress with the young. At the start, only the toolbox of national and local instruments exists. As we shall see in Section 3, the rest has to be constructed, following the "conventional intention" (Goodin, 1988) behind the French Youth Reception Network.

The approach affirms the core message of the public report that gave birth to these agencies: "The whole society is implicated in this goal: *young people will be autonomous only if they become responsible*" (Schwartz, 1981, italics added). Autonomy is thus the common good to be pursued, attained only if the deprived young become individually responsible. But this requires the acknowledgement of a collective responsibility to provide them with the resources they need. The report's author added: "*For some of them [the young people], even if they were given a job, nothing would be resolved*". More than twenty years on, this conviction still underlies the action of the agencies and their staff. The law even made it explicit that the MLs should:

> (...) provide young people with more comprehensive help, *going beyond professional guidance*, and permitting them to elaborate a project of *social and vocational* insertion and to implement it in each aspect of everyday life (1982 Law).

This is not to say that this "philosophy of public action" has been easily implemented. Many difficulties arose from the very beginning of these agencies. These were and still are due to the excessive domination within the French administration (but not only the French one, of course) of a top-down approach that separates issues into vertical domains. Each issue (health, vocational training, employment, housing, etc.) is treated separately from the others. National and standardised instruments are specialised by issue. National institutions that command these instruments compete with each other for power over resources and recipients. They guard their frontiers. This form of perverse co-ordination between administrations can be said to be "conventional" in the sense that the type of action we describe is mutually expected by each actor (by private actors and individuals). As each actor adapts his behaviour to what he expects from others, the process is self-fulfilling and leads to "natural" enforcement. As such, this is a convention between them. All actors, notably the claimants, are accustomed to navigating between administrative "rocks". This is what is called, in Storper and Salais (1997), "the convention of their external State" [3]. In some cases, this convention is efficient and provides people with

---

[3] The State, like other institutions, is essentially a convention between persons. In western societies, we can observe three general conventions of the State. In some societies, each person expects the State to intervene in the economy from a position outside and above the situation of action. This is the convention of the "external State" which is particularly strong in France. In

adequate solutions. But this is not the case for young people at risk of social exclusion. Problems are specific to each person, depending on background and circumstances. Hence solutions are to be found horizontally and at local level, through a process of discovery and adjustment. These are outcomes of what we call a convention of the "situated State" [4].

At the birth of these agencies, existing public administrations were convinced that their traditional methods were perfect and the only possible ones. The creator of the MLs, Bertrand Schwartz, was subject to open hostility from these administrations. For instance, he complained to the 1981 Prime Minister, Pierre Mauroy, that some administrations (namely the Department of Vocational Training) were elaborating, "a monitoring that ought to be very structured and institutionalised".... Such a project will be perceived as technocratic and meaning formal schooling (which was precisely what these young people rejected). He claimed, by contrast, that the failure of policies with regard to youngsters was, above all, due to central implementation of separate strategies of vocational training, employment and social inclusion. "If I have proposed a comprehensive policy of social inclusion managed at a local level, it was precisely to prevent these rocks" [5].

No battle is definitively won. One must be aware that the MLs are conceived as experiments addressed to young people rather than as a matrix to reform social policies. The MLs will remain subject to diverse and probably contradictory influences. Some pessimism may be expressed today. For a long time, French employment policies have been marked by political instrumentalism (how to minimise the figures more than the reality of unemployment) and with dogmatism. The TRACE scheme could be threatened and its public funding reduced in the near future, because its "statistical return" could seem poor. Nevertheless, as Sections 2 and 3 will explain, its practical and theoretical interest is still intact.

other societies, each person expects the State to be absent from situations of economic action, and for individuals to work coordination between themselves. This convention of the "absent State" is particularly marked in the USA A third possibility is that the persons involved in economic action (including State representatives) operate on the premise that the State participates in economic coordination but as an equal, neither superior nor absent. We call this the convention of "situated State", adapting slightly the concept from political philosophy, which terms this the "subsidiary State" (Storper, 1998, p. 11).

[4] More in Section 3.

[5] Bertrand Schwartz, letter to the Prime Minister of 16 November 1981, Archives of Cabinet of the Prime Minister, file 67 (with the authorization of *Fondation Jean Jaurès* and *Archives de France*).

2.   New wine into old bottles:
The TRACE programme
for young people "in difficulty"

The TRACE programme is implemented by the Youth Reception Network mentioned above. It was launched as the employment component of the 1998 Law to Combat Exclusion (*Loi de Lutte contre les Exclusions*), representing a move towards a fundamental rights approach, emphasising the State's responsibility to ease or permit access to "fundamental rights", such as health, housing and employment.

The TRACE programme provides low qualified young people between 16 and 25 with personalised guidance. In most cases, these beneficiaries were already registered with a local agency of the Reception Network. The personalised guidance can last up to 18 months, and has so far covered 180'000 people. As before, it is based on the voluntary involvement of the young, with no compulsion. The institution commits itself to give increased help to recipients, on a positive discrimination basis. Local agencies are instructed that, "once entered in the TRACE programme, the young must notice a change in his or her life. He or she must know what he or she will do during the day, and have the feeling of being taken care of differently" (publication of *Délégation Interministérielle à l'Insertion des Jeunes* — DIIJ, their national administrative supervisor). For the first time, a quantitative target was introduced to guide and control the decentralised action of intermediaries. This target, fixed by the central government services, is that 50% of those in the programme should be guided to steady employment (a permanent job or a contract of more than 6 months) at the end of their course in the scheme. This obviously looks like a new framework for action, condemning non-job-related procedures.

More recently, it has been acknowledged that, in many cases, the lack of monetary resources can undermine the efficiency of inclusion routes for young people. Given the holes in the French social safety net, the "Access to Employment Grant" (BAE, *Bourse d'Accès à l'Emploi*) was created within the TRACE programme. The 1998 law on exclusion was reinforced in 2001, when the volume of possible entries in the programme was doubled to 120'000.

The major feature of the BAE grant is that it acts as a benefit of last resort, when nothing more adequate is available for the young person. According to the decree (3 January 2002), "the attribution decision is taken in respect of *the active participation* of the young in the insertion steps and actions that are proposed to him or her" (Article 2, italics added). But it is limited to young people who have no other income sources whatsoever, its duration is short and the amount of money very low, in order to impede opportunist behaviour and dependent attitudes.

Because provision of a BAE grant is a right, every young person who meets the conditions and who claims the BAE must receive it. Nevertheless, participation and awareness of responsibility is key. "The point is neither to sustain *active* insertion routes nor to provide, without *condition*, a subsistence income to young people with difficulties. This is demanding for the young, and also for the people who have to propose solutions, that is, more particularly, the MLs, their partners and the Public Employment Service" a State notice says. The Government has confirmed that *the BAE should not be a minimum income for youth*. The aim is to consolidate the financial situation of young people registered in the TRACE programme, for periods during which they receive no income at all.

Young people who benefit from any type of income such as wages, paid training, or one of the social incomes referred above — RMI if head of a family; disabled allowance; and single parent allowance — are *not* entitled to the grant. The BAE concerns those participants who oscillate between paid and non-paid periods. The grant can amount to a maximum of €900 a semester, or in practice a maximum of €300 per month. Consequently, at its maximum rate, *it can only be distributed for three months over a six-month period.* Knowing this principle in advance, people who decide to claim this benefit are supposed to be aware that they have to find other sources of income for the other three months. This principle underscores the meaning of the grant — giving minimum resources for the in-between period between work or paid training. A core aspect of the legislative intention is that this *individual* obligation is a *collective* matter, which involves the institution, as well as the young person. The law says, in effect, that the institution has to help the young to find work or paid training.

For recipients, their situation and rights are reconsidered monthly. A local committee examines the benefit payments, rather like the local committees for the RMI. If no income or public subsidy has been provided in the month in question, the grant will be €300. To take part-time jobs into account, the committee can allow part of the grant, based on the *weekly* income obtained from the activity at the end of the considered month. If the individual has not received any such income for three (respectively, two and one) weeks during this month, *and* if the activity is less than 60% of the net SMIC (*Salaire Minimum Interprofessionnel de Croissance*, the legal minimum wage), the grant will come down to €225 (respectively, €150 and €75), i.e. 75% (respectively 50% and 25%) of the maximum monthly amount. The grant will be nil if the young person has not communicated the necessary information.

3. Understanding monetary allowances in a capability perspective

It would be easy to interpret this new grant as a refined form of means-tested benefit, far from income security. There are undoubtedly some aspects that could lead to this type of welfare. Nevertheless, we will argue that, due to the extent the BAE is embedded in the process, along with the way the MLs are accustomed to operate, things are more complicated. Furthermore, to reconstruct the true meaning of such public schemes requires scrutinizing how they work; in favour or against the inclusion needs of their applicants.

Autonomy is rooted in the French solidarity tradition [6]. In political discourse, the BAE was conceived as a rights and responsibility scheme. Empowering young people by giving them more autonomy should make routes to employment more active. However, a look at the ways through which the scheme (ML+TRACE+BAE) operates in practice suggest that making routes more "active" would entail something quite different from the present notion of activation in terms of incentives and individual responsibility. In our view, the scheme still functions as if it remains governed by the "capability intention", that was at the origin of the Youth Reception Network public action (Farvaque, 2002). Thus, the notion of capability, developed by Amartya Sen, is relevant to the problems of public action and income security.

For policies to address these concerns, a substantive priority and a procedural priority, are needed. The substantive priority is to ensure that everyone has the capability to achieve conventionally defined functioning. The procedural priority specifies the intention: to stay alongside the beneficiaries, and to help them to plan their life and build sustainable projects. When fulfilled, these priorities can give birth to a self-realizing process. Working on the assumption that, potentially, people have the necessary capability to achieve their aims, this convention of public action creates an incentive structure (institutional environment, adequate services, cash benefits, continuous evaluations) that progressively makes people more capable.

---

[6] For instance, coinciding with implementation of the BAE, a commission was launched at the beginning of 2002 in order to examine the possibilities of an "autonomy benefit" for people aged 16–25 (see the final report, *Commission nationale pour l'Autonomie des Jenunes*, 2002). Several scenarios were examined that might have manifested a desire to grant more autonomy to the recipients. But no compromise could be reached among the 70 members of this heterogeneous commission. Technically the issue was difficult and full of pretexts for institutional blockages.

According to Sen, the capability a person has over his or her life lies in effective possibilities freely to choose a life path and achieve certain "functionings". These functionings constitute a good life, more or less in line with the Aristotelian sense (see the debate in Nussbaum and Sen, 1993). This entails achieving basic needs (adequate nourishment, shelter, mobility, good health, etc.) *and* social needs (participating in community life, appearing in public without shame and having self-esteem.). In other words, it means achieving a set of "doings" and "beings" (Sen, 1992). The capability a person has to achieve these functionings is synonymous with his or her freedom. It represents the extent of what the person can *do* and *be*.

Thus, the value and quality of inclusion in a given society are tied to a "conventional" definition of basic functionings. These are not some "objectivist" minimalist standards, fixed by a scientific authority. These functionings are conventional in the sense that everybody, at a given period, and in a given society thinks, that they are necessary and that one has reason to value them. Sen (1983) recalls the example given by Adam Smith that "to be able to avoid shame, an 18th century Englishman has to have leather shoes". This capability was necessary, "not so much to be less ashamed than others, but simply not to be ashamed, which as an achievement is an absolute one" (Sen, 1983, p. 159). To have, or not to have, the required capabilities are the question to address for judging situations in which help is needed. The capabilities in question are not minimalist (having shoes), but those everybody in a given society considers as normal (having *leather* shoes) [7]. This poses the difficult question of listing the functionings that, in that period and society are considered necessary.

In this perspective, money has an advantage because it allows achievement of an undefined number of different functionings, as long as the budgetary constraint is respected. It is one thing to have a garden, which permits growth of nutritious food; it is another to have the money that allows the purchase of food, presumably with wider choice. Thus, satisfying one's "nutritional needs" can occur through different strategies of using available money, some requiring more money for current use than others. In all cases, money not only gives choice, but also increases the scope of the choice. By contrast, if welfare recipients are provided with a fixed number of predefined services in kind, the absence of a money allowance (or its very limited amount) could restrict the recipients' choices, and hence their individual freedom. Thus, it can be argued that providing an unconditional minimum income to youngsters is the right way to improve their capabilities. From this (market-based) perspective, providing

---

[7] Recalled in Salais (2002).

money, even on a restricted basis, through the BAE for young people with no resources at all, could be viewed as a criticism of the old way in which the Youth Reception Network operated. Furthermore, it could be conceived as the first step towards the return (or expansion) of liberal incentive/penalty activation policies.

Sen has been aware of the functioning-achievement value of money, if not its evident intrinsic value (as Cohen, 1993, argued). However, such ideas leave aside Sen's main contribution, which has been to emphasise how much people differ in their ability to convert a given amount of money (or basket of commodities) into valued functionings (Sen, 1985, 1990). This is decisive for analysing policies *and* for implementing efficient and fair ones. For instance (keeping our example of food) a young trained cook (A) will not buy the same products at the supermarket as an amateur one (B). The evidence is that the well-being of A will be higher than that of B. Equally, this seems to be due to the access of A to an activity (cooking) that B does not have. Cooking offers a larger set of possibilities to improve his/her well-being than buying products with no idea of the potential of transforming them into good food. This means that, with the same amount, A can do more that B. A has a better rate of converting money into adequate functionings; A has more capabilities than B. For Sen, enhancing capabilities should be the target of welfare (and inclusion) policies. It provides people with more effective freedom of choice and, eventually, with greater well-being.

Thus, unless we can establish that an equal conversion rate (equal capabilities) prevails among people to be helped in their social (or employment) inclusion, monetary provision cannot be synonymous with real freedom. It is misleading to regard the delivery of money as an *a priori* sufficient condition for welfare. In generalizing, it follows that, most often, income security requires money (at a level to be determined) plus other things. The fact that people differ in their conversion possibilities is not a reason why they should not be provided with a certain amount of monetary resources. But such allowances are merely an element of a more comprehensive range of opportunities. This set of possibilities has to be constructed by public action, combining State and non-State resources and actors, and access must be universally guaranteed.

A capability model for welfare provision does not focus on the nature of the instrument itself (in-kind, monetary, etc.) but rather on its appropriateness to the specific personal situation. This means that access must be adjusted to the situation of claimants, raising the question of selectivity in a capability approach.

There are dangers in the search for appropriateness, namely discretion and *ex ante* selection. In the context of asymmetrical power (an individual claimant confronted by a collective organization with large resources and complex rules), it is easy for the provider to exercise discretionary and arbitrary power.

Choosing what he prefers on the basis of criteria obscure to the claimant and providing help at his discretion are likely to be tempting. This is the reason for preferring formal and general rights, guaranteed by law. The problem is how to enforce these rights, given the initial inequality of capabilities between recipients. Some will profit from and mobilize such rights, because they have individual resources to make them effective; the majority cannot. Hence the need to achieve equality of capabilities. But the effectiveness of such a priority requires adequate devices to evaluate individual situations.

The second danger is *ex ante* selection. Frequently, public policies are composed of a large number of specific measures, with different schemes targeted at specific categories of claimants. There is often a kind of implicit (sometimes explicit) hierarchy between these schemes. In the case of employment policies, for instance, one can find, at the top, schemes targeted to the most employable and, at the bottom, to the least employable (above some threshold). The distribution of claimants between the schemes is achieved by local public agencies in France through *ex ante* evaluation of individual employability, the "best" schemes being reserved for the supposedly "best" claimants. Problems arise when, as is usual, there are fewer places than candidates, which means entry selection for each scheme. In such rationing, providers try to maximise *ex ante* the number of people capable of finding a job at the end of the scheme. Managers are often rated according to the percentage of recipients subsequently employed: this conditions the extent of funding and the number of places offered to them the following year. "Good" schemes and "good" recipients are those that maximise this rate of return. This results in perverse effects because agencies aim to maximize their own rating rather than enhance the capabilities of their users. Hence, those deemed most capable are selected at the outset, resulting in more rather that less exclusion.

There are no miracle solutions to discretion and *ex ante* selection, but several lines of thought. One is to implement procedural rights and facilitate participation of recipients in their evaluations and in defining the help they need. Codes of conduct and professional ethics favour such an approach. This could also be done to contest decisions taken by the scheme's officers. Rights can be conferred on recipients or only on representatives (unions, associations, etc.). Rulings may require special jurisdictions or arbitration courts, the existence of which could avert arbitrary behaviour, because scheme managers will soon realise this will be costly, and so will prefer, in most cases, to avoid it. Courts act more as *ex-ante* discipline than *ex-post* correction. Some schemes in France have such rights for claimants, for instance, unemployment benefits and schemes for helping people to create businesses.

Another line is to involve in the scheme's operation a number of actors: public (from several administrations) and private (for instance, associations and other members of civil society). Thus, commissions to access claims will be more broadly based and may shed light on some relevant aspects of the situation of the claimants that would have been missed by using a single set of criteria. A "considered judgment" can be developed by such commissions. They will thus favour fair selection and an effective definition of the help required. For instance, family associations can insist on some aspects of family life while health officers will help to shed light on health deficiencies. Other criteria than employability are thereby introduced. As one knows, family or health problems can impede the return to employability and to employment, more surely than a supposed lack of competence.

However, whatever the "technical" optimality of procedures and criteria, welfare provision implies mutual expectations between the actors (public and private actors, *and* potential recipients) about what is fair and efficient. This is especially visible in the TRACE scheme that emphasises the value of autonomy for young people. Applying a theoretical framework developed in Storper and Salais (1997) to this special case, implementing a capability approach requires a specific type of state action, that of a "situated State". In a convention of a "situated State", the common purpose is to foster the autonomy of agents, achieved through a process different from the liberal or interventionist prescription. As Storper and Salais note:

> [The situated State] views the *general common good as a situation in which actors have autonomy of action.* Autonomy is defined, not with respect to the individual's procedural rights, as in liberal-contractual theory, but (in addition to those rights) with respect to collective action and the rights of groups to deploy different action frameworks in coordination with each other. The State's role is to ensure that these frameworks of action and practices of coordination are treated with respect. (...) The general common good, in other words, is directly linked to the extent to which the state and its policies *grant actors the freedom and resources* needed to draw on diverse possible frameworks of efficient economic action (Storper and Salais, 1997, p. 212, emphasis added).

With this type of public action, people are confident that, if necessary, the State will do something tangible and, if possible, effective to help them. They are not abandoned to their individual limited resources as in the liberal "absent" state [8]. Nor are they cared for through general abstract categories as in the

---

[8] Or "residual" if one takes Epsing-Andersen's typology of welfare states (Epsing-Andersen, 1990).

"external" state (of which the French State is an example). However, what they can expect from the State has to be defined by their situation. The solutions are not definable *a priori*, because developing effective autonomy depends on the singularities of the situation to be dealt with. The actions to undertake and the resources to deliver must be discovered through the collective and cooperative development of the situation.

For instance, for young people participating in the TRACE scheme, although the final objective can be finding them a job, developing autonomy may mean more job offers available, or a better school system, or transport facilities. Similarly, the provision of monetary allowances cannot be isolated from the circumstances of the affected person or from overall policy. The BAE, for instance, is a package of monitoring plus grant. The grant is meant to *secure* the pathway to employment. It is delivered, after the launch of the process or return to employment, with its qualitative aspects focussed on the young. Emphasis is not on incentive effects, and guidance towards employment precedes monetary help. *Money comes last, not first.* It proves useful only if accompanied by additional services. For instance, access to personal housing, central for autonomy and inclusion, may require more money to pay rent. But it is insufficient. Personal housing requires the durable capacity to gain independent income through work and the personal responsibility to keep a house.

We believe that all those features are specific to a "situated State". To understand this type of public action requires not only regard for the political philosophy by which schemes are justified, but also observation of the practical operations. In addition, the assumption is that such a "situated State" tends to act according to a capability approach for they have in common the premise of personal autonomy and the ambition to improve *real* autonomy (Sen's effective freedom).

Formal and abstract rights belong to an "external State", while the mix of incentives and penalties are characteristic of an "absent State". A capability approach appears to require a "situated State"[9]. Autonomy means capability, i.e. the potential effectively to achieve personal goals. As a manifestation of the individual's freedom of will, his actions cannot be considered as separate from him; they are part of his personal development. The conclusion is that progress

---

[9] See Farvaque and Raveaud (2002) for examination of the concepts of the situated State and the capability approach. They propose several forms of situated action, one based on capabilities, the other closer to an incentive-based approach. This helps understand differences between "local" and "situated".

in society towards some common good or general interest (the responsibility for which is a major attribution of the State) cannot be achieved by the State alone. The State must acknowledge that to achieve its goals, for the sake of society it has to leave room for autonomous actions from individuals and collective actors. This is conceivable only if people develop the capability to act and coordinate themselves towards such collective goals. To develop capability through learning, people must be placed in a situation where, due to the expectations of other participants (the State representatives among them), they cannot do anything but commit themselves to act in the expected direction.

What is true at a global level is also true at a local one. Inclusion into society or into a job (the common good we are talking about in this paper) cannot be achieved unless the persons involved develop the capability to do so. If not, public resources would have been wasted. For the State and for all participants, this requires a situation in which incentives are endogenous to the collective game and the associated course of action. Several conditions have to be fulfilled, again not in an *a priori* way, but endogenously created during the process. These include equality of consideration between participants whatever, their resources and potential power; rejection of any *a priori* description of the claimants that will lead to exclusion of those considered as unable to develop capabilities; and generation of an atmosphere of trust. Another major difference with regard to "external" or "absent" States is the view that fair and effective social inclusion cannot proceed simply by creating optimal rules and schemes. It requires the creation of mutual expectations, through conventions between participants. To reiterate these conventions require evaluation procedures that are democratically debated and subject to change, as well as procedures permitting decisions to be challenged and given fair consideration.

4. Conclusions

To conclude, let us ask the same questions: to what extent do allowances for young people in difficulty in France conform to a capability approach, both in their operation and in the conception of the State they mobilise? What can one learn about income security as a right?

The absence of selectivity at entry to the process is essential to such a perspective. Every young person who decides to enter *Mission Locale* or a PIAO guidance centre is free to do so. And he or she will be welcome. His needs and the services he requires will be assessed. Admission into the scheme is voluntary; so is the decision to stay. In return for personal commitment, the agency personnel commit themselves to give him the best help relevant to his situation, not only with regard to the labour market and a job, but also to housing, health and urgent needs, even if the ultimate goal is finding work. This is done by mobilizing the network of local agencies in charge of these different domains; hence the involvement of many public and private actors around each young person that helps to ensure the "considered judgment" discussed earlier. All of this seems to follow a capability approach to a large extent.

So does the BAE monetary allowance. The means-test being satisfied, the young person is free to claim it or not. It comes as help of last resort. It cannot substitute for services in kind, but is in addition. We cannot say that this allowance obeys a principle of selectivity and of exclusion. The relevant feature is the forward-looking condition. A young person who activates the right to this allowance in advance knows it is limited in duration (nine months) and in frequency (three times). That means for him that the scheme and, by deduction, he himself expect that he will succeed in his inclusion. It creates an atmosphere of mutual expectations. What we observed in our empirical work is the self-fulfilling aspects of such an atmosphere. Is it a case of learning to behave rationally? Not in a simplistic standard conception (as in neo-classical economics), but as a capability to plan and execute the future. The paradox is that such rationality cannot be learnt through monetary incentives and penalties advocated by standard economics. By contrast, it needs time and an environment composed of institutional schemes, public resources, trust and conventions, all considered as inefficiencies by standard economics.

There are failures, of course, and there is a need for a rigorous assessment of how far a capability approach is achieved. The same applies for inquiring into the type of State action implemented. The political future of the TRACE scheme is uncertain. The ways in which it operates, however, contrast with the activation debate, and the actions or offers "you can't refuse" (Lødemel and Trickey, 2000). Rather than "activate" people, the grant gives them increased effective freedom to act. Both interpretations are linked with the idea of making the policies "active", but the philosophical and practical attributes of *acting* are different.

The operation of the scheme argues in favour of income security as a right. The need to add a monetary grant to the public mechanism for youth inclusion demonstrates that services in kind, regardless of how well suited they are, are not enough to ensure autonomy in all circumstances. Income security as a right *of last resort* is necessary. But its fairness and efficiency require more than formal rights. It requires collective institutional arrangements that help people enter a process of learning capabilities and gaining effective freedom to plan and to act rationally. Implementation of such arrangements must meet strict requisites. A large range of tools, from services in kind to money must be available. Judgments about claimants have to be deliberated, contestable and adjustable through explicit procedures. They are to be "situated". The methods of developing effective autonomy have to be discovered through the collective and cooperative unfolding of the each individual situation. Finally, implementing a capability approach that could ensure income security requires further reflection about State actions and the variety of their feasible forms. Opposition between State and market, and the debate about their respective merits, are too crude to be relevant. There is a need for analysis and theories of other forms of State action, the ones we label "situated States".

References

Astier, I. 1997. Revenu minimum et souci d'insertion (Paris, Desclées de Brouwer).

Cohen G. A. 1993. "Equality of what? On welfare, goods, and capabilities", in M. C. Nussbaum and A. Sen (eds.) The quality of life (Oxford, Oxford University Press).

Commissariat Général au Plan. 2001. Jeunesse, le devoir d'avenir, Rapport de la Commission présidée par Dominique Charvet (Paris, La Documentation Française).

Commission Nationale pour l'Autonomie des Jeunes. 2002. Pour une autonomie responsable et solidaire, Rapport au Premier Ministre (Paris, La Documentation Française).

Erhel, C. et al. 1996. "Job opportunities for the hard-to-place", in G. Schmid, J. O'Reilly and K. Schömann (eds.) Handbook of labour market policy and evaluation (Cheltenham, Edward Elgar).

Enjolras, B. et al. 2000. "Between subsidiarity and social assistance — the French Republican route to activation", in I. Lodemel and H. Trickey (eds.) An offer you can't refuse. Workfare in international perspective (Bristol, The Policy Press), pp. 41–70.

Epsing-Andersen, G. 1990. The three worlds of welfare capitalism (Cambridge, Polity Press).

Farvaque. N. 2002. The French rights and responsibility system for young people in a European perspective, paper presented at the 2nd COST A15 (European Concerted Research Action, Reforming Social Protection Systems in Europe) Conference on Welfare Reforms for the 21st Century, Oslo, 5–6 April.

———— and Raveaud, G. 2002. Responsibility and employment policies: A 'conventionalist' view, Annual conference of the European Social Policy Research Network on Social Values, Social Policies. Normative Foundations of Changing Social Policies in European Countries, Tilburg University, 29–31 August.

Goodin, R. E. 1988. Reasons for welfare. The political theory of the welfare state (Princeton, Princeton University Press).

Join-Lambert, M.-T. 1995. "Exclusion: pour une plus grande rigueur d'analyse", in Droit social, No. 3, mars, pp. 215–221.

Lodemel, I. And Trickey, H. (eds.) 2000. An offer you can't refuse. Workfare in international perspective (Bristol, The Policy Press).

Nussbaum, M. C. and Sen, A. (eds.) The quality of life (Oxford, Oxford University Press).

Percy-Smith, J. (ed.). 2000. Policy responses to social exclusion. Towards inclusion? (Buckingham, Open University Press).

Raveaud, G. 2001 "Dynamics of the welfare states regimes and employability (A study based on the national action plans for employment, 1998–2000)", in D. Pieters (ed.) Confidence and changes: Managing social protection in the new institution (The Hague, Kluwer Law International), pp. 5–26.

—— and Salais, R. 2001. "Fighting against social exclusion in a ⊓nstitut knowledge-based society: What principles of action?", in G. Mayes, J. Berghman and R. Salais (eds.) Social exclusion and European policy (Cheltenham, Edward Elgar), pp. 47–71.

Salais, R. 1998. "A la recherche du fondement conventionnel des institutions", in R. Salais, E. Chatel and D. Rivaud-Danset (eds.) Institutions et conventions. La réflexivité de l'action économique, Raisons Pratiques No. 9 (Paris, Ed. de l'EHESS).

——. 2002. "Work and welfare. Towards a capability-based approach", in J. Zeitlin and D. Trubek (eds.) Governing work and welfare in a new economy. European and American experiments (Oxford, Oxford University Press).

—— and Villeneuve, R. (eds.). 2004. Towards a politics of capabilities. The agenda for social Europe (Cambridge, Cambridge University Press). Forthcoming.

Schwartz. B. 1981. L'insertion sociale et professionnelle des jeunes. Rapport au Premier Ministre (Paris, La Documentation Française).

Sen, A. K. 1983. "Poor, relatively speaking", in Oxford Economic Papers, Vol. 35, pp. 153–169.

——. 1984. "Rights and capabilities", in Resources, Values and Development (Oxford, Blackwell), pp. 307–324.

——. 1985. Commodities and capabilities (Amsterdam, North-Holland).

——. 1988. "Freedom of choice: Concept and content", in European Economic Review, Vol. 32, pp. 269–294.

——. 1990. "Justice: Means versus freedom", in Philosophy and Public Affairs, Vol. 19(2), winter, pp. 111–121.

——. 1992. Inequality re-examined (Cambridge, Cambridge University Press).

——. 1999. Development as freedom (London, Alfred Knoft).

Storper, M. 1998. Conventions and the genesis of institutions (Paris, Association Recherche et Régulation).

_____ and Salais, R. 1997. Worlds of production (Cambridge, Mass. Harvard University Press).

White, M. 1990. "Information et chômage des jeunes", in Sociologie du Travail, No. 4/90, pp. 529–541.

MINIMUM GUARANTEED INCOME AND BASIC INCOME IN PORTUGAL

5

Alfredo Bruto da Costa [1]

1. The Portuguese minimum guaranteed income (MGI)

Policies against poverty and social exclusion in Portugal have been given a major push since the late 1980s by participation in the Third European Poverty Programme (commonly known as Poverty 3), launched by the European Community in 1989. [2] Projects included in the Programme had to satisfy the principles of multi-dimensionality, participation and partnership, which have provided the opportunity for a new approach to the problem of poverty and exclusion. Due to the limited size of the European programme, Portugal could contribute only four projects [3], out of about 100, which applied. These were designed according to the rules established by the European Commission and, therefore, followed the criteria mentioned above. In an important move, the Government decided to give national funding to all projects that had applied but

---

[1] Portuguese Catholic University, Lisbon.

[2] The Third European Poverty Programme brought together 41 projects: 29 "model actions" and 12 "innovative initiatives". Model actions were broad programmes that emphasized the multi-dimensional nature of poverty and of the action needed to combat it. The innovative initiatives focused on types of poverty that are sufficiently complex to demand specific action (e.g. homelessness). The aim of the Programme was not to eliminate poverty, but to "support innovation, promote an exchange of views on methods and policies to combat poverty, and to contribute, thereby, to a public debate on possible policies to be developed in the future" (*Animation et Recherche*, 1993, Foreword)

[3] Three were Model Actions: The Transformation of a Rural Environment, that covered the whole rural municipality of Almeida in the centre-east of Portugal; Mountain Villages bet in Development, comprising four villages in the municipality of Covilhã in the centre-east of Portugal; and Social and physical rehabilitation of the Historic Zone of Porto. There was one Innovative Initiative (Street Children in Lisbon).

did not gain European support. This group of projects constituted the national poverty programme.

The methodology adopted by the European Commission to monitor and evaluate the projects, and the programme as a whole, fostered considerable progress in understanding and tackling poverty. This approach was extended to the Portuguese national programme that, at the time, comprised more than 100 projects.

The Third European Poverty Programme ended in 1994, and the European Council of Ministers did not approve the subsequent programme, which had been prepared by the European Commission. The formal justification for this was the reinforcement of an interpretation of the principle of subsidiarity, according to which the fight against poverty and exclusion should be a responsibility of member States and not of the European Community as a whole. Admittedly, financial reasons might also have played a part in the decision, since new social and economic problems were arising in the wake of the reunification of Germany. Since 1994, the European Union has had no other specific poverty programme.[4] The Treaty of Amsterdam opened the way for Community competence in the social area, but it was only later, at the European Summit in Lisbon, that poverty and social exclusion regained the status of a European concern. The National Action Plans for Social Inclusion (NAPincl) launched in 2001 seems to be an attempt to restore poverty and exclusion to the European political agenda, albeit gradually.

In October 1995, a general election was held in Portugal. During the campaign, the Socialist Party announced that, if it won, it would establish a minimum guaranteed income scheme. The issue was the subject of debate between the parties, and aroused some suspicion from civil society. The main doubts were the risk of dependency, the possibility of fraud and the increase of public expenditure, in a context of financial constraints faced both by the State in general and the social security system in particular. At that time, the main concern about the existing social protection system was its sustainability. Some commentators foresaw a medium-term financial crisis, while others expected it later. The debate was focused on what should be done in the immediate future, and in the long run, to avoid collapse of the system.

---

[4] Note, however, that various other European programmes were launched, especially related to unemployment and to urban rehabilitation, which had strong, direct and indirect, links with poverty.

The Socialist Party won the most votes in the 1995 elections, and, although it did not gain an absolute majority in parliament, it formed the Government and about six months later launched the scheme.

In the meantime, the Government decided to study the problem of the sustainability of the social security system in a comprehensive way by setting up a pluralistic commission to prepare a White Paper on Social Security. The Commission approved, by majority, a final report, which assessed the situation and made proposals for changes. The four members who voted against the report were allowed to include their dissenting opinion in a single text that came to be known as the Report of the Minority.

The Minimum Guaranteed Income scheme was not a major issue in the proceedings of the White Paper commission. Nor did civil society pay much attention to it. Thus, there was no need to promote a debate about a measure that possibly raised more doubts than opposition. Indeed, dependency and fraud could be avoided or limited, and the financial burden was not significant. The Government therefore succeeded in launching the scheme without resistance. Furthermore, the low level of the guaranteed benefit and the adoption of an experimental phase reduced any potential opposition. Some months later, the scheme was almost unanimously considered a success. This was clear when, in debates on the achievements and failures of the Government, the opposition accused the Government of mentioning the Minimum Guaranteed Income scheme too often, as if it had no other success. Implicitly, therefore, the opposition recognised that the scheme could be considered as successful.

The basic features of the Minimum Guaranteed Income (MGI) (*Rendimento Mínimo Garantido*) are described below. Nevertheless, some of its positive aspects may be summarized here.

First, the scheme covers everyone above the age of 17 years who satisfies the means test. Second, it is defined as a right, and hence is not subject to discretionary decisions about entitlement or the amount of the benefit. Third, it is based on a multi-dimensional approach to poverty, hence the obligatory character of a "social insertion contract". The contract includes all the instruments that may help the beneficiary and family to achieve social and economic autonomy (occupational training, finding a job, job creation, sending children to school, etc.). Fourth, the scheme sets up a network of partners to promote social inclusion of beneficiaries (social labour market, involvement of NGOs, etc.). Fifth, the monitoring system includes institutions at national and local levels. Thus, the actual situation of candidates can be better assessed, changes better followed and fraud reduced.

1.1 Basic features

The MGI was established by Law No. 19-A/96, of June 29, 1996, and Decree-Law No. 196/97, of July 31, 1997.The scheme covers all persons and families in a situation of "serious economic want", which is understood as encompassing the following conditions:

- individual income lower than the social pension;[5]
- household income lower than the sum of the following values:
  - 100% of the value of the social pension per adult, up to two adults;
  - 70% of the value of the social pension per adult, from the third onwards;
  - 50% of the value of the social pension per child.

Other conditions of eligibility:

- age 18 years or above;[6]
- if below the age of 18, the person should be economically independent and in one of the following situations:
  - be emancipated by marriage;
  - have children exclusively dependent on him or her, or on his or her household;
  - be pregnant;
- legal residence in Portugal;
- acceptance of the obligations of a social insertion programme (agreed upon in the insertion contract, mentioned above), namely by active availability to work or to undertake occupational training or integration;
- be willing to apply for social security benefits to which he or she may be entitled, and exercise the right of appeal to recover possible credits or to apply for recognition of the right to alimony;
- provide the means of proof needed to verify the situation of economic want.

---

[5] Social pension is the non-contributory pension of the social security system, set at €138.60 per month from December 2001.

[6] The new Government following the election in March 2002 announced its intention of raising the minimum age of eligibility to 25 years (see below).

1.2 The benefits

The scheme has two components, a non-contributory monetary benefit and a social insertion programme.

The objective is to guarantee individuals and their families the means to meet minimum needs and foster progressive social and occupational insertion. Accordingly, the MGI guarantees the minimum means of subsistence to all those who lack resources and represents an instrument of social insertion. In return for financial benefit, the beneficiaries must accept a social contract aimed at enhancing their prospects of social and economic autonomy.

The amount of benefit is equal to the difference between the amount of the MGI that would correspond to the composition of the household (on the assumption of zero income) and the income actually earned by the household. Furthermore, when housing (or dwelling) expenditures exceed 25% of the household MGI, the benefit is increased according to household size.

The social insertion programme establishes the type of action, the responsible institutions, and the support provided to the beneficiaries and their obligations. The programme is established by agreement between the local monitoring commissions and the members of the household concerned.

In order to facilitate the social insertion component, some complementary measures were taken, such as:

- the establishment of a fund to support the creation of small and easily established self-employment activities aimed at meeting local needs and interests;

- special occupational training programmes for beneficiaries in long-term unemployment;

- a programme aimed at establishing Personal Employment Plans, tailored to the individual needs of each beneficiary and supported by personalised help. This programme includes the following active measures:

  - direct placement in the labour market;
  - creation of one's own job;
  - support to job creation in existing firms; and
  - the "insertion-employment" programme.

1.3 Institutions of management and control

Regional Social Security Centres (CRSS)

The application for MGI benefits may be submitted to the regional social security centre of the area of residence, or to the attendance offices defined by the local monitoring commissions (CLA), and should be presented with the required documents of proof.

The decision on the granting of monetary benefit is taken by the CRSS. The local monitoring commissions take the decisions about the insertion programmes.

Local Monitoring Commissions (CLA)

These commissions are based in the municipality or, when justified, the civil parish. The CLA includes the local representatives of public institutions in the domains of social security, employment, occupational training, education and health. Wherever necessary, the CLA may also include representatives of other relevant public institutions, of local authorities, local non-governmental organization (NGOs) and other non-profit organizations, namely trade unions and employers' associations. Each CLA is co-ordinated by the representative of the social security sector, unless its members unanimously elect another coordinator.

National Minimum Income Commission (CNRM)

The implementation of the MGI scheme is monitored by the National Minimum Income Commission, which is appointed by the Minister of Solidarity and Social Security. The CNRM includes representatives of education, health, qualification and employment, and solidarity and social security Ministries.[7] It also comprises representatives of local authorities, NGOs and trade union and employers' confederations. The functions of the commission focus mainly on monitoring, support, evaluation and proposals for improvement of the scheme's legal framework.

---

[7] The names of some of the ministries have since changed.

2.4 Financing

The scheme — including the financial benefit, insertion programmes and administrative costs — is totally financed by the Government budget through general taxation, as are the other non-contributory social security schemes.

2. How far has the Minimum Guaranteed Income (MGI) succeeded in combating poverty?

2.1 Overall assessment

According to a working document prepared for an evaluation of the MGI: "The implementation of the Minimum Guaranteed Income brought about innovative aspects in relation to the traditional social protection policies" (UPE/DIC, 2002, p.4). It highlighted the three main changes:

- the right to a minimum subsistence income for all persons without resources, irrespective of the reason underlying the want and of any contributions to the social security system;

- the responsibility to make an effort towards social insertion;

- the adoption of a model of partnership that widens the engagement and the collective responsibility of social actors in combating poverty and social exclusion.

Before analysing the implementation of the MGI, it should be stressed that the measure was designed to cover only the most severe forms of poverty and exclusion. Leaving aside the European, and worldwide, debate on the thresholds used to quantify poverty, it is estimated that the poverty rate in Portugal was about 20% at the launch of the MGI. However, the population covered by the scheme is less than 4%of the total population (IDS-CNRM, 2001), given the low level of the entitlement baseline. This means that the "target group" of the MGI did not exceed the poorest fifth of the poor. The scheme's effectiveness in combating poverty can only be assessed within these limitations. In other words, one should not expect more than the MGI scheme can offer or achieve.

The indicator that Eurostat calls the "poverty risk rate"[8] fell between 1997 and 1998 from 24% to 20%. At first sight, one might infer that this progress was partly due to the MGI, although there are more than 100 other local projects also aimed at combating poverty. Such an assumption would seem to be confirmed by the numbers of beneficiaries that left the scheme because they achieved a level of income above the entitlement baseline. However, given the low level of that baseline, moving out of the scheme does not necessarily mean overcoming poverty, although it implies a narrowing of the poverty gap. In some cases, it may have led to moving out of poverty, although there remain questions about the sustainability of such progress.

Using a different poverty line,[9] Rodrigues (2001, p.11) estimated that the threshold applied to data from the Household Budget Survey 1994/95 leads to poverty rates (individuals) of, respectively, 18.1% and 17.8% before and after transfers from the MGI scheme. It should also be noted that the value of the social pension (baseline for the MGI) represents only 34% of the poverty line used by Rodrigues. Furthermore, the data on income in the Household Budget Survey include non-monetary forms of income, which are not considered by the estimates adopted by the MGI scheme.

The impact of a programme on poverty cannot be measured purely in terms of the reduction of the poverty rate. The same study shows that, as a result of the income transfers via the MGI, the intensity of poverty fell by 14.5% and the severity by 29.5%. Thus, it may be concluded that the programme had a considerable role in reducing the hardship of families and individuals covered.

Moreover, the overall effect on poverty is larger than the effect due only to income transfers. Its ultimate objective consists in leading the beneficiaries to a sustainable situation of income self-sufficiency, in which they no longer need income transfers. We will see below the extent to which the scheme may have succeeded in achieving this.

---

[8] Threshold at 60% of the median equivalized income per person.

[9] Equivalent poverty line at 60% of the median disposable income.

2.2 Social and demographic characteristics of beneficiaries of the MGI [10]

The population entitled to the MGI is predominantly female (71%). It is mainly women who represent the households applying for the MGI in most of the country's regions. It seems, therefore, that women are more active in searching for support to enable them to meet the needs of the family. Women also make up the majority of the beneficiaries, though to a lesser degree (53.5%).[11]

The most frequent types of beneficiary are nuclear families with children (33%), female single-parent families (19%), extended families (16%), women living alone (14%), nuclear families without children (10%) and men living alone (8%). Persons living alone (men and women) account for 22% of the beneficiaries. This proportion reflects their vulnerability to poverty and exclusion.

About 61% of households that benefit from the MGI comprise between one and three individuals. About 33% have between four and six members, while those that comprise more than seven represent around 5%. These proportions confirm the figures on poverty in general, which show that poverty in Portugal is mainly caused by low incomes rather then by size of household.

The average number of children of beneficiaries (average age 14 years) is 2.2.

Data on the marital status of persons entitled to the scheme show that 44% are married, most of them living in nuclear families with children. Single persons, the divorced and widow(er)s represent, respectively, 24.3%, 12.4% and 11.5%.

As shown in table 5.1, 89% of those entitled to the MGI are in the economically active age group. More than half (54%) are aged 18–44 years. As stated earlier, youth below the age of 18 years are eligible only in exceptional circumstances (married, pregnant or with dependent children), and therefore their proportion among the entitled population is negligible. The low proportion of the elderly is explained by the fact that they are eligible for other types of

---

[10] Unless otherwise stated, the data used in this section draws on IDS-CNRM (2002).

[11] Persons *entitled* (or *recipients*) are those who apply for the benefit and receive it. *Beneficiaries* include the entitled and their respective households.

benefit (mainly the social pension). Understandably, the distribution of beneficiaries shows a higher proportion of younger cohorts.

Table 5.1   Entitled persons and beneficiaries, by age groups

Age group	Entitled (%)	Beneficiaries (%)
Under 18 years	—	35.2
18-24 years	7.1	10.5
25-44 years	46.6	27.4
45-54 years	17.7	9.5
55-64 years	17.9	9.4
Above 64 years	10.8	7.9
Total	100	100

Source: IDS-CNRM (2002)

The Government that took office in 2002 announced an increase of the minimum age for entitlement from 18 years to 25 years. The change is motivated not by financial reasons but in the words of the Minister of Labour and Social Solidarity, by "a matter of principle".[12] As may be seen in Table 5.1, the corresponding proportion of persons entitled to the MGI under the age of 25 years is only 7.1%.

Table 5.2 shows the health status of beneficiaries. The percentages cannot be added due to double counting. The largest group (21%) suffers from some chronic disease. Physical disability accounts for 8.4%, while drug addiction and alcoholism represent, together, 11% of beneficiaries. When all the so-called "psychiatric diseases" (drug addiction, alcoholism and mental illness) are added, the proportion is around 16%. In all, 40% of households had at least one member with health problems.

The state of health of the beneficiary population causes additional problems in combating poverty and exclusion. Frequently, such situations are long lasting and thus hamper progress.

Bearing in mind that Portugal is a country with long-term poverty that persists along the entire life cycle of the poor and is transmitted from one

---

[12] As the Minister explained in an interview, "The idea is to avoid, as much as possible, delay in the beginning of active life, due to subsidy dependency". The Minister added that in special cases (e.g. persons with serious social situations, such as single mothers, young couples with children, or youth presently undergoing occupational training or qualification activities, etc.) the MGI would continue to be granted to persons below 25 years of age (*Público*, April 27, 2002).

generation to another. It is more resistant than recent or short-term poverty because of the rigidity of its causes and the resilience of its consequences. The large majority (about 86%) of the recipients of the MGI were acquainted with poverty since childhood. Around 67% faced more or less permanent poverty and only 19% occasional poverty. Only 11% of the cases suffered recent poverty (IDS-CNRM, 2002).

Table 5.2   Health problems of beneficiaries

Health situation	(%)
Chronic disease	21.3
Physical disability	8.4
Drug addiction	6.6
Alcoholism	4.6
Mental disease	4.4
Bed-ridden	2.6
Households with at least 1 member with health problems	40.0

Source IDS-CNRM (2002)

Long-term poverty demands well-designed, multi-dimensional and sustained action, which inevitably reduces its immediate effectiveness. Any feasibility study on the introduction of a basic income scheme in Portugal must take this aspect into account. Poverty, defined as a situation of deprivation due to lack of resources, can only be reduced or eradicated by increasing the resources of the poor. However, this necessary condition is not sufficient when one deals with long-term poverty. Since poverty and social exclusion are multidimensional, a policy to combat those problems can only be efficient if it is also multi-dimensional. Action is needed to overcome the obstacles generated by the consequences of poverty (low aspirations, lack of initiative, low self-esteem, lack of self-confidence, specific habits and behaviour, fatalism, cultural bottlenecks, etc.).

One structural cause of poverty in Portugal is the low educational level of the poor, as reflected in the educational profile of MGI recipients [13] (table 5.3). About one fifth are illiterate, more than one-third do not have any qualification, and more than three-quarters have, at most, primary school education (four years of schooling). Some 74% of illiterate recipients are above 45 years of age, and

[13] The use of the educational profile of MGI *recipients* avoids children (who are counted among the *beneficiaries*)

60% of recipients with the basic second cycle (six years of schooling) were below 35 years of age.

Table 5.3 educational levels of recipients of MGI

Level of education	Recipients	
	(%)	Cumulative (%)
Illiterate	19.2	19.2
Read and write	16.1	35.3
Basic 1st cycle (4 years of schooling)	42.2	77.5
Basic 2nd cycle (6 years of schooling	15.2	92.7
Basic 3rd cycle (9 years of schooling)	4.9	97.6
Secondary education	1.6	99.2
Medium or Higher education	0.7	100.0
Total	100.0	

Source: IDS-CNRM (2002)

The figures above show that the solution of the poverty problem in Portugal is not only a question of income transfers. The educational profile has an impact on the labour market situation of individuals, reflected later in the old age pension. Indeed, 21% of recipients belonged to the occupational group of craftsmanship, construction and mining; another 21% were non-qualified workers in services and commerce; 11% worked in agriculture and fishing; and 11% worked in services or were salespersons. Housewives represented more than 29% of recipients.

It is useful to analyse the work status of recipients (see table 5.4). More than 30% are unemployed, of whom 66% are women, 55% are long-term unemployed and 34% have never worked. The recently unemployed represent 10% of unemployed recipients.

It should be stressed that more than one-quarter of the recipients has a job. The very fact that persons in this situation are entitled to the MGI reflects the precariousness of their jobs, both in terms of the level of wages as well as their nature. In fact, 45% of these workers did not have any type of contract (half had seasonal work), 27% had a fixed-term contract and only 24% had a permanent contract. The great majority (73%) worked on a full-time basis and more than half (52%) were in their respective jobs for more than two years.

The above analysis seems to justify the conclusion that the vast majority of the recipients and beneficiaries of the MGI were effectively in need of the scheme. The alleged cases of fraud should not be denied *a priori*, but its scale does not seem to be significant. It is possible that the knowledge of individual cases of fraud has led to a hasty generalization. Nevertheless, closer control of the implementation of the scheme is necessary, not only to identify and eliminate, fraudulent cases but also to rehabilitate its public image.

Table 5.4   MGI Recipients' work status

Work status	Recipients (%)	
Unemployed	30.3	
Domestic tasks	26.1	*
Has a job	25.6	
Pensioner	9.5	
Disabled	6.2	
Other	2.3	
Total	100.0	

Note.   (*) 97% are women.
Source: IDS-CNRM (2002).

2.3 The impact of the MGI in combating poverty

In December 2001, there were 124'456 recipients and 354'258 beneficiaries of the MGI scheme. About 65% of recipients had to leave the scheme because their incomes rose beyond the eligibility baseline. To some extent, this is a global indicator of the effectiveness of the scheme. Approximately 19% of the cases were cancelled, because the recipient failed either to sign or to fulfil the social insertion agreement (Comissão Nacional do Rendimento Mínimo, 2001).

The impact of the MGI scheme may be perceived in four different dimensions:

• improvement of the living conditions of the recipients, mainly due to the regularity of their income;

• changes in lifestyle (previously characterized by "adaptation" to poverty and passivity);

• action towards professional and social insertion (e.g. closer involvement of the parents in the education of children, improvement of educational levels, improvements in the house, etc.); and

• critical attitude towards the relation between needs and the direction of the proposed insertion process.

Perception of the recipients

In a survey on the perception of the recipients about the positive outcomes of the scheme, almost all of them mentioned the "regularity of incomes" as a major improvement in their lifestyles. The other aspects mentioned were the enhancement of self-esteem (32%), access to medical care (14%), better housing conditions (9%) and better job insertion (5%).

A closer analysis of the positive effects of the MGI on the basic needs of beneficiaries leads to the conclusion that the majority succeeded in meeting their respective housing needs, including accommodation, basic facilities (piped water, electricity, sewage, etc.) and equipment (fridge, television, etc.). Nevertheless, 28% of recipients still mention the housing problem as one that must be solved to achieve better living conditions. It should also be underscored that the share of housing expenditure in total expenditure is very high, just next to food, and that housing problem is one of the most serious social problems of Portuguese society, especially young couples.

Another domain in which progress has been registered concerns those who were in arrears and succeeded in normalising their debts, as well as the penalties due to the non-payment of certain bills (house rent, water, electricity, gas, etc.).

The MGI also fostered educational progress, both among children at the basic (compulsory) school age as well as among adults. 17% of the households covered by the scheme, at least one member succeeded in returning to school.

Occupational training seems to be one of the areas with the lowest level of achievement, and one that must be improved in the future. Indeed, the majority of recipients declared that they did not follow any such training. About 68% of the latter mentioned that no training was suggested, and about a quarter was not interested in the skills provided by the courses available.

The job situation of recipients capable of work (i.e. not prevented from working due to health) improved: the employment rate rose from 22% to 40% between application for the MGI and the date of evaluation. The younger age group shows the highest rate of change, though the group of 35–44 years has the highest employment rate. There were also differences between changes registered in urban centres and rural areas (table 5.5).

Some 65% of recipients who could work (between 16 and 55 years of age and without any health problem that prevented work) succeeded in getting a job. They thus achieved economic autonomy and were no longer in need of the benefit. However, the jobs available to recipients are frequently precarious, so the need for stable employment persists in some cases.

Table 5.5   MGI recipients employed

Age groups	Recipients employed (%)	
	At application	At evaluation
18–24 years	12	28
25–34 years	21	40
35–44 years	26	44
45–54 years	23	39
Urban centres	26	38
Rural areas	22	42

Source   DS-CNRM (2002)

The existence of the MGI scheme seems to have facilitated the take-up and use of other social protection benefits by recipients. This is an indirect effect of the scheme that should also be considered, because 64% of recipients had never previously received any support from the social protection system.

Finally, the scheme fostered some improvements in the area of health. The recipients in the survey declared that they now have access to occasional economic support for health care as well as guidance and access to health care. Among families with deeper health problems, those with problems of drug addiction present the greatest improvements as a result of actions focused on de-intoxication, insertion in the labour market and recovery of the family's social relations.

The majority (65%) of recipients consider that their life has improved under the MGI scheme. For 32% there have been no meaningful changes, and 4% consider that life is worse.

The survey distinguishes between recipients that tend to stay in the scheme for a longer time and those who succeeded in achieving autonomy within a relatively short time (table 5.6).

Age is clearly a relevant factor: younger recipients manage to move out from the scheme more easily than older ones. The educational achievements of the former seem slightly higher, although occupational qualifications do not affect the duration of dependence. Health also affects the insertion process. Indeed, around 50% of those who stayed longer under the scheme suffered from health problems that hampered their capacity to work. The health situation is also reflected in the causes of unemployment: about 50% of those with health problems became unemployed for health reasons or never worked due to ill health. Couples with children and single parent families showed higher social mobility than couples without children and persons living alone. Presumably, this is associated with age. The type of unemployment is particularly meaningful: among the unemployed with most difficulty in moving out of the scheme, 39% had never worked and 53% were long-term unemployed.

Table 5.6   Dependence and autonomy

Characteristics	Persist in the scheme	Achieved autonomy
Age group	Higher	Relatively young (63% below 44 years)
Education:		
never went to school	17%	—
has no qualification	about 50%	28%
primary school (4 years)	39%	44%
Qualifications	Low (are not a handicap when compared to those who achieved autonomy)	Low
Health	About 50% have ill health that affects ability to work	Lower proportion of persons with health problems
Reasons for unemployment:		
due to ill health	29.4%	21%
due to age	17.8%	—
need to care for family	14.7%	22%
lack of jobs	—	29.3%
never worked	20% (due to ill health)	—
Type of family	nuclear families without children; persons living alone	Nuclear families with children; single parent families. (Note: 76% are women)
Duration of unemployment	52.6% long-term 39% never worked 8.5% recent unemployment	17%
Expectations	More than half considers that they will need another similar type of support when entitlement to MGI ends.	In general, optimistic. Tend to perceive the scheme as transitory.

Source: IDS-CNRM (2002)

The perception of the staff

A survey covering the technical staff engaged in the implementation of the scheme helps to complement the above analysis (Table 5.7). In general, the evaluation by the staff is not entirely favourable. Fewer than 60% consider that the MGI scheme reduces but does not solve the problems of the poor. This percentage seems compatible with the fact that 65% of recipients left the scheme due to changes in their respective incomes. But the MGI's eligibility baseline (about 20% of the median disposable income) is below any acceptable poverty line, so moving out from the scheme does not necessarily mean moving out of poverty. This is a big shortcoming. On the other hand, it is not clear whether the apparent self-sufficiency acquired by recipients leaving the scheme.

Table 5.7   Positive and negative effects of the MGI scheme, according to staff

Effects	Frequency (%)
Positive effects:	
Higher visibility of the problems of poverty and social exclusion	61.0
Attenuation but not solution of the problems of the poor	57.0
Involvement of new actors in social protection policies	55.0
Need for changes in other social policies	28.0
Fosters innovation in public services	20.0
Negative effects:	
Generates dissatisfaction among those not covered	32.0
Increases dependency on support from State	31.0

Source. CNRM/IDS (2001)

The increased visibility of poverty and social exclusion is a positive, though indirect, effect of the MGI scheme, which benefits not only the present group of beneficiaries but also other current and future poverty programmes. Involvement of new actors in social protection policies, the need for changes in other social policies, and the fostering of innovation in public services — also point to institutional and policy.

Dissatisfaction among those not covered by the scheme concerns those who do not fulfil the eligibility criteria. Considering the notoriously low level of the income eligibility baseline, it is not surprising that poor persons, who have incomes higher than the threshold and still live in poverty, are dissatisfied with the scheme.

Finally, criticism about dependency on support from the State, together with fraud among beneficiaries, was one of the *leitmotifs* of the centre-right and right parties in the 2002 electoral campaign. Objectively, there seems to be reason to improve the control and monitoring systems, both in granting the benefit as well as in following the situation of the beneficiaries. The campaign against those irregularities has claimed the name of justice. However, it seems biased by an individualistic political philosophy, a "conservative" notion of social rights, a superficial understanding of poverty and exclusion and insensitivity towards deeper and more damaging forms of injustice that stain Portuguese society, such as tax evasion.

As shown in table 5.8, the perception of staff is that the population in general has a sharply negative opinion of MGI beneficiaries. Only 5% of staff believe that the population considers beneficiaries deprived and entitled to the MGI, whereas 57% believe they are dependent on the MGI, and 38% believe MGI recipients are privileged and without work habits. This must be taken into account when trying to assess the possibilities of introducing any basic income programme in Portugal.

As regards staff assessment of the effects of MGI on beneficiaries (table 5.8), a relatively high proportion say that the scheme provides better access to information and services. Around 40% mentioned the improvement in domestic organization brought about by a regular income, and the development of personal and school skills. Other positive effects are the improvement of occupational integration, development of social and occupational skills, and improvement of health and of housing conditions. One aspect that emerges from this perception is the multi-dimensional character of the MGI scheme. It is clear that the income transfer is only one of the components of the scheme, included in a set of measures that try to face the multi-dimensional nature of poverty and exclusion.

Staff perceptions also revealed factors hampering implementation of the MGI: weak participation of the partners, accumulation of functions by the staff, and insufficient resources.

Partnership is a relatively new concept and practice in Portugal. It was launched in the late 1980s, fostered by the Third European Poverty Programme 1989–94. Although the principle may be accepted, progress is still needed in practice. The other two bottlenecks concern resources (including human resources).

Almost half of the staff in the survey (41%) mentioned that they knew persons who satisfied the eligibility criteria but did not apply for the benefit. However, there is no information on the relative size of non-take-up.

Table 5.8   General public perception of MGI beneficiaries, according to staff

Perception	% of staff
Dependent on the system	57.0
Privileged and without work habits	38.0
Deprived and entitled to the MGI	5.0

Source CNRM/IDS (2001)

The survey also includes proposals by staff to improve implementation of the MGI. The most frequent recommendations was the need to foster new types of action aimed at social insertion, and to adapt solutions more closely to the needs of beneficiaries. Two other recommendations refer to more efficient use of the resources available, and closer monitoring of beneficiaries (CNRM-IDS, 2001).

Table 5.9 also shows some negative effects: dependency, dissatisfaction with the social insertion processes and indebtedness.

Table 5.9   Positive and negative effects of the MGI scheme on beneficiaries, according to staff

Effects	%
Positive effects:	
Better access to information/services	62 0
Improvement of domestic organization, due to regular income	42.0
Development of personal skills	42.0
Development of school skills	39.0
Better occupational integration	34.0
Development of social skills	30.0
Improvement of health	29.0
Development of occupational skills	26.0
Improvement of housing conditions	21.0
Easier access to housing	3.0
Negative effects:	
Higher dependency on State support	35.0
Dissatisfaction with regard to social insertion processes	22.0
Indebtedness	8.0

Source. CNRM/IDS (2001).

3. Reflections on introduction of a basic income in Portugal

The introduction of a basic income scheme in any society requires a number of pre-conditions, contextual as well as practical, that have to be fulfilled to make the measure feasible. It is, therefore, useful to summarize some aspects of poverty and the MGI scheme, and add other relevant features of the Portuguese social security system and society.

The idea of a basic income is, in many respects (cultural, financial, economic, etc.), too far removed from the thinking of policymakers and public opinion to be feasible in the short-term. Furthermore, given the tendency towards retrenchment of the welfare state all over Europe, and the fact that the reduction of public deficits has been selected as the primary concern of socio-economic policy, any innovation in this field will need sound and convincing arguments to be acceptable. In this sense, it is important to obtain greater awareness of its capability to combat and/or prevent poverty and social exclusion, as a substitute to the minimum guaranteed income.

The aspects that particularly relevant in this context are:

• poverty as a multi-dimensional problem;

• specific features of poverty in Portuguese society;

• the debate about the MGI, social security and the role of the State;

• financial and "developmental" problems of the social security system;

• influence of neo-liberal thinking in Portugal and in Europe, competitiveness and globalization.

3.1 Poverty as a multi-dimensional problem

Poverty is defined as "deprivation due to lack of resources".[14] This definition has the virtue of highlighting the two related dimensions of poverty

---

[14] See, e.g. Townsend (1979).

— deprivation and lack of resources. Deprivation is a state of want, of unmet basic needs. Usually, it is a state of multiple deprivations. Since it is related to basic needs (food, shelter, health, etc.) it demands emergency measures.

However, action against deprivation is not sufficient to solve the problem of poverty. Indeed, the poor person only moves out of poverty when, having solved the problem of deprivation, s/he also succeeds in achieving self-sufficiency with regard to resources. Self-sufficiency means that the person earns his or her income from one of the sources considered as "normal" in a given society. In European societies, "normal" relates only to flows from the primary distribution source in the form of labour or capital income. Transfers are not considered as a "normal" source of income, except in the case of old age, invalidity or survivor pensions. Any other type of transfer usually has a transitory nature (e.g. unemployment benefit, sickness benefit, etc.). Apart from these cases, redistribution is not considered a "normal" source of income, especially when the benefit is non-contributory.

The MGI scheme stems from this basic understanding. The monetary benefit is meant to help overcome deprivation and meet other expenses until the beneficiary achieves self-sufficiency (e.g. gets a job).

3.2 Some features of poverty in Portuguese society

In order to combat poverty in Portugal, one must distinguish recent poverty from long-term poverty. When dealing with recent poverty, action normally includes emergency measures to end deprivation, and measures to tackle the individual and structural causes of lack of resources.

By long-term poverty, we mean persistent poverty throughout the life cycle, often passed on through generations. Recall that a large majority (about 86%) of MGI recipients has been acquainted with poverty since childhood, and that around 67% faced chronic poverty. Recipients suffered recent poverty only in 11% of the cases, and 19% poverty occasionally.

Long-term poverty is a more complex problem than recent poverty. Besides facing deprivation and lack of resources, the long-term poor suffer handicaps that are a consequence of poverty and affect important aspects of the personality such as self-esteem, self-confidence, aspirations, initiative, social identity, values, behaviour, etc. Whatever the income support available, if these factors are not integrated into a multi-dimensional action programme, the outcome may be very different from expected. From the point of view of combating poverty, therefore, the mere introduction of a basic income would not solve or reduce the phenomenon. One must envisage complementary forms of interdisciplinary action. Should, as seems unavoidable, the transfer assume the form of a right, independent from any obligation, it is difficult to imagine how such complementary action may be made acceptable to the poor and implemented.

3.3 The debate about the MGI, social security and the role of the State

Even before the previous socialist Government launched the MGI in 1996, there was a wave of criticism centred on the possibilities of fraud, prompted by fears about how to verify information provided by applicants about their current situation and potential changes. This objection continued during the implementation period, backed by examples of fraud and "misuse" of the benefit. The underlying idea was that the beneficiaries were accountable to society with regard to how they spent the benefit. The March 2002 electoral campaign exacerbated the debate, with heavy criticism from the centre and right parties, which are both in the coalition currently in power. With regard to the Centre PSD, which received most votes, it was not clear whether they advocated revision or abolition of the MGI. For the right-wing CDS/PP, the MGI was a prize for laziness. As mentioned above, the new Minister of Labour and Solidarity promptly announced that the MGI will not be abolished but will undergo changes, including an increase in the minimum age for eligibility from 18 years to 25 years.

One principle underlying the attitude of society towards non-contributory benefits for the poor is that they should not be unconditional. Since such benefits are financed by general taxation, the beneficiary is deemed accountable to society with regard to a certain number of rules and behavioural norms, even though, as is the case for the MGI, there are no legal obligations. Only in the case of labour or capital incomes is the ethical right to them considered to be unconditional. In spite of the progress in Portugal in understanding poverty during the last 15 years, the impact of scientific findings on politicians and public opinion has been limited. It is difficult to shift the blame from the poor themselves to the social and economic system.

This cultural background explains the lack of proportionality between the true extent of fraud in the MGI scheme and the sanctions suggested (namely its abolition). It should be noted that, in 1999, total expenditure on the MGI amounted to 1.4% of total expenditure on social protection. Furthermore, as mentioned earlier, the baseline for eligibility corresponds to one-third of the threshold amount considered by Eurostat as the "risk of poverty".

In such a cultural context, it is apparent that society does not recognize the ethical, moral or other grounds for a basic income that would cover every citizen equally and unconditionally. One should not expect society to accept that the poor are net receivers, and most other social strata net payers.

One of the changes in the social security system announced by the present Government is the introduction of a wage ceiling above which workers will be given the possibility of opting for public social security or private insurance. This opening to the private sector of the field of protection against risks mirrors trends in the health services. In both cases, the policy seems based not only on pragmatic reasons of efficiency and access to a wider range of services (private and public), but also on a political philosophy that supports the reduction of the role of the State and enhancement of the private sector. Such a trend seems incompatible with notions of solidarity and social rights that provide the ethical and political grounds for a basic income.

3.4 Financial and "developmental" problems of the social security system

One of the main topics under debate during the last ten years about the "crisis" and the future of social security in Portugal has been its financial sustainability. The discussion is limited by the fact that social security continues to be conceived basically as a system of solidarity among workers. Except for the non-contributory sub-system, which is financed by general taxation, the system is entirely supported by contributions from labour income. Given the major changes in the labour market, it is essential to widen the solidarity base to the entire society. This would entail financing the system by contributions on all forms of income, including capital. However, the need for major changes in the political philosophy underlying the understanding of social security, and problems related to competitiveness, capital mobility and the tax system, hamper the feasibility of such changes. Furthermore, it is indispensable that the problem be analysed within a wider economic area (in the case of Portugal, the European Union). If trends towards the reduction of the relative weight of human work in the economy persist, then the widening of the contributory base may be the only way to ensure financial sustainability of the social security system. Until such a change takes place, the system will be threatened by insolvency.

The share of social protection expenditure in GDP in Portugal has been rising steadily since the second half of the 1990s and is close to the EU average (Figure 5.1). Other major reforms related to sources of income and changes in the labour market may thus be necessary.

Figure 5.1   Social protection expenditures as percentage of GDP

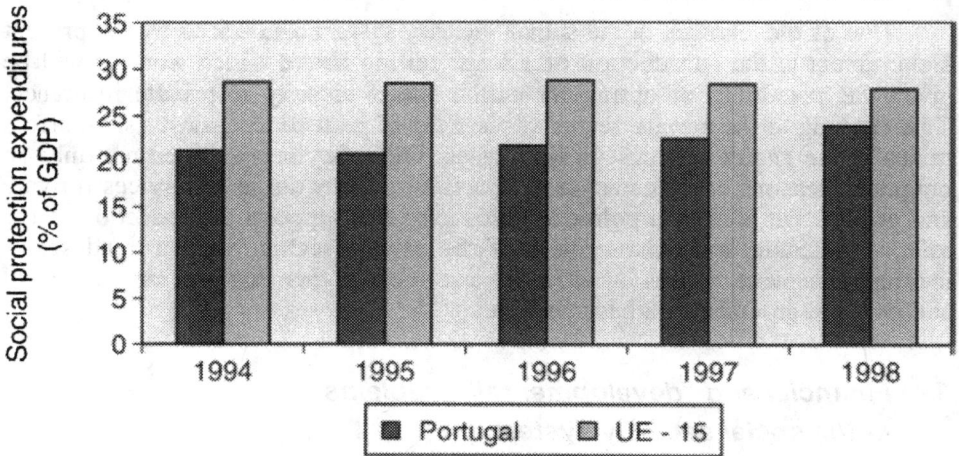

Source National Institute of Statistics

First, the democratization of access to capital. The distribution of capital from larger sections of society in order to reduce economic instability among households that depend on labour incomes could be an important factor of income stability. Second, the labour market is undergoing so many fundamental changes that there is a need for reflection on their consequences and durability. It is true that different scenarios have been presented about the future of work. The most optimistic believe that the changes are transitory and that the apparent excess of labour in some societies will be absorbed by an increase in new activities. This would be similar to what happened in the industrial revolution: manpower made redundant in agriculture was ultimately absorbed by industry. However, less optimistic authors raise the possibility of other scenarios that assume deeper, more lasting changes in the labour market. It is useful to analyse some of these.

In its 1993 Green Paper, *European Social Policy — Options for the Union*, the European Commission called attention to what it considered a major trend in European society: the progressive increase of the proportion of self-employed in total employment. It is not clear whether this tendency is already affecting Portuguese society. Figure 5.2 shows the long-term trend in the share of employees in total employment. The share increased steadily from the 1950s until the early 1980s, followed by a fall until 1987, after which it rose. Finally a sharper decrease of the share occurred during the first half of the 1990s. Though it is too early to say whether this last trend will persist, it is advisable not to ignore the forecast of the Green Paper.

Figure 5.2   Employees as percentage of total employment

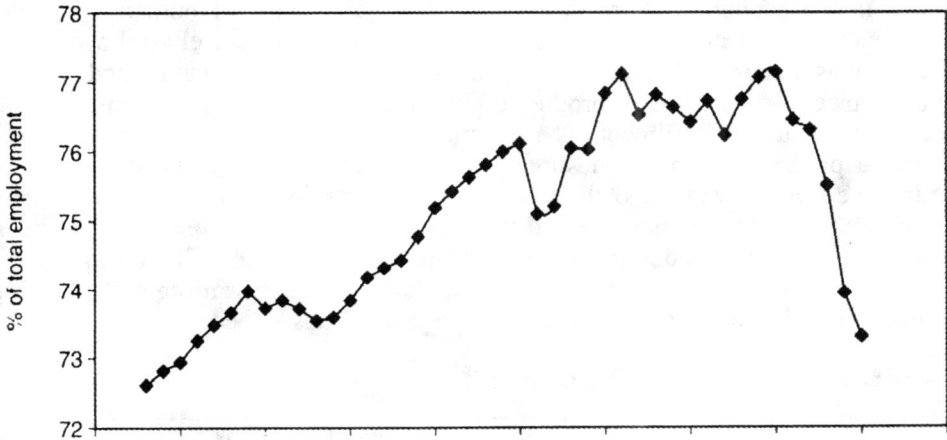

Source. Bank of Portugal.

An increase in self-employment may mean an increase in job instability. Indeed, it is difficult to know to what extent self-employment is a free choice or a disguised form of unemployment or underemployment. There is no information about the degree of stability of recent forms of self-employment. Estimates that refer to 1995 show that 33% of the heads of poor households were self-employed.[15].

Second, low-paid jobs are another relevant problem of the Portuguese labour market. According to the above-mentioned estimates, 18% of the heads of poor households were employees. Yet, a study published by Eurostat (2000a) shows that "poverty risk index" of a working household (i.e. with at least one member working for an income) is 82 (where index 100 corresponds to the average poverty rate).

A third aspect concerns job stability as reflected by the type of contract. A high percentage (84%) of job contracts in Portugal are permanent. However, the proportion of fixed-term contracts has risen steadily during the second half of the 1990s (Table 5.10).

[15] Data obtained from the project "Family Structures, Labour Market Participation and the Dynamics of Social Exclusion", within the Targeted Socio-Economic Research programme.

Finally, the changes that have occurred in the labour market suggest that attention be given to future developments in the role and importance of human work in the economy. Work is a fundamental dimension of human existence. However, one may question whether it should be so closely related to its function as a source of income. Irrespective of changes in the nature and relative importance of the factors of production, work will always constitute an essential element of human fulfilment. The question is the extent to which work should mean a paid job, primarily designed to serve economic objectives. Bearing in mind the type of work and the working conditions of most workers, one may also ask how many workers regard their jobs a means of personal fulfilment. In this context, the introduction of a basic income could be a liberating factor. People would then have some freedom to choose more rewarding and fulfilling work rather than accept a job purely as a means of subsistence.

Table 5.10   Employees by type of contract

	1992	1993	1994	1995	1996	1997	2001
Permanent contract	87.9	89.1	89.4	88.9	87.5	85.8	83.9
Fixed term contract	12.1	10.9	10.6	11.1	12.5	14.2	16.1
Total	100.0	100.0	100.0	100.0	100.0	100.0	100.0

Source: National Institute of Statistics

This suggests a clearer distinction between work and employment. However, this has to be worked out from the perspective of political philosophy, and its implementation demands changes in society and the economy, both cultural and organizational, which can only be envisaged in the long term.

Moreover, the political profile of the present Government does not seem compatible with reforms aimed at developing and expanding social protection. Specifically on social security, the Government's programme emphasizes the principle of social co-responsibility of the State, firms and families in sharing risks; a better balance is the solidarity between the economically active and the inactive, on one hand, and obligatory and voluntary savings, on the other; positive discrimination in favour of the most vulnerable groups; incentive to work and save; the indivisibility of social risks; and co-ordination of the reform of social security with those in the areas of taxes, labour and health.

The main general guidelines on social security that may imply changes in the political philosophy and are of interest to our study seem to be the following:

• an overall reform of the social security system, aiming at a fair balance between social rights and duties, between public and contractual actions, and between social equity, economic efficiency and freedom of choice, generating the conditions for inter-generational sustainability of the public social security system;

• development of the different pillars (public, entrepreneurial, family and individual) of social security. This implies complementarity with:

› the introduction of a contributory ceiling, with the corresponding establishment of stable mechanisms of public, private and social capitalization;
› more consistent tax benefits in order to encourage complementary pensions (public and private);
› reinforcement of the supervision of pension funds and establishment of mechanisms to guarantee complementary pensions and ensure their portability;

• diversification of the sources of finance for the social security system, through reductions in the contributions based on labour incomes aimed at greater economic and fiscal neutrality;

• coordination between social security, tax and the labour reforms, to foster savings, eliminate distortions in the economy and enhance labour market flexibility;

• revision of the minimum guaranteed income, in order to implement a new philosophy based on the principles of:

› effective control in the granting and monitoring;
› social, professional and community insertion;
› coordination with active employment and training policies;
› positive discrimination in favour of more serious social and family situations; and
› promotion of activity and prevention of social vices;

• implementation of the principle of subsidiarity, encouragement and protection of local, voluntary, private and mutual social protection initiatives.

As in many other European countries, with the exception of the political parties at the extremes of the ideological spectrum, differences rarely take the form of clear alternatives. Insofar as the programme indicates the preferences of the Government, one might infer that the basic tendency goes towards reducing the role of the state in social protection and fostering the role of firms, families and individuals. This trend goes in tandem with preferential treatment of the most vulnerable. Such a perspective does not seem favourable to the introduction of a universal basic income.

Public statements have focused on the minimum guaranteed income. This was the first policy to be revised in a draft law sent by Government to parliament. The scheme was renamed "Social Insertion Income", presumably to underscore the relevance of its insertion dimension. Some of the main changes in relation to the MGI, described and analysed earlier, are the following:[16]

- the minimum eligibility age for new applicants will be 25 years, excepting pregnant women and those with dependent children. This age limit does not apply to existing beneficiaries;

- the elderly, handicapped and couples or single parents with a child below one year of age will benefit from positive discrimination;

- the introduction of social vouchers, up to 50% of the monetary benefit, must be used to pay services provided by NGOs;

- revision of the model of partnership, in order to accelerate the social and occupational integration of the recipients;

- better control and monitoring.

3.5 Influence of neo-liberal thinking in Portugal and Europe

The neo-liberal context of the European and world economy runs counter to major changes towards broadening and deepening social solidarity. Calls for deregulation are still strong in Portugal and find support in the trend of European common policies on competitiveness. The levers that existed at national policy level (exchange rates, interest rates, public deficit, etc.) have vanished, especially within the Euro-zone to which Portugal belongs.

The target of attaining a zero-deficit State budget in 2004 is a commitment that binds the Euro-zone, and small countries such as Portugal cannot afford to differ. This is the central objective of the present Government, which makes any policy that might translate into a higher deficit unthinkable. From the revenue side, any increase in taxes has a negative impact on competitiveness and

---

[16] The final version of the law will only be known after it is approved by parliament and promulgated by the President of the Republic.

investment, and encourages capital mobility towards countries with higher rewards. Thus, restrictive policies and the "postponement" of social progress seem to be the sole prescriptions.

4. Conclusions

The Minimum Guaranteed Income scheme introduced in Portugal in 1996 can only be partially evaluated after just a few years. The philosophy underlying the scheme consists in recognising the right to a monetary benefit, linked to the right and obligation of a social insertion contract for all those with incomes below the established baseline.

Access to the MGI scheme is limited only to extreme forms of poverty due to the low level of the eligibility baseline. At about 20% of the median disposable income, the baseline represents one-third of the European "risk of poverty" threshold. Accordingly, the population covered by the MGI does not exceed the poorest fifth of the poor in Portugal.

About 40% of households had at least one member with health problems, and 21% of beneficiaries suffered from chronic disease. Low educational levels and low qualifications also hinder progress. Furthermore, about 86% of the recipients had experienced poverty since childhood, and 67% faced permanent (or near permanent) poverty. Thus, long-term persistent poverty is a dominant feature of recipients.

Long-term poverty demands well-designed, multi-dimensional and sustained action, which reduces the short-term effectiveness of the action.

The overall assessment of the scheme leads to a positive conclusion about its implementation. About 65% of recipients moved out of the scheme because their incomes increased beyond the eligibility baseline, and there were improvements in the living conditions of beneficiaries. However, given the low baseline, moving out of the scheme does not necessarily mean overcoming poverty and, even in the latter case, the data do not contain information on the sustainability of the progress achieved.

The evaluation suggests that management of the MGI should be improved in various ways, namely, in closer control of the information provided by the candidates, better monitoring of their situation, more coherent involvement of the partners, and more effective social insertion. Furthermore, the improvement of the image of the scheme, in a cultural context that is still largely insensitive to the social rights of the poor and the societal causes of poverty, is essential.

This attitude seems incompatible with the introduction of a basic income scheme in the near future. Public opinion has to be convinced, *inter alia*, of the ethical grounds for permanent incomes that stem from transfers, beyond old age, invalidity and survivor pensions. Labour and capital incomes are the only types of income considered as "normal" for citizens in the economically active age group.

The financial limitations of the social security system — still based mainly on solidarity within the labour market (except for the non-contributory benefits), compounded by the constraints of European Monetary Union, provide a pragmatic justification to avoid measures that imply higher public expenditure. The neo-liberal philosophy and economic policies that dominate the European scene and the unregulated global economy are obstacles to the promotion of solidarity. Furthermore, the high degree of interdependence between countries and economies hampers the adoption of major policies at the national level.[17]

Basic income constitutes a potentially powerful instrument against poverty and the growing economic uncertainties that affect Portuguese society. However, any progress in this field would require a medium-term or long-term strategy aimed at promoting a public debate on the cultural, political and practical aspects of the scheme.

References

Animation et Recherche. 1993. *Poverty 3 — Directory of the Projects* (Lille).

Comissão Nacional do Rendimento Mínimo-Instituto para o Desenvolvimento Social (CNRM-IDS). 2001. *Estudo de Avaliação de impactes do RMG — Inquérito por questionário aos técnicos que fazem acompanhamento directo às famílias RMG* (Lisboa, not yet published).

Comissão Nacional do Rendimento Mínimo. 2001. *Execução da Medida e Caracterização dos Beneficiários, Dezembro 2001* (Lisboa, CNRM).

European Commission (EC). 1993. *Green Paper: European Social Policy — Options for the Union* (Brussels).

Eurostat. 2000a. *European social statistics — Income, poverty and social exclusion* (Luxembourg).

_____. 2000b. *Low-wage employees in EU countries, Statistics in Focus, Theme 3 — 11/2000* (Luxembourg).

---

[17] For example, the introduction of a basic income could lead to lower relative wages and, thus, be qualified as a form of "social dumping".

Instituto para o Desenvolvimento Social-Comissão Nacional do Rendimento Mínimo-(IDS-CNRM). 2002. *Estudo de Avaliação de Impactes — Inquérito aos Beneficiários RMG, Dezembro 2000-Março 2001, Versão de Março de 2002* (Lisboa, not yet published).

Rodrigues, C. F. 2001. *Anti-poverty effectiveness and efficiency of the Guaranteed Income Programme in Portugal*, Working Paper (Lisboa, Instituto Superior de Economia e Gestão).

Townsend, P. 1979. *Poverty in the United Kingdom* (Harmondsworth, Penguin).

UPE-DIC. 2002. *Resultados do Inquérito por Questionário aos Técnicos que fazem acompanhamento directo às famílias RMG, Doc. De Trabalho, Janeiro 2002* (Lisboa, not yet published).

TESTING THE *REDDITO MINIMO D'INSERIMENTO* IN THE ITALIAN WELFARE SYSTEM

6

David Benassi and Enzo Mingione [1]

1. The Italian welfare system and its continuing transformation

After a long period of standstill, the Italian welfare system is finally undergoing a process of change marked by the introduction in 1998 of the *Reddito minimo di inserimento* (RMI — Minimum Insertion Income) as an experiment, and the passage of the general policy law on social assistance at the end of 2000. While it is still not possible to assess fully the impact of this new legislation, we can discuss the changes to the Italian welfare system. In the first part of our analysis, we focus on the significance of these changes for the specific characteristics of the Italian welfare system. Then we piece together the fragmented picture of the fight against poverty in Italy, against which the innovatory measures have to be viewed. Lastly, we discuss the RMI on the basis of results of an evaluation of the first two-year experiment. [2]

The current innovations are instances of a more general transformation of welfare systems, motivated by the need to respond to changes in the structure of social protection deficits (Esping-Andersen, 1999; Ferrera, 1998). In the countries of the European Union, the adaptation of welfare has become intertwined both with restraints on the management of public finances imposed through the treaty of Maastricht prior to the introduction of the single currency, and with the increasingly urgent calls for the standardization and coordination of

---

[1] University of Milano-Bicocca, Italy.

[2] The evaluation was carried out by an independent body drawn from three research institutes (the *Istituto per la ricerca sociale* (IRS) from Milan, the Fondazione Zancan from Padua and the CLES from Rome).

social policies. In Italy, a strategy of putting its financial house in order has had important consequences for the organization and funding of welfare – this at a particularly difficult time due to profound social, demographic and occupational changes and to the chronic crisis in the Mezzogiorno. The link between restoring order to public accounts and the necessity to reorganize welfare was explicitly referred to in Italy in the work of the Onofri Commission. This was a team of experts nominated by the Prodi Government in 1997 to propose cuts in social spending that would enable public finances to comply with the Maastricht parameters.[3] The Commission did not confine itself to suggesting cuts in welfare expenditure (the only area in which substantial savings could realistically be made, which were implemented by the Dini Pensions reform)[4] but also pointed to structural weaknesses and explicitly recommended the introduction of a national scheme for the *Minimo Vitale* (minimum subsistence income).[5] This recommendation was accepted by the Government, which applied it on an experimental basis in 1998–2000 and then extended and broadened it to include other municipalities in which the experiment is continuing.

The introduction of the experiment with RMI, in contrast with France 10 years before, took place amid a low-profile political and public debate: the struggle against poverty and social exclusion has never been a political priority in Italy. When the Onofri Commission, following the 1992 recommendations of the European Union, suggested the introduction of a national income scheme the political coalition supporting the Prodi Government was divided. Part of the Left and the moderate parties of the Centre were in favour, whereas *Rifondazione Comunista* and other sections of the Left were against. Meanwhile, the Treasury opposed any immediate substantial expenditure on social policies. The main trade union federation, the *Confederazione Generale Italiana del Lavoro* (CGIL), was also opposed, favouring giving priority to the reform of labour policies. However, the Prodi Government finally decided to go ahead with a tiny experiment: the cost of the investment was extremely small (about €246 million) and thus did not pose an alternative to other innovations in social policies; there

---

[3] This is shown in the Commission's name: Commission for the Analysis of Macro-economic Compatibility in Social Spending.

[4] The so-called Dini Pensions reform was carried out in 1995 to overcome the structural imbalances of Italian expenditure on pensions. The main changes were increased age for retirement, introduction of a new method of calculating pensions, and support for voluntary retirement schemes.

[5] For more information on the debate surrounding the Onofri Commission see, among others, Mingione (1998).

has been no serious public debate (even now few people even know there is a RMI experiment); the scheme was presented in parliament as necessary to meet the European recommendation, as a measure to be included in the Reform of Social Assistance [6]. The more radical, but easier to implement, alternative of a Basic Income scheme was never seriously considered (though at the time of the Amato Government's approval of the second two-year RMI experiment at the end of 2000, some ministers and economic consultants raised the issue).[7] The main reason is that the high level of tax evasion and informal activities would create problems and distortions. But it is also true that a basic income would not help to improve the supply of social services, which is weak and underdeveloped. Moreover, it would reinforce the family-based and informal nature of the Italian welfare system.[8]

1.1 The main features of the Italian welfare system

Italy is today one of the few remaining countries in Europe that does not have a universal [9] programme for combating social exclusion and, as we see below, the transformation of its welfare system starts from a historically fragmented and divided base (Kazepov, 1996; Negri and Saraceno, 1996). Protection against the risk of poverty is characterized by the subsidiarity of public welfare to the protection provided by family and kin; by a structural deficit in professional skills and coordination in the public sector and by the chaotic and uneven participation of old and new private operators in local social provision.

---

[6] However, as the Reform Law on Social Assistance was still far from final approval, the architecture of the RMI experimental scheme, as discussed later, has features inconsistent with the Law. There is no mention of the role of the regions or of the territorial division into zones that characterizes the Master Plan for Social Intervention and Services.

[7] The debate has been, as usual, out of public view, and never even reached parliament, which had just approved the Social Assistance Reform Law with provisions for extending the RMI scheme nationwide.

[8] This helps to explain why social policy innovators, on the Left, in the Catholic Centre and even on the Right, favour more complex policies that involve upgrading of third-sector institutions in providing support services.

[9] By "universal", we mean programmes accorded to everyone, even though they may be subject to means-testing, rather than be totally unconditional.

As in much of Europe, the construction of a regime of welfare capitalism in Italy rested a great deal on the family, which had to adapt its own solidaristic operations to the needs arising from the division of labour with State and market. Furthermore, this took place in a country still strongly characterized by self-employment and family-run businesses, a pronounced North-South economic dualism, and the State's long-standing difficulty in managing social dynamics.[10] Unlike in other European countries, the "defamiliazation" of care and protection systems has occurred only in part. Instead, the modernization of lifestyles and family organization has pivoted around the woman's role of care-(professionalization of motherhood, innovations in everyday lifestyles and so on), and on kinship networks and formal and informal support institutions, from community and neighbourhood networks to charitable organizations, Italian welfare, public and private, has developed as a complement to this situation (Mingione, 2002).

There are various features of public welfare that reflect the central role of the family: a universal health service and a part-time school system; weakness of policies that impinge on family responsibilities;[11] a preponderance of income-supplementing programmes; the shrinking of services for individuals and families; local and category-based fragmentation of programmes; tolerance of informal relations etc. (Negri and Saraceno, 1996; Ferrera, 1998; Benassi, 2000). Given this picture, it is not by chance that in 1998, 64% of spending on social protection in Italy was on the elderly (old-age pensions and survivors' annuities) as against a European average of 45.7 % (Table 6.1).

The principle on which the Italian welfare state rests is that the nuclear family and, in a subordinate role, the kinship network take prime responsibility for protecting the individual against socio-economic risks. The State is assigned residual tasks mainly in the form of monetary handouts to family heads. The combination of social rights and family responsibilities takes shape in the expectation of recourse to the extended family before public welfare. As a consequence, public welfare has remained fragile and fragmented and has not

---

[10] These are structural aspects of Italian society that are too wide-ranging and complex to describe here. As regards administrative distortions, a single example will suffice to show how the instruments of welfare can be used to obtain political consent: the use for political patronage of some income-support measures as in the case of certain kinds of invalidity pensions given to non-invalids living in less developed areas (Ascoli, 1984).

[11] For instance, pre-nursery and nursery schools are not very widespread; national policies for the young are weak; there is no support for the non-breadwinner unemployed; and there are no national norms for care services for the elderly and other vulnerable groups.

fully "secularised" the private charity establishment, which has brought about large-scale welfare reorganization.[12]

Table 6.1 **Social expenditure by function, selected EU countries, 1998**
(percentage distribution of total expenditure)

	EU 15	Germany	Spain	France	Italy	Netherlands	Sweden	United Kingdom
Sickness/health care	26.8	28.1	29.2	29.2	23.4	28.5	23.4	25.2
Disability	8.3	7 9	8.1	4.9	6.2	11.8	11.6	11.6
Old age	40.6	40 4	41 9	37.9	53.3	35.8	37.2	39.9
Survivors	5.1	1.9	4.3	6.1	10.7	5.3	2.3	3.9
Family/children	8.3	10 1	2 1	9.8	3.6	4.5	10.8	8.6
Unemployment	7 2	8.7	13.5	7.6	2.7	7.3	9.3	3.6
Housing	2.1	0.7	0.3	3.2	0.0	1.6	2.5	6 2
Social exclusion	1.6	2.2	0.7	1.4	0.1	5.2	3.0	0 8

Source Eurostat (2000)

Faced with the socio-economic changes of the last few decades (Benassi and Mingione, 2001), the Italian welfare system has been subjected to increasing tensions. In particular, the following tendencies need emphasis:

- an over-burdening of responsibilities on the family as the population ages, and the prolonged cohabitation of parents and adult offspring — one cause of the big fall in the birth rate (Barbagli and Saraceno, 2000);

- a weakening of the supportive capacity of kinship and community networks, because of the decline in births and in solidarity because of increased individualism (Micheli, 1997, 2001; Andreotti, 2002);

- an over-extension of economic protection for the elderly (Benassi, 2000) — the only group for whom family support is not taken for granted. This is offset by the poor provision of services for this group, especially in some regions, in the face of population ageing;

- a cultural resistance by families, transmitted to the political class and political-administrative systems, to the outsourcing of care. This in turn leads to fewer job opportunities for women and young people, combined with the development of domestic services supplied by immigrants;

---

[12] See the classic works of Flora (1986-7), and also Alber (1986) and Ritter (1996).

- a widening of the differences between North and South, a dominant Italian characteristic, which has had an impact on social exclusion, social policies and the RMI.

Welfare protection has been stunted in the face of these changes, essentially unable to make up the deficit in protection caused by the weakening of the market-family combination typical of southern European welfare, and diversified at local level (Fargion, 1997). Secularization and professionalization have been weak and uneven. This means that the majority of local agencies lack the strategic capacities for organization and coordination that are indispensable to formulate interventions based on the mobilization of public and private institutions and on participation of citizens-users — the network of home assistance for the elderly or activation of insertion procedures envisaged by the minimum income scheme.

The divergence between conditions in the North and those in the South is the biggest hurdle to social policy reforms in Italy, including making the RMI generally applicable. We must, therefore, dwell briefly on the resulting problems: the concentration of people in difficulty in the South; the enduring difference in types of social vulnerability in the two halves of the country; and the growing unpopularity of social policies openly benefiting the South.

The fracture between North and South is long-standing.[13] Here we confine ourselves to mentioning the widening gap that emerged after the end of the economic miracle, the wave of emigration from the South and investments aimed at closing the North-South divide. The post-war economic miracle was also the result of a mutually beneficial relationship between North and South. This period coincided with the development of welfare institutions. The South supplied the North with a reserve army of workers, with new consumers freed from rural poverty but unable to compete locally in industrial production, and with conservative electors guaranteeing political stability. In exchange, the South benefited from investments to consolidate the domestic market, from agrarian reform and modernization of infrastructure, from involvement, though

---

[13] The history of the Southern question consists of two phases. From the formation of the Italian State in 1860 to the Second World War, the South was an agricultural society founded on large landed estates with many landless peasants and limited exposure to market production and consumption. In spite of the break-up of the agrarian regime and the region's integration into an economic area subject to market pressures, the second phase did not see the South develop a social model based on market competition. For the first phase, see the authoritative interpretation of Gramsci (1966), Villari (1966) and Caizzi (1970); for the second phase, see Castronovo (1975) and Rossi Doria (1956).

of a discriminatory kind, in the modernization of welfare, and from a substantial dose of State, and to a lesser extent private, investment in industry.[14]

The impact on the South of the post-Fordist transition during the 1980s and 1990s was negative. Jobs crisis affected the majority of young people entering working age. There were structural difficulties in innovation for small enterprises, which were traditional and not very productive, while in the rest of the country they were the engines of the "second industrial divide" (Piore and Sabel, 1984). Lack of investment caused deterioration in economic infrastructure and welfare services when elsewhere they acted as a driving force in the creation of new opportunities in terms of human and social capital.[15] As a result, the southern regions, where 36% of the Italian population live, accounted for over 65% of unemployment, of people below the poverty line, of informal and precarious occupations, and of school drop-outs.[16]

In the period before the State's finances were put in order to comply with the Maastricht parameters, the growth in public spending and the State deficit were used more to buy political consent (not only in favour of the South) than to promote adaptation to the social transformations. Management of the labour market, youth training, education and "insertion" into work, assistance for the poor, modernization of transport and other infrastructures, and policies for housing and the family all remained inadequate. The vicious circle that concentrates the critical problems in the South has made the situation even worse. In other words, the crisis in Italian welfare is concentrated in the South where it is more difficult to find answers to the jobs crisis, the chronic poverty in the big cities, the deficit in public services and so on. Today, Italian welfare reform means paying new attention to the social problems of southern regions, which conflicts with political dominance exercised by "northern" interests. In the sphere of policies to combat social exclusion, a further complication arises from the fact that it is the traditionally local character of Italian assistance that

[14] Concentrated in the chemical, iron and steel sectors, State investment did not foster an adequate increase in employment, though it helped to boost consumption. Graziani and Pugliese, 1979; Del Monte and Giannola, 1978; Trigilia, 1992 and 1996.

[15] As Trigilia notes, "there are serious signs that economic and social infrastructures have grown less than the increase in income and that, therefore, the quality of the environment in the South today is worse than in other places with a smaller per capita income and less private consumption." (1996, p. 167).

[16] For instance, 66.5% of poor people and 64.7% of the unemployed were in the Southern regions.

constitutes a resource for innovation, which is more effective in central and northern regions.

1.2 Innovations in assistance: Localism, professionalization and third-sector agencies

Our reading of Italian welfare rests on two assumptions. The first is that alongside the major national components of social insurance and health, which historically has absorbed a large part of social protection spending social assistance, is re-emerging. An aspect of the social assistance system is that, unlike health and social insurance, access does not depend on a contractual rationale in the narrow sense. It is in this area that the idea of citizenship, at the core of the modern relationship between the individual and the State is founded, finds its broadest application in as much as the right to receive services to maintain a minimum standard of living is justified by the fact of belonging to a national community (Benassi, 2002). At a time when the struggle against social exclusion assumes increasing importance, this connection between citizenship and assistance runs counter to the rationale of privatising public services. Public responsibility in guaranteeing an equal right to a minimum living standard entails keeping control over such programmes.[17] One of the consequences of the important role of social assistance within the welfare framework is that it forces us to grasp the relationship between the production of the conditions of need and ways of meeting the requirements of social protection.

This is connected to the second assumption in our approach. Marginalization takes on features and implications only at a local level, where social policies are adapted to the resources available, the institutional structure and the mobilization of different participants.[18] Variability in local social conditions, especially as regards forms of marginalization, does not end with divergence from a national general model. In reality, we are dealing with

---

[17] The argument concerns the area of assistance we are focusing on, i.e. policies for combating social exclusion and, to a lesser extent, the other two crucial sectors of care for pre-school children and the non-self-sufficient elderly. In these cases, the guarantee of quality and equity in the service under public control is an important factor in relation to the development of intervention by the private social sector and the market (see, e.g. Gori, 2001).

[18] This is developed in Mingione and Oberti (forthcoming), Benassi (2002), Benassi and Mingione (2001). See also the interesting remarks in Bagnasco and Negri (1994) and results from Saraceno (2002).

complex historical processes of social, political and economic structuring through which a character is imparted to the local features of social assistance (for instance, in the selection of the most "deserving" or in the division of tasks between the public and third sectors) and the characteristics of those lacking social protection. Local factors are decisive in the implementation of assistance, independent of the national welfare regime and public policy, be it a question of universal versus free market policies or local autonomy versus a centralized national system.

This dichotomy between national policy and local implementation of social assistance is central to the present reform of welfare in Italy. The key role accorded to the public guarantee of a minimum living standard as a citizenship right necessitates a strong nationwide system of control, which underpins the philosophy of the law on social assistance. At the same time, however, varying local need-generating mechanisms and implementation models[19] require wide margins of operational autonomy for the municipalities. At this point, difficulties arise that cannot be dealt with by appealing to "subsidiarity" in its various forms. We cannot here go into the detail, but it is worth mentioning the powers of the regions, crucial in the Italian institutional framework.

The national institutional mechanism to ensure minimum standards for services and the control exercised over local agencies were complicated by constitutional reform in 2001, giving exclusive power over welfare policies to the regions. This reform was introduced after the RMI experiment and the social assistance reform. Moreover, enhancing the role of the regions in drawing up the operational and financial framework for welfare policies, constitutional devolution may trigger tensions between regions and municipalities. Take, for example, the potential dispute between regions that decide to give priority to social policies based on care vouchers and municipalities that prefer instead to boost direct personal services (e.g. home assistance).

Within this controversial picture, the RMI experiment is important in allowing us to grasp the local variability of a welfare programme that aims to guarantee last-resort universal intervention for individuals and families excluded from other forms of social protection.[20] The RMI is managed at local level in

[19] For these it is impossible to envisage the standardized regulation found in social security and health.

[20] Interpretations of Italian welfare have long emphasized the inequity in the national system of social protection, stemming from the fact that operational responsibility has been delegated

favour of poor people with different characteristics and, at least as far as "insertion" contracts are concerned, brings into play varying social and institutional networks and competences.[21] But on the question of the local diversity of people at risk and the local approaches to policies against social exclusion, it is important to mention more general parameters, inspired by evaluations made by the commission set up to examine social exclusion and by national and comparative research into social vulnerability and interventions against poverty.

Social exclusion — or new forms of poverty — affects population groups in different ways. Broadly, we can identify four main vulnerable groups:

- socially isolated, low-skilled individuals who do not manage (or unable, as is the case of the elderly) to return to stable employment and/or rebuild social networks (the extreme case being the homeless);
- immigrants and minorities who face difficulties gaining access to stable jobs (and adequate incomes) as well as social discrimination;
- one-parent families unable to combine sufficient access to work (and income) with looking after their offspring;
- (relatively) large families for which a single precarious income is not enough to maintain a suitable standard of living.

In Italy, the second and third groups are less important than elsewhere in Europe, where the share of immigrants and minorities is traditionally higher and divorce and children born out of wedlock are more frequent. Nonetheless, these groups are on the increase, especially in the big cities of the Centre and North. The socially isolated group is also more widespread in the Centre and North. These regions have more single old people (especially women) or elderly couples with pensions too low to maintain an adequate standard of living; however, this group is declining thanks to increases in the minimum pension and the spread of home assistance services. In contrast, the proportion of younger isolated individuals is rising, though their characteristics vary according to

without a national framework for minimum rights of assistance. The intention was for the RMI to be the first step towards a national standard, with all the difficulties and doubts mentioned below.

[21] It is perhaps no accident that in the framework of the RMI experiment little space is given to the intermediary powers of regions between the State and municipalities. The Italian programme is directly inspired by the original French scheme, notoriously highly centralized. It would be possible to adjust the institutional framework and, taking the constitutional reform into account, enhance the role of the regions along the lines of the Spanish model.

features of local labour markets. An example is the difference between Milan and Turin (Saraceno, 2002; Andreotti and Mingione, 2001). In Milan, unemployment is low and people at risk of social exclusion are affected by accumulation of problems leading to "unemployability". In Turin, unemployment has remained slightly higher and is more complex in composition, thus fostering a build-up of needs in which the main difficulty is finding employment.

The fourth group — large families supported by an income too low and intermittent to guarantee an acceptable living standard — accounts for most of the population below the poverty line in Italy, though these are not always affected by social exclusion. They are concentrated in the southern regions, fed by the chronic crisis in employment — combined result of high levels of joblessness, precarious and informal occupations and a low employment rate. They have widely varying characteristics and needs, but tend to live in badly run-down quarters of the big cities, where environmental factors aggravate conditions of hardship.

The spread of new types of social marginalization demonstrate the inadequacy of the traditional instruments of intervention, which seem unable to solve the problem of social exclusion. Italy has increasingly unacceptable — and politically indefensible — imbalances between citizens enjoying a high degree of protection, unlikely to slide into a precarious condition, and those with inadequate social rights, more exposed to social exclusion. This is encouraging an innovative approach to policies to supplement inadequate income, combat social exclusion and ease social reinsertion, in which the recipient of interventions is increasingly viewed as an active subject and actor in his/her own reinsertion path.

In this climate of institutional innovation, there are three key questions: the professionalization of an intervention that attaches more value to giving users responsibility and to social reinsertion practices, and thus cannot be confined to a bureaucratic assessment of the means and the provision of monetary support; the mobilization of a mix of old and new institutions in the third sector; and the organization, control and coordination of historically inefficient public intervention. In Italy, local areas have answered these questions in very different and unequal ways. In some cases local councils with a long tradition of intervention are at the fore in adapting the assistance sector to the new requirements, while others are unable to go beyond a traditional incapacity to deal with the demand for social protection As seen above, the more macroscopic differences have to do with the division between North and South, but significant differences are beginning to be recorded within these macro-regions, for example, between Milan and Turin: both with regard to income-support programmes — untouched by the RMI experiment that did not cover big cities in the North (Saraceno, 2002; Mingione and Oberti, forthcoming) — and to initiatives to help the homeless (Mugnano, 2002). Turin has shown greater capacity for coordination and public intervention, especially through active labour policies. In Milan, the autonomy and initiative taking of the private social sector is still strong.

2.   A picture of anti-poverty policies in Italy

To understand the impact of the RMI and the role it could play in the Italian welfare system, we need to look at existing anti-poverty income support provisions. We will dwell on a series of national measures even though welfare interventions to support income and social services for the poor (such as night shelters for the homeless, provision of hot meals or rent subsidies) are the task of the municipalities.[22] We will not go into the details of municipal welfare here, mainly because its variability makes it impossible to identify any common standard. This is a reason for introducing the RMI to replace the jungle of local measures that leaves many of the poor in the hands of municipalities that lack the financial and professional resources for effective assistance. The wide variation in local interventions is the result of various factors. First, prior to the welfare reform law (L.328/2000), which will take years before it becomes fully operative, the absence of regional or national standards left the municipalities free to formulate welfare programmes with their own rules and intervention and service thresholds. This was done independently, or in cooperation with (and sometimes duplicating) private assistance. See tables 6.2a and 6.2b for synoptic data on the minimum programmes in the RMI municipalities before the experiment.

Another factor giving rise to inequality and diversity in intervention is the mechanism for autonomous funding that has penalised municipalities with scarce economic resources, especially at times of economic crisis, when the need to intervene in favour of the poor is even stronger. Lastly, and this is important because it affects the capacity to implement the RMI, almost all the small municipalities and many of the larger, especially in the South, have not managed to develop the professional capabilities of social workers, information

---

[22] Public responsibility at municipal level became established in the 19th century through the Municipal Welfare Agencies, which also had the task of breaking the Roman Catholic hold over charity. After various difficulties and changes with, as always, wide local variation, the agencies came under the competence of the municipal offices for social services in the 1980s.

technology services, health, family and psychology consultants, etc., required for a modern welfare service.

Moving to national anti-poverty measures, two factors broaden analysis for two main reasons:

- these are implicit policies in that they are inserted into the fragmented social protection panorama without forming a systematic, integrated approach to poverty intervention (Negri and Saraceno, 1996);

- these are, in most cases, indirect policies in that they are not explicitly or exclusively designed to fight poverty or, at least, reach people or groups not necessarily in economic difficulty.

These aspects make it difficult to reconstruct the domain of anti-poverty policies because it is unclear whether a given policy belongs to a given domain and because it must be taken into account that not all beneficiaries of a given instrument are necessarily in poverty or at risk of falling into it.

In order to find a precise criterion to identify the services that cut poverty, let us consider means-tested instruments designed to improve the economic condition of the low-income population. As will be seen, these are fragmented and unsystematic, and in many respects unjust and ineffective. For this reason, the RMI represents a true innovation in the social protection system and fills a gap that has been poorly defended at the national level.

Table 6.2a   Social assistance prior to the RMI experiment

Macro-region	Municipality	Number of households	Average amount per year €
NORTH	Nichelino	29	1 264.3
	Limbiate	24	667.1
	Cologno Monzese	125	1 241.4
	Rovigo	120	1 200.8
	Genova Voltri/Pra	507	1 002.3
	Massa	186	833.0
	Civita Castellana	65	341.7
	Corchiano	n. a.	n. a.
	Monterosi	n. a.	n. a.
CENTRE	Onano	n. a.	n. a.
	Gallese	n. a.	n. a.
	Fabrica di Roma	n. a.	n. a.
	Canepina	n. a.	n. a.
	Pontecorvo	n. a.	n. a.
	Alatri	259	n. a.
	Caserta	194	143.8
	Orta di Atella	n. a.	n. a.
	Napoli	292	245.8
	L'Aquila	180	926.8
	Isernia	n. a.	n. a.
	Foggia	n. a.	n. a.
	Andria	n. a.	n. a.
	Bernalda	n. a.	n. a.
	Grassano	n. a.	n. a.
	Isola Capo Rizzuto	n. a.	n. a.
	Cutro	n. a.	n. a.
SOUTH	San Giovanni in Fiore	n. a	n. a.
	Reggio Calabria	n. a.	n. a.
	Nardodipace	n. a.	n. a.
	Enna	n. a.	n. a.
	Barrafranca	256	103.3
	Leonforte	46	696.5
	Catenanuova	n. a.	n. a.
	Agira	n. a.	n. a.
	Centuripe	35	1 032.9
	Catania VII, IX, X	3 600	1 147.7
	Sassari	1 407	378.0
	S. Nicolò d'Arcidano	n. a.	n. a.
	Oristano	63	564.1
	Total	7 388	736.8

Note: n. a. = not available
Source: CIES (2001)

Table 6.2b   Italian and RMI municipalities and population

	No.	%
Italian Municipalities	8 101	100.0
RMI municipalities	39	0.5
Residents in Italy	57 844 017	100.0
Residents in RMI municipalities	2 361 782	4.1

Source: CIES (2001) and Istat

2.1 Benefits for those at risk of impoverishment

Whether direct or indirect, explicit or implicit, anti-poverty policies act as regulatory factors in several areas of society. Essentially, there are areas of social life where (not only monetary) resources are produced and distributed, to which some people have insufficient access. In following the principles of the welfare state, policies of social protection or amelioration intervene, or should intervene, in these areas to restore a balance or compensate people affected by deprivation. Given the difficulties previously mentioned, our analysis includes benefits designed for direct intervention in favour of poor individuals and families, as well as those that alleviate the economic hardship of vulnerable people at risk of impoverishment.

Benefits can be grouped into three categories: direct income-support policies, labour market policies and policies in favour of the family.[23] The Minimum Insertion Income (RMI) cuts across all three.

Direct income-support policies

These are measures aim to guarantee an adequate income to particularly socially disadvantaged groups, the elderly and disabled, who are unable to secure an income due to old age or invalidity, and have no right to a pension or

---

[23] Housing policy — (public housing and rent support) —should also be included. Public housing involves mixed local —national policies. Two measures on rent support deserve attention: the creation in 1999 of the National Fund for Access to Rented Accommodation and, also in 1999, tax relief for holders of rent contracts. There are not yet aggregate national data on these measures.

insurance benefit. Here we are dealing with social assistance or mixed benefits.[24]

The social allowance paid to the over-65s (replacing the social pension for the elderly from 1996) is the main benefit for topping-up inadequate incomes. The other social assistance measure consists of civil invalidity payments to the disabled who do not meet the conditions for obtaining invalidity pensions. These payments comprise a monthly welfare benefit, disability pension and escort allowance; the first two components are replaced by the social allowance at the age of 65.

The minimum pension, disability pension[25] and ordinary invalidity allowance, are social insurance benefits that require beneficiaries to have paid contributions. The minimum pension covers the largest group (4,405,476 in 2000).

Labour market policies

This encompasses services connected with the individual as a worker (in or out of employment). Unlike direct income-support measures, these services cannot be viewed as "pure" instruments for combating poverty since they are not linked to beneficiaries' incomes. Nonetheless, given the lack of general income-support policies, many regard these instruments as a solution to their scarce economic resources. They safeguard against risks from lack of work, in some cases by acting as a stopgap in emergencies, in others, by encouraging entry or re-entry into the labour market.

Unemployment benefit (both ordinary and with reduced conditionalities),[26] labour mobility lists,[27] socially useful jobs and "jobs in the public interest"

---

[24] By mixed we mean services where access depends on a contributory right to some form of pension, they are given on a social assistance basis.

[25] There are two disability pensions: one paid out by INPS (National Institute of Social Insurance) on an insurance basis, the other by the Ministry of the Interior on a social assistance basis.

[26] We have not taken into account three other unemployment allowances (ordinary and special for agricultural and special for building workers) as these are for workers in sectors with particular characteristics or specific problems.

[27] We have not included the *Cassa Integrazione Guadagni* (Unemployment Benefits Fund or, more exactly, Wage Support Fund) because it cannot be seen as an instrument against poverty, even though it often enables recipients to avoid sliding into hardship. Workers benefiting from the Fund keep their jobs and so are employed to all intents and purposes, unlike workers placed on the

(being phased out) belong to the area of labour policies with poverty-reducing effects.

Policies in favour of the family

Family benefits and allowances for the nuclear family are services of the social insurance kind but also have social assistance characteristics since they are redistributive and mostly benefit needy families (large, with disabled members, single parent).

Strictly of a social assistance kind, by contrast, are benefits to nuclear families with three or more children, given according to family composition and certain income requirements. The same parameters are applied to maternity benefit (for women who do not receive a maternity allowance for working women). The latter was introduced as a citizenship right, namely maternity, but is now subject to means-testing in order to contain costs.

Minimum insertion income

In view of its particular and innovative nature within the Italian welfare state, the RMI cannot be placed in any of the above social policy areas. Together with the central role of services for reinsertion of the individual, its universal welfare character makes it the only instrument for combating poverty and social exclusion on a national scale in Italy.

2.2 *Main characteristics of the benefits*

The lack of a systematic approach in the welfare state's system of anti-poverty instruments goes with the lack of a unified approach to socio-economic hardship. This is reflected in the use of multiple criteria to identify potential beneficiaries and calculate the size of handouts. The non-coherent development of the Italian welfare system has caused unevenness in the regulation of services, which translates into a high degree of inequality in citizenship rights and an institutional division between "insiders" and "outsiders" hazy and shifting.

labour mobility lists in the phase subsequent to the Fund when reinsertion in his/her job becomes more uncertain.

Access requirements

Qualification for anti-poverty benefits envisaged by the national welfare system is dependent on having specific individual or family characteristics, though nearly all measures require compliance with income thresholds.[28]

The parameter that distinguishes the different kinds of service is whether they are based on insurance or social assistance principles, which determines the range of potential beneficiaries. The measures are not rigidly of an insurance kind; none is based solely on paid contributions. Rather, various measures presuppose a minimum number of years of insurance payments – that is, an "insurance biography" that is sufficiently long to enjoy a right that is also social assistance in nature.

This area covers the minimum pension payment, disability pension, assistance benefit, ordinary invalidity benefit, unemployment and mobility benefits, and family and nuclear family allowances. The minimum pension payment envisages compliance with the requisites of age and number of contribution years (15); in addition, there is a right to welfare if the old-age pension calculated is less than a pre-set minimum (€4,961 per year in 2001).

The National Institute for Social Protection (INPS)[29] disability and invalidity benefits require at least five years of contributions, including at least three of the last five years. The disability pension is given to those who are definitively unable to do any kind of work, and the amount is calculated by adding to the existing periods of contributions the period up to pension age (calculated on the average wage received in the last five years). The ordinary invalidity benefit is given to those with a residual capacity to work of less than one-third; it is calculated according to contributions paid. Where the amount is very low, it can be raised to a sum equal to the social allowance or minimum pension.

Ordinary unemployment benefit is paid to workers made redundant [30] with at least two years of insurance contributions against involuntary redundancy, including at least one year in the two years before termination of employment. It

---

[28] Exception is made for unemployment benefits, mobility lists and socially useful work.

[29] The INPS administers the majority of private sector pensions and social assistance benefits.

[30] Before 1 January 1999, workers who left their jobs voluntarily could also apply for this benefit; the same goes for ordinary unemployment benefit with reduced conditionality.

amounts to 30% of the wages received in the preceding months, independent of personal or family income, and is paid for a period of six months. Ordinary unemployment benefit with reduced conditionalities differs in that an applicant without the required 52 weeks of contributions over the last two years can still file in a request if he has worked for at least 78 days in the preceding year. The benefit paid is based on the number of days worked in the preceding year. The mobility benefit has a similar rationale to unemployment benefit, but last longer (from 12 to 48 months) and is based on the worker's age and locality of his workplace (North, Centre or South). To qualify, the worker must have been employed by his company for at least 12 months and have worked there for at least six months.

Employees, pensioners who are ex-employees, and workers drawing on the Wage Support Fund, mobility benefit or doing socially useful work are entitled to benefits for nuclear families. The amount due is calculated according to the number of family members and their characteristics. From 1 January 1999, those enrolled in the separate fund for the self-employed [31] can also obtain benefit for the nuclear family, although the access criteria are more demanding than for employees. Family allowances, on the other hand, are awarded to tenant farmers, sharecroppers and pensioners covered by special funds for the self-employed. They have to meet income limits and receive a fixed sum of €10.2 per month for each beneficiary.

Benefits intended for the entire population with given individual or family requisites, regardless of occupation or insurance contributions, belong to the strictly social assistance category. This comprises old-age benefits, socially useful jobs, civil invalidity payments, maternity benefit and benefit for large families. Old-age benefits are given to the over-65s with incomes below a fixed threshold and who are not entitled to other pension payments.

Various groups of employed or unemployed workers can apply for socially useful jobs and those in the public interest: young first-job seekers, those on the unemployment lists for at least two years, those on the mobility lists; and those drawing on the Wage Support Fund but not working. There are no proper income requirements in order to engage in socially useful jobs, but the benefit —for those who receive no other welfare payment —is incompatible with a fixed-term full-time job. It is compatible, on the other hand, provided a set

---

[31] This fund has been created for people with new types of job contracts such as, like solo self-employed (*collaboratori coordinati continuativi*).

income threshold is not crossed, with income from self-employment or a fixed-term part-time job.

Disabled with a minimum 74% disability rate who meet certain income conditions are entitled to civil invalidity payments, which do not exclude engaging in work. The escort allowance is only conceded to invalid pensioners with limited mobility and in need of constant care; there is no income limit since it is an entitlement due to disability.

The maternity benefit goes to resident mothers with Italian citizenship who do not receive the maternity allowance for working women and have incomes below set thresholds. The benefit for households with at least three children is for families made up of resident Italian citizens who satisfy certain income requirements.

Income thresholds and equivalence scales

Anti-poverty policies generally select recipients so as to direct the benefits to the poor or those at risk of impoverishment.[32] For nearly all the services envisaged, income thresholds are set above which the risk of poverty is considered to be non-existent. These income thresholds are often applied using equivalence scales according to household size and characteristics.[33]

Some services apply only income thresholds, above which there is no access to the service, without any reference to equivalence scales. This is the case with the social allowance, the social pension and the minimum pension, for which the annual amounts are €4,428.8, €3,650.0 and €4,960.9 respectively (in 2001).

The social allowance is different from the social pension since it is given even if the applicant's personal income is above the threshold, provided the combined household income is below the required limit.

---

[32] Anti-poverty policies are usually based on selectivity whereby the granting of services depends on ascertaining the applicant's economic condition. For a discussion of this point, also in relation to the debate between supporters of the selective and the universal approaches, see S. Toso (2000), in particular the chapter on "Selectivity or Universalism? The Dilemma of Welfare Policies".

[33] Unemployment, mobility and socially useful job benefits made no reference to income threshold or equivalence scales.

Table 6.3   Annual income thresholds for access to social allowance, social pension and minimum pension, 2001

Retired, living alone	Full	Reduced		Not eligible
		From	To	
Social allowance	0	0.1	4 428.9	4 428.9
Social pension	0	0.1	3 650.0	3 650.0
Minimum pension	4 960 9	4 960 9	9 921 9	9 921.9

Retired, married	Full	Reduced		Not eligible
		From	To	
Social allowance	4 428.9	4 428.9	8 857.7	8 857.7
Social pension	8 927.6	8 927.6	12 577.6	12 577.6
Minimum pension	14 882 8	14 882 8	19 843 7	19 843.7

Source: National Institute for Social Protection (INPS)

INPS benefits (excluding disability payments, based on insurance) and civil invalidity payments do not apply equivalence scales, but only refer to maximum thresholds for personal income.[34]

The benefit for nuclear families is calculated according to size, composition (orphans, brothers/sisters, etc) and characteristics (non-problem, single-parent, with disabled). As a consequence, there are a large number of tables for calculating the benefit, of which table 6.4 is just one example.

Table 6.4   Income thresholds for access to INPS and civil invalidity payments, 2001

	Individual annual threshold (€ a year)	Monthly amount (€)
Invalidity pension INPS	None	Insurance-based
Invalidity ordinary allowance INPS	8 857.7	Insurance-based
Assistance allowance	3 650.0	212.5
Civil invalidity payments	12 435.5	212.5
Escort allowance	None	422.1

Source   National Institute for Social Protection (INPS).

[34] Only the INPS ordinary invalidity payment makes provision for increasing the threshold where the applicant is married (€13,286.6 in 2001).

Table 6.5   Benefits for the nuclear family (households with both parents, at least one child and no disabled), 2001

Household yearly income (€ a year)	Monthly amount by household size				
	3	4	5	6	7
0–11 122.4	130.7	250.5	358.9	492.2	619.7
11 122.4–13 763.1	114.7	220.5	339.8	481.3	600.6
13 763.1–16 403.2	92.4	190.6	313.0	473.1	584.1
16 403.2–19 042.3	65.6	158 0	283.0	454.0	565.0
19 042.3–21 683.4	43 9	111.6	241.7	407.5	507.7
21 683.4–24 323.6	25.8	81.6	217.4	391 0	488.6
24 323.6–26 964.7	15.5	57.3	176.6	364.1	466.9
26 964 7–29 603.8	15.5	38 7	135.8	339.3	439.5
29 603.8–32 244.0	12.9	25.8	102.8	317.6	426.1
32 244.0–34 883.6	12.9	25.8	91.9	225.2	398.7
34 883.6–37 525.2	12.9	23.2	91.9	154.4	292.8
37 525.2–40 165.4	—	23 2	78.5	154.4	219.0
40 165.4–42 806.0	—	23.2	78.5	132.2	219.0
42 806.0–45 446.1	—	—	78 5	132.2	189.0
45 446.1–48 087.3	—	—	—	132.2	189.0
48 087 3–50 728 5	—	—	—	—	189.0

Source: National Institute for Social Protection (INPS).

Benefits for those enrolled in the separate fund for the self-employed are subject to greater restrictions in terms of income limits and family types. Total family income — subdivided by the number of members — cannot be greater than €4,131.6 per member, which is raised to €5,164.6 in the case of units with one parent or a disabled member. Furthermore, the amount of income from permanent freelance work, door-to-door sales and self-employed professional occupations must not be lower than 70% of total family income.

Unlike the benefit for the nuclear family, family allowances provide a fixed amount for each family member (€10.2), with entitlement also based on set income limits according to household size.

Those entitled to maternity benefit and benefit for nuclear families with at least three children are selected using the *indicatore della situazione economica* (ISE — economic situation indicator). This indicator, introduced on an experimental basis for the period 1999–2002, defines unified criteria for assessing the economic situation of those applying for welfare or health services not intended for all. The ISE is now applied only to a few benefits, excluding widely paid benefits such as minimum pensions, social allowance and pension, invalidity payments, etc.

Table 6.6 **Income limits for family allowance, 2001**

Number of members	Yearly income threshold (€)
2	14 620.4
3	18 795.9
4	22 463.8
5	26 103.8
6	29 584.7
7 or more	33 065.1

Source National Institute for Social Protection (INPS)

The following equivalence scale is used to weight family size in determining their economic situation.

Table 6.7 **ISE equivalence scales**

Household size	Coefficient
1	1.00
2	1.57
3	2.04
4	2.46
5	2.85

Weighting 0.35 for each extra member; 0.2 for a spouse with children; 0.5 for each member with permanent disability or more than 66% invalidity; 0.2 for nuclear families with children in which both parents work

A family's economic situation is obtained by adding together total tax income and investment income.[35] If the family lives in rented accommodation, the annual rent up to a maximum of €5,164.6 is deducted from the aggregate income.

Maternity benefit applies the ISE criteria starting from a basic annual income of €27,644.9 (2002) for a nuclear family of three members (Table 6.8). The amount of benefit is €265.2 for five months.

[35] If a nuclear family lives in its own property, the value of the property is deductible up to €51,645,7.

The ISE indicator is also applied for the benefit to nuclear families with at least three members, starting from a basic annual income of €18,889.9 (2002) for a nuclear family of five (Table 6.9). The amount of benefit is € 1,437.5 per year.

Table 6.8   Yearly income thresholds for access to maternity benefit, 2002

Household size	Equivalence scale		Equivalent income (€)
	Dlgs 109/98 scale Base: 1 comp. = 1	Art. 56 L 448/98 coefficients Base: 3 comp. = 1	
2	1.57	0.87*	24 051.1
3	2.04	1.00	27 644.9
4	2.46	1.21	33 450.4
5	2.85	1.40	38 702.9

* (1.57 + 0.2 single parent household weight): 2.04 = 0.87

Source: National Institute for Social Protection (INPS)

Table 6.9   Yearly income thresholds for access to benefit for large families, 2002

Household size	Equivalence scale		Equivalent income (€)
	Dlgs 109/98 scale Base: 1 comp .= 1	Art. 56 L 448/98 coefficients Base: 3 comp. = 1	
4	2.46	0.93*	18 511.5
5	2.85	1.00	19 904.3
6	3.20	1.12	22 292.9
7	3.55	1.25	24 880.4

(2.46+0.2 single parent household weight)· 2.85 = 0.93.

Source National Institute for Social Protection (INPS)

2.3. Recipients and expenditure

The number of beneficiaries from anti-poverty measures is very high, though it is not possible to arrive at a definitive figure for at least three reasons: one person may receive two services concurrently; for some services (nuclear family benefit) it is impossible to know the precise number of beneficiaries; and some instruments have been introduced only recently so there is insufficient data.

Apart from these methodological problems, numbers benefiting from the various measures considered here, almost 4.5 million pensioners to fewer than 100,000 on the mobility lists (Table 6.10).

The total number of beneficiaries from pension payments (social allowance, social pension and minimum pension) is over five million of whom a very significant share has incomes below the poverty threshold indicated by *Commissione d'Indagine sull'Esclusione Sociale* (CIES — Commission for Studying Social Exclusion). The income requirements for receiving these pensions are in fact very strict.

Table 6.10 Recipients and monthly and yearly amount of benefits, various years

Measure	Number of recipients	Average monthly amount (in €)	Average yearly amount (in €)
Social allowance (1999)	127 922	272.0	3 264.1
Social pension (1999)	525 755	266.8	3 201.4
Minimum pension (2000)	4 405 476	407.5	4 889.9
Invalidity pension INPS (1998)	70 526	850.1	10 200.7
Invalidity ordinary allowance INPS (1998)	2 977 753	446.6	4 946.9
Benefit for nuclear family (1998)	~3 430 000	37.8*	453.0*
Ordinary unemployment benefit (2000)	191 712	410.8	4 930.0
Ordinary unemployment benefit – reduced conditionality (2000)	387 133	208.0	2 496.4
Mobility allowance (2000)	93 542	657.1	7 885.3
Socially useful jobs (2000)	119 520	733.5	4 529.6
Civil invalidity benefit (1999)	1 263 277	476.7	5 720.7
Maternity benefit (2000), (5 months)	172 742	134.0	669.8
Benefit for large nuclear families (2000)	243 637	103.1	1 237.0

* Retired only

Source. National Institute for Social Protection (INPS), Ministry of Labour.

There are more than three million people (1998) on INPS benefits, while those on civil invalidity benefit number 1,263,000 (1999). It is difficult to estimate the proportion that is in serious economic difficulty since INPS invalidity payments and the escort allowance for civil invalids may be cumulated with other incomes.

There are only 119,520 people engaged in socially useful jobs, to which can be added the 93,542 receiving mobility payments. These are services independent of income thresholds, so it may be that a significant share of beneficiaries is not in serious economic difficulty.

Social assistance benefits (maternity benefit and benefit for large nuclear families) [36] are highly specialized services that cover well-defined population groups: women who have given birth and have no right to maternity leave, and families with at least three children. They are nonetheless forms of income support, which, although recently introduced, have spread rapidly to reach 172,742 mothers and 243,637 large families, slightly reducing the rate of poverty among the latter.

Data relating to the average amounts paid out with these benefits is not easy to compare since the goals differ. However, we believe that only in a few cases are the interventions sufficient to resolve economic difficulties that lead to poverty. In the case of instruments for supplementing incomes, if we take those beneficiaries who have no other source of income, the conclusion is that only the disability pension, the mobility allowance and, perhaps, the civil invalidity payment guarantee an adequate income.

Table 6.11 shows the total expenditure for each service. At nearly 55 billion euros, the figure for overall spending is not in itself a significant indicator of the financial commitment involved in the fight against poverty. This is because a considerable part of this spending goes to nuclear families that are not poor and, besides, other interventions that we have not considered have an impact on poverty. [37] Nevertheless, it is interesting to note that social insurance benefits absorb 81.3% of national anti-poverty funding, while social assistance benefits account for 18.7%. The minimum pension and ordinary invalidity benefit, both social insurance measures, account for 68.2% of total spending. If we add the nuclear family benefit, the three services together make up 75.2% of total spending and almost 95% of social insurance benefits. In the area of social assistance, by contrast, the largest part of the resources (70.3%) is absorbed by civil invalidity payments; together with the social allowance and the social pension they take up 90.7% of expenditure on social assistance.

Aggregating expenditure on beneficiary categories helps to understand the internal balances. A large part (€23.9 billion) goes on invalidity benefits, equal to 43.5% of the total. Equally high is the spending on the elderly, at €23.6 billion covering 43% of the total. The upshot is that 86.5% of anti-poverty resources are concentrated on two categories of beneficiaries: the elderly and the disabled. This is particularly worrying because those in a condition of poverty have social

---

[36] To these must be added, the RMI, which is discussed in more detail in the next section.

[37] Bear in mind also that the amounts for the single benefits are for different years.

insurance rights to claim, and thus often find themselves deprived of protection. The strengthening of the assistance component is thus a desirable goal in the reform of Italian welfare.

Table 6.11   Expenditure on social benefits, various years

Benefit	Expenditure in thousands €	%	A/S*
Social allowance (1999)	417 553.3	0.8	A
Social pension (1999)	1 683 171.4	3.1	A
Minimum pension (2000)	21 542 148.3	39.2	S
Invalidity pension INPS (1998)	719 424.5	1.3	S
Invalidity ordinary allowance INPS (1998)	15 958 156.7	29.0	S
Benefit for nuclear family (1998)	3 827 410.4	7.0	S
Ordinary unemployment benefit (2000)	945 140.2	1.7	S
Ordinary unemployment benefit — reduced conditionality (2000)	966 438.8	1.8	S
Mobility allowance (2000)	737 606.7	1.3	S
Socially useful jobs (2000)	541 377.8	1.0	A
Civil Invalidity benefit (1999)	7 226 828.7	13.1	A
Maternity benefit (2000)	115 708.4	0.2	A
Benefit for large nuclear families (2000)	301 387.7	0.5	A
Total	54 982 352.9	100.0	

Nature of the benefit. A = social assistances, S = social security
Source: Benassi (2000)

Table 6.12   Distribution of expenditure by type of instrument, various years

Benefit kind	Expenditure (thousand €)	%
Social insurance	44 696 325.6	81.3
Social assistance	10 286 027.3	18.7

Source: Author's calculation

Gender

It is interesting to look at the distribution of beneficiaries and spending in respect of gender (Table 6.13). All these benefits are strongly female-oriented: the share of female beneficiaries is respectively 70.1%, 83% and 74.9%. Note that these benefits are paid to people with limited or no social insurance rights, that is those with a limited employment record due to interruptions for household duties. What we have, therefore, are benefits intended for people who cannot receive work-related pensions, which are more generous.[38]

Table 6.13   Beneficiaries and average monthly amounts for the social allowance, social pension and minimum pension by gender, 1999 and 2000

	Males		Females		%F
	Number	Average monthly amount (in €)	Number	Average monthly amount (in €)	
Social allowance (1999)	38 244	291.2	89 678	263.8	70.1
Social pension (1999)	89 267	279.5	436 488	264.2	83.0
Minimum pension (2000)	1 105 088	409.5	3 300 388	406.8	74.9
Total	1 232 599	396.4	3 826 554	387.2	75.6

Source: National Institute for Social Protection (INPS).

Equally interesting are the data for beneficiaries of INPS invalidity payments, which are tied to a sufficient number of previous contributions, and of payments on an assistance basis from the Ministry of the Interior. Here we can see that benefits dependent on contributions go predominantly to men while those of an assistance kind go predominantly to women (Table 6.14). The first types of payment are more generous than the second; moreover, within the first type there is a marked difference in average amounts received by males and females. The latter receive about 30% less and the two invalidity benefits are even lower than the civil invalidity payments (due to award of the escort allowance).

A greater equality in the treatment of the sexes emerges, on the other hand, from analysis of payments for mobility and socially useful jobs (data for 1998) (Table 6.15).

In short, a gender analysis of benefits mirrors labour market inequalities: "strong" social rights are acquired through participation in the labour market. The alternative is to rely on much less generous instruments. This explains the clear prevalence of women in anti-poverty welfare for the elderly and why, conversely, the more generous invalidity payments (social insurance) go less to women than the less generous kind (assistance).

---

[38] The average monthly pension in Italy was €638.5 in 1999. Taking only private old-age pensions, the average rises to €743.7, and if only public sector pensions are considered, the average goes up to €1,372.8.

Table 6.14   Beneficiaries and average monthly amounts for invalidity pension, ordinary invalidity pension (INPS) and civil invalidity benefits (Ministry of Interior) by gender, 1998–99

	Males		Females	
	Number	Average monthly amount (in €)	Number	Average monthly amount (in €)
Invalidity pension INPS	55 081	912.6	15 445	627.0
Invalidity ordinary allowance INPS	196 171	530.6	86 698	381.2
Pre-law 222/84 allowance	1 078 135	514.7	1 616 749	394.5
Civil invalidity payments	481 895	485.0	781 382	471.8

Source: National Institute for Social Protection (INPS).

Table 6.15   Beneficiaries of mobility allowances and socially useful jobs by gender, 2000

	Males		Females	
	Number	%	Number	%
Mobility allowances	53 898	62.0	32 964	38.0
Socially useful jobs	76 196	54.1	64 540	45.9

Source: Ministry of Labour

The RMI is a turning point for the welfare system since it could overcome historical imbalances. The lack of a systematic approach in national policies for dealing with poverty leads to unjustifiable inequalities in the welfare system. In particular, the weakness in Italian social protection is due to the subordinate role of social assistance measures. Although the ongoing process of reform is trying to redress this, the crux of the question is the mixture of social insurance and social assistance: the majority of (national) anti-poverty measures depend on the beneficiary's contributions, thereby excluding many people in economic difficulty. The most contradictory aspect is that social insurance measures are in part applied on a social assistance basis. Hence, two assistance circuits exist: a more generous one based on the principle of contributions and a more unsystematic and deficient one, based fully on social assistance.

This situation produces widely known imbalances in the effectiveness of spending, given that poverty largely derives from the impossibility (unemployment) or incapacity (illness, invalidity, family responsibilities) to participate fully in the labour market. The fundamental requisite for acquiring social insurance rights is missing. This leads to the formation of a group excluded from the core of social protection policies — a form of institutionalized social exclusion.[39] Only a small part of expenditure goes to benefit those who are most in need.

The last few years have witnessed the beginning of a response through the introduction of measures directly aimed at supporting individuals and families in — or at risk of — poverty. The first signs of a more coherent approach can be seen in measures to ease the burden of rent, to help deprived families (benefit to numerous large families) and the Minimum Insertion Income (RMI), currently on an experimental basis. The latter, in particular, would bring Italy in line with other EU countries if it became permanent and would provide Italian welfare with an explicit and universal instrument to combat poverty.

3. The challenges to the RMI in Italy

Introduced in the 1998 budget law and defined by a series of legislative provisions up to its (presumed) definitive implementation envisaged by the social assistance system reform law (328/00), the RMI "is a measure for combating poverty and social exclusion by providing economic and social support for people exposed to the risk of social marginalization and unable to maintain themselves or their offspring for psychological, physical or social reasons" (DL 237/98, Article 1). As originally stated by the Onofri Commission and then confirmed several times by the *Commissione d'indagine sull'esclusione Sociale* (CIES), the RMI is a last resort service, aimed at those people who are incapable of independently meeting the needs of a dignified existence and are not eligible for any other programmes (for example, allowances linked to unemployment, invalidity or old age). It hinges on a means test to verify a potential beneficiary's economic resources. On the Italian welfare scene, the RMI is an innovation — even if still on a provisional basis [40] — in that for the

---

[39] It is a well-known feature of the Italian welfare system. See, for example, Saraceno (1993) and Ferrera (1998).

[40] Whether the RMI is provisional or definitive is not easy to establish since, although article 23 of Law 328/00 envisages the prolongation of the measure (without indicating until when), it is also the case that the political climate is not favourable. This is demonstrated by, among other things, the failure to meet the deadlines provided for by article 23: the Government was supposed to have reported to Parliament on the progress of the experiment by May 30, and issue a legislative decree on the reorganization of payments for civil invalidity, deaf-mutism and blindness. The RMI

first time a universal income-support benefit has been created that is not based on the beneficiary belonging to a particular category — workers, the unemployed, pensioners, the elderly, invalids, etc. — but simply on the existence of economic need.

The sections below analyse the operation of the RMI in the 39 municipalities involved in the experiment, mainly using data contained in the CIES (2001) since the evaluation report, drawn up by independent bodies in mid-2001, has still not been made public by the Government. Our aim is not to examine in detail all the phases of the experiment and the aspects involved in this complex process. We will concentrate on several aspects that we consider to be central for formulating judgments on the progress of the experiment and on possible adjustments to the RMI with a view to its generalization: the penetration of the RMI in the target population; the role of reinsertion programmes; the impact of the RMI in different local contexts; and the capacity of municipalities to manage a service of this kind.

3.1 The design of the RMI

The RMI experiment started in October 1998 through three legislative measures (the Budget Law of 1998 No. 449/97 which laid down its introduction, the DL 237/98 regulating its features, and the Ministerial Decree of 5 August 1998, which named the municipalities involved. The objectives were:

- to check the modes of carrying out the experiment and the costs in different parts of the country;

- to study its effects in the fight against poverty and promotion of social integration;

- to evaluate its possible extension to the whole country.

Management of the RMI is entrusted to the municipalities, which receive the resources directly from the Ministry of Labour and Social Policies.

experiment was extended up to the end of 2002 in all the municipalities covered by the territorial pacts containing one of the original 39 municipalities (see article 80 of the 2001 Finance Act [388/2000], by which approximately €181 million was allocated for 2001 and approximately €222 million for 2002, and the decrees of the Ministry of Social Solidarity of April 20, 2001 and May 7, 2001, listing the municipalities involved). The number of municipalities covered was 267, to which the original 39 must be added. Our analysis here necessarily refers to the first experiment, now concluded.

The recipients of the RMI are:

- Italian or other EU citizens resident for at least 12 months in one of the municipalities involved in the experiment;

- non-EU citizens or stateless persons resident for at least three years in one of the municipalities involved in the experiment.

Those of working age who are jobless but able to work are required to attend occupational training courses and accept job offers.

The maximum income threshold allowing access to the RMI for a one-person household was €258.2 in 1998, €263.4 in 1999 and €268.6 in 2000. An equivalence scale was used to determine the RMI amounts in the case of families of different sizes and compositions (Table 6.16).

Table 6.16   Monthly income thresholds for access to the RMI by family size, 1998-2000

Number of members	Ratio	1998	1999	2000
1	1.00	258.2	263.4	268.6
2	1.57	405.4	413.5	421.6
3	2.04	526.8	537.3	547.9
4	2.46	635.2	647.9	660.7
5	2.85	736.0	750.7	765.4

Weighting: 0.35 for each extra member, 0.2 for a spouse with children, 0.5 for each disabled member; 0.2 for large families with children in which both parents work.

The amount of the RMI is calculated as the difference between the set threshold and the monthly income. This base income is the total of the single incomes earned by the recipient's nuclear family. Incomes from work, net of taxation, are calculated at 75% to reduce the risk of the poverty trap. In addition, recipients must have no assets or property apart from their own home.

The municipalities are charged with formulating personalized integration programmes taking into account the personal and family characteristics of beneficiaries. These are aimed at improving and promoting personal abilities and rebuilding social networks; in the case of minors, priority is given to completing compulsory schooling and occupational training.

The cost of the experiment has amounted to just under €246 million (Table 6.17).

Table 6.17   Cost of the experiment by geographical area, 31 December 2000

	Expenditure (in €)	%
North	8 515 044.4	3.5
Centre	11 996 222.1	4.9
South	225 445 539.1	91.7
Total	245 956 805.6	100.0

Source: CIES (2001)

3.2. The recipients of the RMI

In designing the experiment, municipalities in the South were over-represented since poverty is much more widespread there than elsewhere. Of the 39 municipalities selected, 24 were in the South, 10 in the Centre and only five in the North. Although this decision is justifiable, it limits the assessments that can be made about the northern and central municipalities.[41] This seriously complicates the attempt to gain an idea of the impact of the RMI on social structures and poverty typologies that vary widely throughout the country.

Table 6.18   Population, poverty and RMI beneficiaries by geographical area, 2000

	Population (%)	Poverty (%)	RMI (%)
North	44.7	18.9	2.8
Centre	19.3	14.6	4.0
South	36.0	66.5	93.2
Total	100.0	100.0	100.0

Source Istat for population, CIES (2001) for poverty and RMI

[41] Nine of the 10 municipalities in the Centre are in the region of Lazio; of the five municipalities in the North only Rovigo has (just) over 50'000 inhabitants, even though poverty is known to be concentrated in the bigger cities. Moreover, in many regions — even very populated ones like Emilia Romagna — the RMI has not been tested in any municipality. This is a very serious failing because it limits the possibility of evaluating the experiment in the context of different local welfare systems.

In the first two-year period of the RMI experiment, 55,522 applications were made of which 34,730 were accepted, covering a total of 25,591 families and 85,818 individuals (see Table 6.19). One of the most interesting considerations arises from observing the penetration of the service among the target population. The incidence of beneficiaries among the population is an indicator, however rough and ready, of the role that the RMI could play in widely differing socio-economic contexts.[42] It is of course to be expected that the incidence of applications and beneficiaries is greater in the areas with bigger employment problems (South) compared to those where conditions are more favourable (Centre and North). Aside from this, however, it is important to remember that the RMI should not be viewed as an instrument either for providing income support to the unemployed or for fostering employment, but as an instrument that can help rebuild a subject's capacity to find employment and work.[43]

---

[42] Here is not the place to address the complex question of Italy's economic dualism (see among others Mingione, 1998; Mingione and Pugliese, 2002). The table below is a condensed summary of some labour market indicators and shows very clearly that there are in Italy at least two distinct employment regimes: one in the North and one in the South.

Leading labour market indicators by gender and geographical area, January 2002

	Males				Females				Males and females			
	N	C	S	I	N	C	S	I	N	C	S	I
Employment rate 15–64	75.6	73.9	71.1	73.7	54.9	50.5	36.5	47.4	65.4	62.1	53.7	60.5
Overall unemployment rate	2.6	5.2	14.5	7.1	5.7	9.7	27.2	12.5	3.9	7.0	18.8	9.2
Long-term unemployment rate	0.9	2.8	9.3	4.1	2.3	5.5	19.3	7.7	1.5	3.9	12.7	5.5
Unemployment rate 15–24	8.5	23.1	44.0	25.4	11.3	26.3	61.4	31.5	9.8	24.6	51.0	28.1

N= North, C=Centre, S=South; I=Italy.
Source Istat

[43] Here is not the place to address the complex question of Italy's economic dualism (see among others Mingione, 1998; Mingione and Pugliese, 2002). The table below is a condensed summary of some labour market indicators and shows very clearly that there are in Italy at least two distinct employment regimes: one in the North and one in the South.

Table 6.19   Applications made and accepted and total beneficiaries (31 December 2000)

	Residents*	Applications	Admitted	Total recipients	Recipients/ residents
North	217 793	2 050	1 466	2 415	1.1
Centre	143 112	2 674	1 789	3 406	2.4
South	2 000 877	50 798	31 475	79 997	4.0
Without Naples	965 042	31 925	22 580	62 661	6.5
Total	2 361 782	55 522	34 730	85 818	3.6

* In the municipalities testing the RMI

Source   CIES (2001)

In the southern municipalities, 4% of the resident population was granted access to the RMI, against a quarter of that figure in the North and half in the Centre. Therefore, a significant proportion of households in the southern municipalities possessed the rigorous and selective requisites for receiving the RMI. This figure is heavily affected by the case of Naples, where only 1.7% of the resident population has been granted the service, which nevertheless represents a high absolute number of beneficiaries (17,336) in respect of the total for the South (79,997).[44] Excluding Naples, we discover that the share of beneficiaries in the South's population rises dramatically to 6.5% - that is, six times the figure recorded in the northern municipalities. It is not so important to discuss here whether the RMI is financially sustainable; the cost of generalizing to cover the entire Italian population is estimated at between €2.22 billion and €2.94 billion per year (CIES, 2001, p. 47), which is surely a sustainable commitment if there were sufficient political will.[45] It is interesting to consider the consequences that could ensue from a "revolution" of this kind in Italian

[44] The experiment in Naples has with all probability been affected by the very order of magnitude of the intervention that the municipality has had to manage. To begin with, the experiment was only supposed to be carried out in some of the city's districts, as happened in Catania and Genova. Reasons of expediency and the fear of unrest in the excluded districts then brought the experiment to be extended to the entire city without, however, increasing the budget proportionately. In the two-year period, in Naples about €46 million were spent out of a total expenditure for the South amounting to €201 million: namely Naples accounted for 22.8% of the total destined for the South but held 51.8% of the aggregate population in the municipalities where the RMI was tested. It thus seems obvious to us that it was necessary to carry out a more rigorous selection in this city than elsewhere.

[45] By way of comparison, €2.1 billion were spent on old-age benefits and pensions in 1999 and €21.5 billion on minimum pensions in 2000.

welfare on beneficiaries and local social systems and on social protection regime and its capacity to manage a service of this type.

There are differences in the incidence of RMI among the local population that are hard to understand without reference to the role of local Government bodies. It is in fact difficult to believe that such differences in the extent of hardship and social marginalization can exist in socio-economically homogeneous areas: in the five municipalities in Calabria the incidence of beneficiaries fluctuated between 3% and 24.9% of inhabitants; in the six municipalities in the province of Enna, between 6.7% and 15.8%; and in one municipality in Campania it reached a peak of 50.9% while going no higher than 6.2% in the nearby provincial capital.

Table 6.20   RMI beneficiaries (head of household) by labour market status (%)

	Employed	First job seekers	Unemployed	Not in labour force	Total
North	16.9	4.0	36.7	42.5	100
Centre	8.6	8.3	64.2	18.9	100
South	12.4	18.5	53.5	15.9	100
Total	12.2	15.7	53.0	19.0	100

Source: CIES (2001).

In the institutional channels for implementing the RMI, a very strong role has been played by factors connected with local "styles" in social reproduction and by the relationship between citizens and institutions. In particular, we want to highlight contextual factors, especially the quality of human and social capital and that of the labour market, and the marked persistence of policy distortions due to practices based on patronage. These factors have exerted great pressure on the management of the scheme, which in many municipalities has been their first experience of "modern" income support, based on the concept of citizenship as a right. Predictably, the introduction of such a big innovation has given rise in the "weaker" social contexts to difficulties in perceiving and managing demand for the service. Proof of this are the protests organized in some Calabrian and Sicilian municipalities against the local councils over merit lists — which undermine the spirit of the RMI — and delays in handing out benefits. Investigations by the financial police in the province of Enna (Sicily) led to 859 beneficiaries out of 7,969 (11%) in six municipalities being charged with defrauding the State and falsifying personal documents. This is an extreme case but it clearly shows the difficulty of implementing a measure like the RMI in settings that epitomize widespread poverty, high levels of joblessness and "black" work, rudimentary systems of assistance, a long tradition of patronage politics and, last but not least, a longstanding presence of organized crime. Such factors risk undermining the spirit of the RMI and turning it into a general economic benefit, dropping the innovative commitment to reinsertion of beneficiaries.

The type of nuclear family most favoured by the RMI was larger than average. This imbalance was due to two interconnected factors. On the one hand, poverty in Italy affects mostly larger families, above all those with five or more members; on the other, these same families are typically found in the South. It follows that the experiment gives fewer indications of its efficacy for other poverty profiles more widespread in the North, such as single people [46] and childless couples.

Table 6.21   Comparison between RMI beneficiary families and families in general by type and size (%)

Size	RMI	Italy	Type	RMI	Italy
1	13 6	22 9	Single person	13.6	22.9
2	13 5	25.8	Couple with children	64.2	44.2
3	24.6	23.2	Single parent	14.6	7.7
4	28.4	20.8	Couple without children	5.4	19.5
5 or more	19.1	7.3	Other	2.2	5.7
Total	100.0	100.0	Total	100.0	100.0

Source Istat, *Indagine sui consumi della famiglie*, 1997, own calculation

3.3 The insertion programmes and their outcomes

One of the prerequisites for a correct functioning of the RMI is that local government bodies are able to formulate and implement measures to help an individual improve his situation and climb out of deprivation. As shown above, Italy suffers from a considerable historical deficit when it comes to interventions aimed at supporting individuals. Apart from the widespread weakness of municipalities on this front — and these functions are their legal prerogative [47] — this territorial fragmentation is magnified by the varying extent to which third-sector bodies have put down roots (see Table 6.22) in a political climate that gives strong encouragement to subsidiarity.

[46] In reality, these are mainly the elderly, who have benefited very little from the RMI since they are already "protected" by the old-age benefit and pension.

[47] Confirmed and strengthened by the recent general policy law on social services (328/00).

Table 6.22   Voluntary organizations and volunteers by geographical area, 1999

	Residents (%)	Organizations		Volunteers	
		No.	%	Number	%
North	44.7	9 257	61.4	386 973	57.7
Centre	19.3	3 018	20.0	162 86	24.2
South	36.0	2 796	18.6	121 667	18.1
Total	100.0	15 071	100.0	670 826	100.0

Source: Istat

Leaving aside the effects on the rights of individual resulting from a welfare service, which widely delegates to the third sector the organization and provision of services, there are still questions arising from the division of responsibilities between the public and private spheres. In those municipalities that are less well equipped and have fewer non-profit organizations, the difficulties in organising systems that meet demand tend to loom larger. In this instance too, the southern regions, already burdened by a greater incidence of people in need of assistance and with less capacity for government, have far fewer third-sector initiatives.

This is even truer of the RMI with its emphasis on the social insertion of beneficiaries, which requires both a greater organizational capacity to involve all parties active in supplying specialist services and good managerial ability to prevent improper or fraudulent use. As pointed out in other studies (Kazepov, 1996, 2000; Fargion, 1997; Kazepov and Orientale Caputo, 1998; Mingione, 1999), local Government bodies are very uneven in their planning and managing abilities, in particular in the field of assistance services where many municipalities have only rudimentary structures or none at all. In the case of the RMI, therefore, many southern municipalities are in a double bind — the weakness of the assistance sector and the scarcity of third-sector organizations comes on top of a greater demand for social protection and social progression and more widespread employment problems.

The result is poor participation in southern municipalities by beneficiaries in social insertion programmes, the key component of the RMI. Thus, while 43.2% of all beneficiaries have taken part in social insertion programmes, the proportion in the South is far lower than in Centre and North, especially if we exclude Naples where all the members of households concerned were involved.

The data on those in insertion programmes (Tables 6.23 and 6.24) clearly reveal the gap between the magnitude of demand and the capacity for supply [48]. This poses the problem of the administrative efficiency of municipalities faced with social decay, a problem that raises a lot of doubts as to their ability to manage a complex measure like the RMI. This aspect, furthermore, does not depend solely on either the above-mentioned Italian institutional weakness in governing social dynamics or on the disparity in administrative efficiency between North and South. The case of France is emblematic here in as far as it has a highly centralized and efficient administrative system in which, nonetheless, territorial differences entirely comparable to those in Italy are to be found. The empirical evidence drawn from the experience of the *Revenu Minimum d'Insertion*, managed by a top-down policy approach, shows that in France too there are varying outcomes in relation to the quantity and quality of insertion paths and the proportion of beneficiaries involved.[49] In short, the local variability in the outcomes of policies is manifest even in institutional systems different from the Italian one, which prompts us to avoid simplistic explanations based on the passiveness or negligence of institutional bodies.

Table 6.23   Recipients included in insertion programmes, 31 December 2000

	Number of recipients	Included Number	% included
North	2 415	1 549	64.1
Centre	3 406	1 985	58.3
South	79 997	33 553	41.9
Without Naples	62 661	16 217	25 9
Total	85 818	37 087	43 2
Source CIES (2001)			

[48] Although the data are not definitive; they seem to express a different managerial and administrative capacity in the various territorial districts. Moreover, evaluation of quality and of the activities effectively undertaken is not currently possible due to the lack of precise data for each city. It is however justifiable to consider with scepticism several occupational or training "reinsertion" activities where these involve a few hours in socially useful work such as the upkeep of green spaces or three months helping municipal staff.

[49] See the observations on Rennes and Saint-Étienne in Saraceno (2002, pp.61-2) which clarifies the importance of the local conditions onto which the RMI is grafted: in Rennes a very old tradition of intervention and collaboration between the public and the third sectors, a dynamic economic system with an expanding tertiary sector and little incidence of poverty and social exclusion; in Saint-Étienne a long and deep-rooted industrial crisis leading to employment problems for generations of workers which has pulled apart the old locally-based forms of mutual aid. The result is that 75% of RMI beneficiaries sign an insertion contract in Rennes whereas the figure in Saint-Étienne is only 24% (Saraceno, 2002, p 77).

Table 6.24   Distribution of beneficiaries by type of programme [50] and geographical area (%)

	North	Centre	South	All
Occupational	21.7	7.8	15.1	14.9
Socially useful	9.6	4.4	10.0	9.6
Training	3.9	19.1	11.5	11.6
Schooling	17.9	28.3	13.5	14.5
Health care support	12.8	12.4	1.2	2.3
Family care support	12.6	12.1	21.4	20.5
Socio-relational support	1.5	9.8	26.5	24.5
Other	19.9	6.1	1.0	2.1
Total	100.0	100.0	100.0	100.0

Source: CIES (2001)

The data from the RMI experiment in Italy are not unequivocal, making their interpretation particularly difficult. This is highlighted by the data on beneficiaries who have exited the RMI measure, even if the period of the experiment is too short for an accurate assessment of the impact of service and the insertion programmes (see Table 6.25).[51]

The data here point along the same lines as the preceding data and show that southern municipalities find greater difficulty in tackling poverty: only 7.5% of beneficiary nuclear families have exited the measure as against almost one third in the municipalities of the Centre and North. We go along with the observation of the CIES (2001, p. 35) according to which "given that the RMI selects individuals and families in a state of serious economic hardship and in general with a limited social capital, it is no surprise that most of its beneficiaries are still recipients two years on from its inception, even more so for being concentrated in the less dynamic parts of the country." Emblematic is the fact that over a quarter of those who have found employment are resident in one of

----

[50] Examples of types of programmes: *occupational* — orientation, on-the-job learning, apprenticeship; *socially useful* — upkeep of green spaces, office work in local council; *training* — basic and occupational training; *schooling* — learning to read and write, completion of compulsory education; *health care support* — courses for drug-addicts, the disabled and alcoholics; *family care and support* — looking after old people and children, supporting parental responsibilities; *socio-relational integration* — voluntary social work.

[51] No longitudinal analysis of beneficiaries is envisaged so it is not possible to consider in detail the impact of the RMI and insertion programmes on their economic situation.

the northern municipalities, where however less than 3% of the beneficiaries are located. On the other hand, we should view in a positive light the fact that almost 20% (5,701) of southern beneficiaries have obtained a school or professional diploma, enriching their cultural capital so that they have a better chance in the labour market. The data in this respect are provisional in that at the end of the evaluation window (31 December 2000) more than 900 individuals in a school completion programme in addition to actions to combat truancy and encourage attendance by minors of school age. Together with the reduction in rent arrears, this is probably the most significant achievement in the first two-year period of the RMI experiment, confirming that it is possible to set in motion programmes of social progression and (re)acquisition of socio-economic autonomy.

Table 6.25   Recipients and departures from the RMI, 31 December 2000

	Application admitted	% left	Reasons for leaving (No.)			Recipients by outcome (No.)		
			No more need	Abandoned	Other*	New job	School diploma	Training diploma
North	1 466	32.0	252	113	104	232	59	101
Centre	1 789	28 3	285	134	87	114	28	43
South	31 475	7 5	1 181	198	820	527	2 257	3 444
Total	34 730	9.7	1 718	445	1 011	873	2 344	3 588

*change of city, death, ...
Source CIES (2001)

4.   Concluding remarks: Critical evaluation and prospects

We can draw only some limited partial conclusions about the outcomes of the RMI. We will look at this aspect in the first part of this section and then discuss some critical points relating to the prospects for applying the RMI over the whole of the country.

Among the positive outcomes of the experiment it must be underlined that numerous situations of poverty were resolved: the standard of living was raised for families with a serious lack of monetary resources [52] and without income support. Especially in the South, the introduction of the RMI represents a

---

[52] Serious because the income threshold envisaged for access to the service was very low: in 2000 €268.6 for a one-person household, €421.6 for a two-person household and so on.

significant step forward, even if only towards providing a last-resort assistance cushion.[53] This is an aspect of the minimum income measures that certainly takes precedence over any criticisms that may be made. The notes contained in CIES (2001,VI-VII) point to other important positive signs emerging in the first two-year period of the experiment, chiefly related to the effect of the RMI on the organization of services and on citizen-institution relations as well as to some specific problem areas (truancy, rent arrears, indebtedness). The critical factors, also indicated in CIES (2001,VII), concern above all management problems (identification of territorial areas, control instruments), difficulties in inter-institutional collaboration, and the problems in integrating the RMI with other social policies (employment and local development).

Significantly, little or nothing emerges on the effective solution to poverty, namely the removal of the causes giving rise to poverty. But this is the main fundamental objective of the RMI: the insistence on insertion through the establishment of binding contracts between the local Government body (which commits itself to activating individual paths for retraining, school and health education, etc.) and the beneficiary (who commits him/herself to undertaking the activities stipulated in the contract) is one of its defining elements. The experimental period has been too brief to allow a proper evaluation of the measure's capacity to provide a definitive solution to poverty hinging not only on money but more generally on capacity to meet the needs of a dignified life.

However, even from such a partial and brief experiment, there emerge faint positive signs of the effects on the organization of local welfare. The implementation of the programme produces important changes in the organizational structure of local assistance: a more professional approach by operators enabling a shift from the standardized assessment of means-testing to the formulation of insertion programmes; the agreements with private third-sector institutions, which entail the involvement of new participants and an increasing professionalism compared to traditional forms of charity intervention and social solidarity; the promotion of intermediary institutions which represent the interests and needs of a diverse range of beneficiaries; the development of multi-faceted coordination by local Government to keep control over a complicated apparatus. On this front, besides the faint positive signs, there are

---

[53] See table 6.2a on pre-existing levels of municipal assistance in the municipalities involved in the experiment; it shows the very low amount for subsistence incomes (where they existed) in the South. In the ESOPO study (Saraceno, 2002) the case of Cosenza was particularly difficult to compare as the subsistence minimum was a derisory sum (between €100 and €200) and given once a year to a few applicants, often chosen according to highly discretional criteria.

also marked signs of difficulties that will have to be taken into serious future consideration. Both the small municipalities and nearly all the southern ones reveal a substantial deficit in competence and professionalism, of their own departments and of the auxiliary institutions required for implementing the insertion programmes.

While the RMI does resolve the distortions resulting from the independent and cyclical nature of local financial support, it is not able to deal automatically with problems such as inadequate professional resources, the uneven presence of the third sector at local level or the capacity to coordinate among public institutions. This last element will undoubtedly have to be addressed when the programme is given general application.

Dealing now with the integration the RMI into the Italian welfare system, the indications emerging from its implementation raise a delicate question. As it is conceived as a last-resort instrument for re-establishing acceptable life conditions, the RMI should not be managed as a mere income support for those in a weak employment position. In other words, it cannot substitute for employment policies or compensate for the weakness of employment-related measures or occupational training programmes. Several episodes connected with the RMI reported in the media, such as the occupation of town halls in the South, seem to point to a different significance given to the service in local contexts where unemployment and "black" work are rife. Here the RMI risks assuming the character of an allowance for the essentially unemployable with family responsibilities,[54] a practice that risks perverting the nature of the RMI and creating an expectation of a generalized welfare handout. In order to avoid this and the return to the old rationale of patronage and personal influence in Italian welfare, the assistance sphere must be kept clearly distinct from that of labour market policies whilst building institutional links that permit the re-construction of a person's capacity for work.[55] Hence, application of the RMI presupposes a strengthening of the system of interventions and benefits in the sphere of employment, so that only those people who have no recourse to other support reach the RMI.

---

[54] We could witness a repeat of the old invalidity benefit, which was granted to those unable to work for social reasons (Boccella, 1982).

[55] For those who preserve a capacity for work. Something entirely different is required for those who are no longer able to work and, for them, an insertion path deals with recovery of the capacity to meet day-to-day needs on one's own or as far as possible.

A first critical remark on the prospects for the RMI is that its general application cannot be an alibi for not tackling other deficiencies in the Italian welfare system — above all in the southern regions afflicted by chronic unemployment — such as the weakness of labour policies, instruments to cushion unemployment and occupational training. On the contrary, the general application of the programme without a parallel strengthening of these welfare sectors risks leading to its degeneration, beginning in the South. It is in this part of the country that introduction of a minimum income measure is most urgent, but what must be avoided is the transformation of a welfare instrument into a palliative for historical labour market difficulties.

A second critical question concerns the institutional design of the programme and, in particular, the role attributed to the regional Governments. The experiment has been based on close cooperation between central Government, which provides funding and lays down the regulations and norms for implementation, and local Government, which implements measures. In legal terms, this design has been superseded by the welfare reform law and the constitutional devolution of welfare responsibilities to the regional Governments, approved by parliament in 2001. It will therefore necessary to establish a role for the regional Government, to interpret the RMI's basic features according to local needs without losing sight of its significance as a universal measure. However, some problems remain that are not easy to solve: the role to be attributed to the regional governments; the organization of the consortia of municipalities to overcome implementation difficulties due to their small size; and the modalities whereby the central State guarantees universal activation of the basic right to a minimum standard of living, even in local contexts with widely differing poverty features and profiles. Local Government must be granted a certain degree of autonomy at both regional and municipal level in defining the local framework and implementing the RMI — for example, in calculating certain aspects of income, such as rent, or managing relations with the third sector. This must be accompanied by close and rigorous national control.

The third critical area is that of possible polarization when putting the programme into effect as, in this regard, the medium-sized municipalities of the Centre and North are at an advantage and many municipalities in the South are penalised. In the first case, the further exploitation of public administrative competence, the development of agreements with private bodies and the third sector, and the effective management of complex insertion programmes lead to an increase in already abundant intervention resources and capacities, whereas in the second case exactly the opposite may occur. In this sense, the general application of the RMI must be accompanied by measures that permit an improvement in organizational, professional and third-sector potential in deficit areas. The small municipalities should be able to operate through consortia or associations linking them together, even though deep-rooted parochialism has always made this difficult. There are some organized multi-municipal arrangements such as the mountain communities or the health districts, but the problem has to be tackled at a general level, probably by using the regional authority to set up effective homogeneous aggregations of municipalities and give them the operational instruments required for an efficient implementation of the RMI.

In conclusion, the introduction of the RMI in Italy could have very positive effects under the following conditions:

- it is accompanied by, and is not made an alternative to measures for strengthening employment welfare (labour and work insertion policies, unemployment benefits and occupational training);

- its institutional design is calibrated so as to guarantee sufficient autonomy to the two local tiers of municipal implementation and regional organizational control without damaging the universal right to a standard of living allowing integration into the community; and

- the present organizational and professional deficiencies and lack of third-sector support in the small municipalities, and especially in the most southern municipalities, are eliminated before they undermine the programme.

The second biennial testing of RMI ended in December 2002 and the centre-right Berlusconi Government is expected to take a decision soon. There are three possibilities:[56]

- cancellation of the scheme;

- its implementation on a national scale as foreseen by the Reform Law on Social Assistance;

- continuation of the experiment for a further biennium.

The third option is the most likely because its cost is very limited, because the southern municipalities where the experiment is taking place are particularly

---

[56] A fourth option of shifting to a completely different income support scheme, like basic income, is extremely unlikely for the same reasons that we raised at the beginning of this chapter (the uncontrollable distortions produced by tax evasion and the informal economy and the necessity to promote the expansion of social services).

keen and mobilized in favour of its continuation, and because it reasonably fits European recommendations for convergence in social policies and the content of the national Social Plan on Social Inclusion for 2001–03.

Under the third condition, the national implementation of the measure would be better. However, implementation should take place under the new legal and political background with different financial and institutional features based on regional supervision and on a local social action plan. Assuming that a more decentralized phase of testing will be difficult, the definitive implementation under a "federalist" institutional structure, shifting from the French model to the Spanish one, better fits the political orientation of the Government majority. But this option raises financial and political difficulties that the new majority is probably unable to solve. There is no open ideological opposition[57] on its part against the scheme, due to the fact that the issue continues to have very low practical priority and visibility (compared, for instance, to labour market and pension reforms or immigration policies). The political background within the new majority coalition resembles the one that characterized the Prodi Government in 1997. The Treasury is against new investments in social policies, while a large part of the coalition is favours other policy priorities (like tax cuts, higher unemployment benefits and labour market innovations, particularly if they are seen as directly connected with economic growth) and oppose financial redistribution in favour of the South. However, as in the case of the D'Alema Government coalition in 1998, another part of the present coalition, mainly elected in the South and strongly linked to Catholic third-sector institutions, is pressing for the continuation and extension of the RMI scheme. This is the main reason why the compromise around the third option is currently the most likely.

Our final remarks are on the general lesson to be drawn from the RMI experiment. The measure will not have the desired effects if it is introduced mechanically into a public welfare structure that is weak, unbalanced, inequitable and ineffective like the one in Italy.[58] The RMI can function effectively to defend the welfare of the most disadvantaged groups only if it is supported by a new vision of welfare, in which the national responsibility for

---

[57] The new Minister of Welfare is a member of the Northern League, and his collaborators have shown little interest in the issue: the evaluation report after nearly one year had not been made official and discussed in parliament as the law would require; the previous Government Commission on Social Exclusion was forced to resign and a new one nominated, with a stronger presence of Catholics.

[58] As emphasized in many studies; see among others Ascoli (1984), Paci (1989) and Ferrera (1984 and 1998).

fundamental choices and the role of local institutional actors to give expression to the general principles are asserted together. It is in this direction that the welfare reform law is moving. The intention of the legislation is to restructure the welfare system with regard to its range of services, its approach to management and lastly the way it is funded. The law outlines institutional mechanisms for governing the welfare sector in which the various levels of Government (State, regions and municipalities) intervene at different stages and with different functions. It gives formal recognition to the role of the third sector in both planning and implementation. It is undoubtedly the right approach to the new need for social protection and, in the RMI, it has a necessary and potentially effective response. The indications that emerge from the experiment, however, seem to call for some important adjustments to give local Government greater flexibility in defining the details of the RMI and to give central Government institutions greater control over its efficacy.

References

Alber, J. 1986. *Dalla carità allo Stato sociale*, (Bologna, Il Mulino).

Andreotti, A. 2002. *Le reti come vincolo e risorsa. Le donne in condizione di bisogno economico a Milano*, Tesi di Dottorato, Università di Trento.

———— and Mingione, E.. 2001. "Esclusione urbana e sistemi locali di welfare in Europa", in *Argomenti*, No. 2 (maggio–agosto), pp.23–43.

Ascoli, U. (ed.). 1984. *Welfare State all'italiana* (Roma-Bari, Laterza).

Bagnasco, A. and Negri, N.. 1994. *Classi, ceti, persone. Esercizio di analisi sociale localizzata* (Napoli, Liguori).

Barbagli, M. and Saraceno, C. (eds.). 1998. *Lo stato delle famiglie in Italia* (Il Mulino, Bologna).

Benassi, D. 2000. *Le politiche nazionali contro la povertà in Italia* (Roma, Poligrafico dello Stato).

————. 2002. *Tra benessere e povertà* (Milano, Angeli).

———— and Mingione, E. 2001. *Tendenze al mutamento della società italiana negli anni '90* ,(Dipartimento di Sociologia e ricerca sociale, Università di Milano-Bicocca), mimeo.

Boccella, N. 1982. "Il Mezzogiorno sussidiato", in Angeli, Milano Caizzi, B. (ed.) *Nuova Antologia della Questione Meridionale (1970)* (Milano, Feltrinelli).

Castronovo, V. 1975. "La storia economica",, in *Storia d'Italia,* Vol. IV, I, (Torino, Einaudi).

Commissione d'indagine sull'esclusione sociale (CIES). 2000. *Rapporto annuale sulle politiche contro la povertà e l'esclusione sociale 2000* (Roma, Istituto Poligrafico e Zecca dello Stato).

————. 2001. *Rapporto annuale sulle politiche contro la povertà e l'esclusione sociale 2001*, mimeo.

Del Monte, A. and A. Giannola. 1978. *Il Mezzogiorno nell'economia italiana* (Bologna, Il Mulino).

Esping-Andersen, G. 1990. *The three worlds of welfare capitalism* (Cambridge, Polity Press).

————. 1999. *The social foundation of post-industrial economies* (Oxford, Oxford University Press).

Eurostat. 2000. *European social statistics. Social protection. Expenditures and receipts 1980-1998* (Luxembourg, Office for the Official Publications of the European Communities).

Flora, P. (ed.). 1986–87. *Growth to limits. The western European welfare states since World War II* (Berlino-New York, de Gruyter).

Fargion, V. 1997. *Geografia della cittadinanza sociale* (Bologna, Il Mulino).

————. 1984. *Il welfare state in Italia* (Bologna, Il Mulino).

————. 1998 *Le trappole del welfare* (Bologna, Il Mulino).

Gori, C. (ed.). 2001. *Le politiche per gli anziani non autosufficienti : analisi e proposte* (Milano, Franco Angeli).

Gramsci, A. 1966. *La questione meridionale* (Roma, Editori Riuniti).

Graziani, A. and Pugliese, E.. 1979. *Investimenti e disoccupazione nel Mezzogiorno* (Bologna, Il Mulino).

Kazepov, Y. 1996. *Le politiche locali contro l'esclusione sociale*, Commissione d'Indagine sulla Povertà e sull'Emarginazione, Roma, Istituto Poligrafico e Zecca dello Stato.

————. 2000. "Italia, Europa: reddito minimo di inserimento", in *Prospettive Sociali e Sanitarie*, No. 20–22 (Nov.–Dec.).

———— and Orientale Caputo, G. 1998. "No organization no money no services: About the social exclusion of the poor from welfare benefits in Italy", in R. Van Berkel, H. Coenen and R. Vlek (eds.) *Beyond marginality? Social movements of social security claimants in the European Union* (Aldershot, Ashgate Press).

Micheli, G. A. 1997. "Spezzare il retaggio, forse assecondarlo : intrecci tra dinamiche di povertà e modelli familiari", in *Polis*, XI, 2, pp. 277–298.

———. 2001. "La configurazione dei legami forti e la gestione delle emergenze", in *Irer, Quattro studi sulla vulnerabilità* (Milano, Guerini Associati).

Mingione, E. 1998. "Riforme del welfare o tagli della spesa : una incompatibilità dimenticata", in L. Paganetto (ed.) *Lo Stato Sociale in Italia : quadrare il cerchio* (Bologna, Il Mulino), pp. 65–80.

———. 1999. (ed.) *Le sfide dell'esclusione: metodi, luoghi, soggetti* (Bologna, Il Mulino).

———. 2002. "Il lato oscuro del welfare : trasformazione delle biografie, strategie familiari e sistemi di garanzia" in *Atti del Convegno "Tecnologia e Società II"*, Roma, Accademia dei Lincei, 5–6 aprile.

——— and Oberti, M. 2003. "The struggle against social exclusion at the local level: Diversity and convergence in European cities", in *European Journal of Spatial Development*.

Mugnano, S. 2002. *From local to multi-tiered social policies: Exploring provision for homeless people*, PhD dissertation, Bristol University.

Negri, N. and Saraceno, C. 1996. *Le politiche contro la povertà in Italia* (Bologna, Il Mulino).

Paci, M. 1989. *Pubblico e privato nei moderni sistemi di welfare* (Napoli, Liguori).

Piore, M.J. and Sabel, 1984. *The Second Industrial Divide*, New York, Basic Books.

Ritter, G. A. 1996. *Storia dello stato sociale* (Roma-Bari, Laterza).

Rossi Doria, M. 1956. *Riforma agraria ed azione meridionalista* (Bologna, Il Mulino).

Saraceno, C. 1993. "Alla ricerca di una difficile legittimazione: il welfare italiano nella prospettiva dell'Europa di Maastricht", in *Stato and Mercato*, No. 37.

———. (ed.) 2002. *Social assistance dynamics in Europe. National and local poverty regimes* (Cambridge, Policy Press).

Toso, S. (ed.) 2000. *Selettività e assistenza sociale* (Milano, Angeli).

Trigilia, C. 1992 *Sviluppo senza autonomia. Effetti perversi delle politiche nel Mezzogiorno* (Bologna, Il Mulino).

Villari, R. 1966. Il sud nella storia d'Italia (Bari, Laterza).

APPENDIX

Main characteristics of poverty in Italy

According to estimates of the *Commissione d'indagine sull'Esclusione Sociale* (CIES, 2001) based on Istat data, in Italy in 2000 there were 2,707,000 families, comprising 7'948'000 individuals, in relative poverty representing 12.3% of all families and 13.9% of all individuals. The poverty threshold was set at €810.30 a month for a two-person family.

About two-thirds of the poor are concentrated in the southern regions, where just over one third of the population lives. In this part of the country the incidence of poverty is 25.5% (individuals) as against 5.9% in the North and 10.5% in the Centre. The tables below summarize the features of poverty in Italy, thus providing an empirical framework for the analysis of national policies to deal with the phenomenon.

Table 6.A1   Expenditure for social benefits by function, selected EU countries, 1998

	EU 15	D	E	F	I	NL	S	UK
Sickness/health care	26.8	28.1	29.2	29.2	23.4	28.5	23.4	25.2
Disability	8.3	7.9	8.1	4.9	6.2	11.8	11.6	11.6
Old age	40.6	40.4	41.9	37.9	53.3	35.8	37.2	39.9
Survivors	5.1	1.9	4.3	6.1	10,7	5.3	2.3	3.9
Family/children	8.3	10.1	2.1	9.8	3.6	4.5	10.8	8.6
Unemployment	7.2	8.7	13.5	7.6	2.7	7.3	9.3	3.6
Housing	2.1	0.7	0.3	3.2	0.0	1.6	2.5	6.2
Social exclusion	1.6	2.2	0.7	1.4	0.1	5.2	3.0	0.8
Total	100.0	100.0	100.0	100.0	100.0	100.0	100.0	100.0

D=Germany; E=Spain; F=France; I=Italy, NL=Netherlands; S=Sweden; UK= United Kingdom
Source: Eurostat (2000).

Table 6.A2   Equivalence scale and poverty thresholds, 2000

Household members	Ratio	Threshold (€ per month)
1	0.599	485.4
2 (standard)	1.000	810.3
3	1.335	1 081.8
4	1.632	1 322.4
5	1.905	1 543.7
6	2.150	1 742.2
7 and more	2.401	1 945.6

Source. CIES (2001).

Figure 6.A1 Poverty (individuals) by region, Italy, 1997–2000

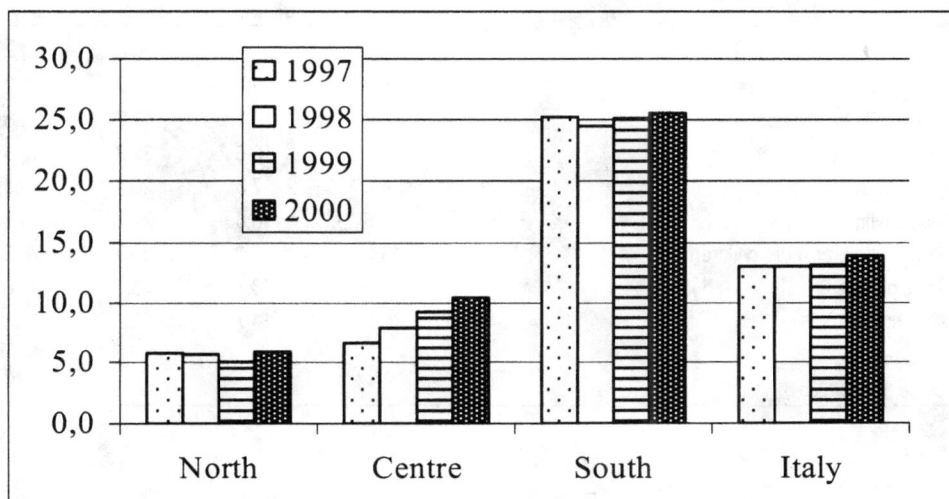

Table 6.A3 Poverty distribution and incidence by geographical areas, 2000 (%)

	North	Centre	South	Italy
Distribution				
Households	22.0 (47.8)	15.3 (19.4)	62.7 (32.8)	100.0
Individuals	18.9 (44.5)	14.6 (19.2)	66.5 (36.3)	100.0
Incidence				
Households	5.7	9.7	23.6	12.3
Individuals	5.9	10.5	25.5	13.9

In brackets: households or individuals resident in the area
Source CIES (2001)

Table 6.A4 Poverty incidence by household size and geographical areas, 2000 (%)

Household size	North	Centre	South	Italy
1	6.1	6.2	17.5	9.3
2	4.9	11.9	24.2	11.7
3	4.9	8.5	21.6	10.5
4	5.9	10.7	25.0	14.7
5 or more	11.3	16.2	33.4	24.3

Source CIES (2001)

Table 6.A5   Poverty incidence by household type and geographical area, 2000 (%)

	North	Centre	South	Italy
Single person under 65	3.1	*	9.0	4.4
Single person 65 or more	8.7	9.4	23.2	13.2
Couple with head under 65	1.9	*	12.7	4.8
Couple with head 65 or over	8.0	18.5	32.8	18.5
Couple with 1 child	4.4	7.3	20.4	9.5
Couple with 2 children	5.6	10.0	24.4	14.5
Couple with 3 or more children	11.3	*	33.3	25.2
Single parent	5.9	13.7	23.5	13.0
Other households	9.6	14.7	32.4	17.6

*Not significant

Source. CIES (2001).

FROM POVERTY RELIEF TO UNIVERSAL ENTITLEMENT: WELFARE, MINIMUM INCOME AND BASIC INCOME IN IRELAND

7

Sean Healy and Bridig Reynolds [1]

1. The present income support system in Ireland

In Ireland there are a range of income supports for people in specific situations such as unemployment or in specific groups such as children. This system is usually called the "social welfare" system. Until 1997 the Government department responsible for making most of these payments and administering the system was called the Department of Social Welfare. Since then it has changed its title to the Department of Social, Community and Family Affairs.

1.1 From small beginnings

The system has been evolving for almost a century. Schemes have been introduced at various times in response to particular perceived needs and/or demands. Nobody would claim that the system has had a coherent evolution and, although it has been much improved in recent years, it is still far from fully integrated.

The Poor Law system was introduced in 1838. This was not an income support measure and was never intended by its initiators to be such. However, it was drawn into the income support system over time, and was the only support available to people on low incomes at the beginning of the 20th century.

The first social welfare scheme to provide income support was the old age non-contributory pension, introduced in 1909 following the passing of the Old

---

[1] Conference of Religious of Ireland Justice Commission.

Age Pension Act in the British parliament in 1908.[2] The pension for the blind was the next payment, introduced in 1920. Ireland became independent in 1922. Unemployment assistance was introduced in 1933 and other schemes followed. Of special significance was the introduction of the Children's Allowance in 1944, today called Child Benefit. The Department of Social Welfare was established in 1947. It was 1961 before the contributory old age pension — an insurance-based payment — was introduced. We will return to the distinctions between assistance and insurance-based payments in the next section.

Since the 1960s, a range of schemes has been introduced, though with no particular underlying philosophy. Indeed, it is clear that there has been no coherent plan for the development a social welfare schemes. Different needs were highlighted and different schemes were developed in response. For example, the unemployment benefit scheme introduced in 1911 provided payments for a short period to those who became unemployed. The prolonged and extensive unemployment of the 1930s led to the introduction in 1933 of the unemployment assistance scheme, which provided payments (at a lower rate and subject to a means test) to those whose entitlement to unemployment benefit had been exhausted.

1.2 The income support system today

Today there are three main kinds of income support payments in the Irish social welfare system — social insurance, social assistance and universal.

Social insurance schemes are financed by compulsory contributions from both employers and employees (including the self-employed). Once the insurance payments have been made, the entitlement is established and the social insurance scheme payments are made irrespective of any other income the person may receive.

The use of the term insurance is a misnomer in this context. The social insurance system is not insurance in the commercial or actuarial sense. There is no proportional link between the contributions paid by individual insured persons and what these individuals receive in payments under any of the social insurance schemes. In practice, the schemes are based on the principle of solidarity and are organized on a pay-as-you-go basis.

---

[2] Ireland was then under direct British rule and decisions on issues of this nature were taken in the British parliament in which there were elected Irish members.

The State provides the additional funding required if there is a shortfall between what has been provided by employer and employee payments and the total cost of the schemes in any particular year. In reality, the social insurance fund represents a tripartite arrangement between employers, employees (including the self-employed) and the State. In the late 1990s and subsequently, there has been an exceptional situation because due to the performance of the Irish economy, the State has not been required to provide any funding for social insurance payments. The years since 1994 have seen reductions in the main rates of social insurance contributions paid by employers and employees as well as the introduction of a threshold below which an employee pays no social insurance contribution.

In 2002 the social insurance contribution threshold for an employee is €38,740 a year. Below that level the employee pays a social insurance contribution (plus a levy) of 6% (with the qualifications listed later in this paragraph). Above that level the employee pays no social insurance but does pay a levy of 2%. If a person's income is €287 a week or less he/she pays no social insurance payments. If a person's income is between €287 and €356 a week he/she pays no social insurance payments on the first €127 and pays a rate of 4% on the balance. On incomes above €356 a week a rate of 2% is paid on the first €127 and 6% on the balance.

For an employer there is no ceiling and the rate is 10.75%. However, there is a lower rate of 8.5% for employers of people who earn less than €356 a week.

The rates paid in 2002 for the main categories of social insurance are listed in table 7.1. For single people they range from €153.70 a week for a (contributory) old age pensioner over 80 years of age, to €118.80 a week for a person receiving unemployment benefit. For couples, they range from €267.50 a week for a pensioner over 80 years of age with a qualified adult over 66, to €197.60 for a couple on unemployment benefits.

The total number of recipients of social insurance payments in 2000 was 440,057 and the total number of beneficiaries was 649,463. Details of the numbers of recipients and beneficiaries in each of the sub-categories of social insurance payments are listed in table 7.5.

Table 7.1   Maximum weekly rates of social insurance from 2002

Personal and qualified adult rates	Euros
Retirement pension/old age contributory pension:	
(i) *Under 80.*	
Personal rate	147.30
Person with qualified adult under 66	245.40
Person with qualified adult 66 or over	261.10
(ii) *80 or over.*	
Personal rate	153.70
Person with qualified adult under 66	251.80
Person with qualified adult 66 or over	267.50
Widow's/widower's contributory pension:	
(i) Under 66	123.30
(ii) 66 and under 80	144.80
(iii) 80 or over	151.20
Invalidity pension:	
(i) *Under 65:*	
Personal rate	123.30
Person with qualified adult under 66	211.30
Person with qualified adult 66 or over	228.70
(ii) *65 and under 80·*	
Personal rate	147.30
Person with qualified adult under 66	235.30
Person with qualified adult 66 or over	252.70
(iii) *80 or over.*	
Personal rate	153.70
Person with qualified adult under 66	241.70
Person with qualified adult 66 or over	259.10
Carer's benefit	
Personal rate	132.70
Occupational injuries benefit — death benefit pension:	
(i) Personal rate under 66	146.60
(ii) Personal rate over 66	151.70
Occupational Injuries benefit — disablement pension:	
Personal rate	148.90
Disability/unemployment benefit:	
Personal rate	118.80
Person with qualified adult	197.60
Injury benefit/health and safety benefit.	
Personal rate	118.80
Person with qualified adult	197.60
Orphan's contributory allowance	91.00

Source: Developed from tables contained in Department of Finance (2002) Budget Documents.

For **social assistance,** eligibility is determined on the basis of an assessment of needs. These are means tested schemes, in which, the claimant becomes eligible for payments only if his/her means are less than a set the threshold. People receiving payments from these schemes have either no social insurance record, or have used up their entitlement, or their social insurance payments are inadequate, e.g. their contributions have not been paid for an adequate period of time.

The rates for social assistance payments for single people range from €118.80 for long-term unemployed people to €140.40 for old age non-contributory pensioners 80 years and over. For couples they vary from €197.60 for the long-term unemployed to €228.90 for non-contributory old-age pensioners. Full details of the various rates of social assistance in 2002 are contained in table 7.2.

The number of recipients and beneficiaries in the social assistance system in 2000 are contained in table 7.5. The total number of recipients was 429,937 and the total number of beneficiaries was 783,311.

Combining social insurance and social assistance, 2000 there were 869,994 recipients and 1,432,774 beneficiaries.

Table 7.2   Maximum weekly rates of social assistance, 2002

Personal and qualified adult rates	Euros
Old age non-contributory pension:	
(i) *Under 80:*	
Personal rate	134 00
Person with qualified adult under 66	222.50
Person with qualified adult 66 or over	222.50
(ii) *80 or over:*	
Personal rate	140 40
Person with qualified adult under 66	228.90
Person with qualified adult 66 or over	228.90
Blind person's pension:	
(i) *Under 66:*	
Personal rate	118.80
Person with qualified adult under 66	197.60
Person with qualified adult 66 or over	207.30
(ii) *66 and under 80:*	
Personal rate	134.00
Person with qualified adult under 66	212.80

Personal and qualified adult rates	Euros
Person with qualified adult 66 or over	222.50
(iii) *80 or over:*	
Personal rate	140.40
Person with qualified adult under 66	219.20
Widow's/widower's non-contributory pension:	
(i) Under 66	118.80
(ii) 66 and under 80	134.00
(iii) 80 or over	140.40
One-parent family payment (including one child)	
(i) Under 66:	138.10
(ii) 66 years and over	153.30
Carer's allowance:	
(i) Under 66:	122.60
(ii) 66 years and over	137.80
Disability allowance:	
Personal rate	118.80
Personal with qualified adult	197.60
Supplementary welfare allowance:	
Personal rate	118.80
Person with qualified adult	197.60
Unemployment assistance (short-term):	
Personal rate	118.80
Person with qualified adult	197.60
Unemployment assistance (long-term):	
Personal rate	118.80
Person with qualified adult	197.60
Pre-retirement allowance/farm assist	
Personal rate	118.80
Person with qualified adult	197.60
Orphan's non-contributory pension	91.00

Source   Developed from tables contained in Department of Finance (2002) Budget Documents

Universal schemes require neither insurance contributions nor a means test. Payments are made without reference to the income of either the recipient or the beneficiary (where these are not the same as with child benefit).

Child benefit is the most important universal social welfare scheme in Ireland. It is paid in respect of all children under the age of 16. It is also paid in respect of 16, 17 and 18 year-olds if they are in full-time education or has a physical or mental disability. The rates in 2002 are €117.60 a month for the first and second child and €147.30 for the third and subsequent child (Table 7.3), paid on a monthly basis. In 2000 there were 510,840 families receiving child benefit in respect of 1,018,175 children (Department of Social, Community and Family Affairs, 2000, table D7, p. 39).

Table 7.3   Monthly rates of child benefit, 2002

Child benefit	Euro
First and second children	117.60
Third and subsequent children	147.30

Source   Developed from tables contained in Department of Finance (2002) Budget Documents.

Table 7.4   Maximum weekly rates of health allowances, 2002

Supplementary allowance payable to blind persons	Euros
In receipt of a blind pension	
(i) Blind pensioner	36.90
(ii) Blind married couple	73.80
Infectious diseases maintenance allowance	
(i) Personal rate	118.80
(ii) Persons with qualified adult	198.80

Source   Developed from tables contained in Department of Finance (2002) Budget Documents.

While these numbers are substantial, the actual level of payments is not adequate to address the issue of poverty. In fact, in recent years, despite the dramatic economic growth Ireland has experienced, the percentage of people living with incomes below the poverty line has increased significantly. The next section presents the reality of poverty in Ireland, given the present income support system. We will go on from there to present the basic income debate in Ireland and outline the pathways we see this taking in the period ahead.

Table 7.5   **Number of recipients and beneficiaries of weekly social welfare payments by payment type and insurance or assistance, 2000**

Type of payment	Recipients	Beneficiaries
Old age (contributory) pension	86 217	109 832
Retirement pension	78 370	104 244
Widower's (contributory) pension	100 374	116 030
Deserted wife's benefit	12 654	25 174
Maternity benefit	6 130	6 130
Health and safety benefit	30	54
Adoptive benefit	10	10
Orphan's (contributory) allowance	1 148	1 148
Disability benefit	46 940	95 038
Invalidity pension	48 663	83 271
Injury benefit	828	1 643
Interim disability benefit	488	914
Disablement benefit	10 925	11 888
Death benefit pension	665	893
Carer's benefit	50	114
Unemployment benefit	46 565	93 080
TOTAL SOCIAL INSURANCE	440 057	649 463
Old age (non-contributory) pension	90 652	96 828
Pre-retirement allowance	12 521	19 675
Widow/er's non-contributory pension	17 367	17 367
Deserted wife's allowance	1 613	1 613
Prisoner's wife's allowance	3	3
One-parent family payment	74 119	192 755
Orphan's non-contributory pension	749	749
Disability allowance	54 303	70 885
Blind person's pension	2 229	2 910
Carer's allowance	16 478	30 901
Unemployment assistance	69 504	132 212
Family income supplement	13 062	44 336
Back to work allowance	34 506	87 481
Back to work enterprise allowance	4 503	11 510
Back to education allowance	4 237	5 932

Type of payment	Recipients	Beneficiaries
Part-time job incentive scheme	474	474
Farm assist/smallholders	8 051	21 760
Supplementary welfare allowance	25 094	45 448
Rent allowance	472	472
Total social assistance	429 937	783 311
GRAND TOTAL	869 994	1 432 774

Source   Department of Social, Community and Family Affairs (2000), *Statistical Information on Social Welfare Services*, Tables A10 and A12.

2. Poverty and the income support system in Ireland

The extent of poverty in Ireland has been highlighted by the United Nations Human Development Report (UN Development Programme, 2001), which shows that of 17 industrialized countries, Ireland ranks 16th on the poverty index. Only the USA has a higher percentage of its population living in poverty. The United Kingdom is ranked 15th, while Sweden, Norway and the Netherlands have the lowest levels of poverty. The variables used in this measurement of poverty are the percentages of people likely to die before age 60, people who are functionally illiterate, people with disposable incomes less than 50% of the median, and those unemployed for more than a year.

In the context of sustained levels of record economic growth, the scale of poverty in Ireland can surprise many. Taken as a whole, the Republic has become a much more prosperous place. However, the distribution of that prosperity has denied many people a share in the "Celtic Tiger" dividend.

How many people are poor? On what basis are they classified as poor? In trying to measure the extent of poverty, the most common approach has been to identify a poverty line (or lines) based on relative income. The most commonly used poverty line in Ireland is *half average income, adjusted for family size and composition*. Alternatives set at 40% and 60% of average income are also used to lend robustness to conclusions that could have an impact on policy. The Economic and Social Research Institute (ESRI) have conducted the major studies on poverty lines in Ireland.

- in financial terms the ESRI discovered that the income-per-adult equivalent averaged over households in 1998 was €237.73 (£187.23). The income poverty lines for a single adult derived from this average were:
  - 40% line - €95.09 (£74.89) a week;
  - 50% line - €118.86 (£93.61) a week;

  ° 60% line - €142.64 (£112.34) a week;

- updating the more generally accepted poverty line (i.e. 50% of average income) to 2002 levels, using actual (Central Statistics Office, 1998-2001) and predicted (Department of Finance, 2002) increases in average industrial earnings, produces a relative income poverty line of €157.71 (£124.21) for a single person. This is €38.91 (£30.65) more than the level of most social assistance.

The most up-to-date data available on poverty in Ireland come from the 1998 Living in Ireland Survey, conducted by the ESRI, and is shown in table 7.6.

Table 7.6   Percentage of households and persons below relative income poverty lines, 1994/1997/1998

	Households			Persons		
	1994	1997	1998	1994	1997	1998
40% line	4.8	6.3	10.5	5.2	6.3	9.1
50% line	18.6	22.4	24.6	17.4	18.1	20.0
60% line	34.1	34.3	33.4	30.4	30.1	28.6

- overall the 40 and 50% lines show a continued increase in the numbers below those lines for the whole period. Only the 60% line shows a minor decrease;
- using the more generally accepted poverty line (50%) the percentage of persons under this line rose from 17.4% in 1994 to 18.1% in 1997, and to 20% in 1998;
- similarly, households experiencing poverty increased, with the equivalent numbers being 18.6%, 22.4% and 24.6% respectively;
- using the 50% line, we may conclude that one in four households and one in five persons live in relative income poverty.

The depth of poverty declined between 1994 and 1998. Even though people remain relatively poor, they do have more money in their pockets. Therefore, those below relative-income poverty lines moved closer to these lines than in the past. Consequently, the share of national income needed to bridge the poverty gap, to bring everyone up to these lines, has been greatly reduced.

The Government's National Anti-Poverty Strategy, published in 1997, adopted the following definition of poverty:

People are living in poverty if their income and resources (material, cultural and social) are so inadequate as to preclude them from having a standard of living that is regarded as acceptable by Irish society generally. As a result of inadequate income and resources people may be excluded and marginalized from participating in activities that are considered the norm for other people in society.

This definition of poverty is, effectively, ignored by government when it focuses principally on reducing "*consistent* poverty" and does not give priority to providing poor people with sufficient income to live life with dignity.

What does "consistent" poverty mean? Income alone does not tell the whole story concerning living standards and command over resources. As we have seen in the National Anti-Poverty Strategy definition of poverty, it is necessary to look more broadly at people's exclusion from the life of a society because of a lack of resources. This involves looking at other areas where "as a result of inadequate income and resources people may be excluded and marginalized from participating in activities that are considered the norm for other people in society".

What are these activities? In seeking to answer this question, the ESRI, in various poverty studies, has measured access to 23 non-monetary indicators. These have subsequently been divided into three subsets, focusing on the basic dimension, the housing/services dimension and the secondary dimension. In the "basic dimension" the indicators included by the ESRI are:

- a meal with meat, chicken or fish every second day;
- a warm, waterproof overcoat;
- two pairs of strong shoes;
- a roast joint of meat or its equivalent once a week;
- new, not second-hand clothes;
- going without a substantial meal;
- going without heat;
- going into debt for ordinary living expenses.

The proportion of households experiencing income poverty who are also experiencing basic deprivation declined from 9% in 1994 to 6.2% in 1998 (see table 7.7). The percentage is likely to have fallen further since then. While these improvements are welcome, they should not be excessively praised. The group being measured as "consistently" poor is a sub-set of those who live in poverty. The ESRI studies identify this group as having a series of psychological characteristics that set them apart from others who live in relative income poverty. The challenge facing the Irish Government is not simply to reduce the proportion of the population living in "consistent" poverty but to eliminate all relative income poverty. The resources to do this have existed for some time.

Table 7.7   Percentage of households below the 50% income line and experiencing basic deprivation in 1994/1997/1998

	1994	1997	1998
50% line	9.0	6.7	6.2

Source: Derived from Layte *et al.* (2001), p. 35.

When poverty is being analysed it is important to distinguish between the risk facing a particular type of household (i.e. the proportion of households of that type found to be in poverty) and the incidence of poverty (the proportion of all those in poverty who belong to that group).

Table 7.8 provides a breakdown, for the period 1973-98, of those below the 50% poverty line (i.e. *incidence* of poverty), classifying them by the labour force status of the head of household.

• this shows that 60% of households who experience poverty are households whose head is either on home duties (39.2%) or retired (21.2%);

• households headed by an unemployed person make up the next largest group at 15.4%.

Table 7.8   Composition of households under 50% relative poverty line by labour force status, 1973–1998

	1973[a]	1980[a]	1987[b]	1994[c]	1997[c]	1998[c]
Employee	9.0	10.3	8.2	5.3	7.3	4.0
Self-employed	3.6	3.5	4.8	6.6	6.2	5.2
Farmer	26.0	25.9	23.7	8.0	5.0	6.2
Unemployed	9.6	14.7	37.4	30.3	18.9	15.4
Disabled / ill	10.2	9.3	11.1	9.6	9.1	8.8
Retired	17.0	18.9	8.1	10.1	17.9	21.2
Home duties	24.6	17.4	6.7	30.2	35.7	39.2
Total	100.0	100.0	100.0	100.0	100.0	100.0

Notes: a. Household Budget Survey Data — b: ESRI Data — c: ESRI Living in Ireland Survey Data
Sources: Derived from Nolan and Callan (1996), p. 95 and Layte et al. (2001), p. 24.

The *risk* of poverty for each of these categories over the same 1973–98 periods is outlined in Table 7.9, which shows that

• since 1997 the overall risk of poverty has increased further to 24.3%;

- the risk of poverty has increased for five out of the seven classifications. Households whose head is a farmer, unemployed, ill/disabled, retired or on home duties have all seen an increase in their risk of being exposed to poverty;

- only households whose head is an employee or self-employed have experienced reduced risk;

- the risk of poverty has decreased dramatically for households headed by a farmer; however, the number of full-time farmers has fallen substantially.

Table 7.9   Risk of relative income poverty (50% poverty line) by labour force status, 1973–1998

	1973[a]	1980[a]	1987[b]	1994[c]	1997[c]	1998[c]
Employee	3.9	3.7	3.5	2.8	4.0	2.3
Self-employed	10.1	8.6	10.5	15.1	17.1	15.8
Farmer	21.2	27.0	32.8	21.5	16.3	22.0
Unemployed	61.9	63.1	57.2	57.3	54.9	56.2
Disabled / ill	42.8	48.2	33.7	50.0	60.4	72.6
Retired	29.5	23.3	9.1	10.2	23.3	28.7
Home Duties	42.2	32.2	9.8	33.2	48.6	58.4
Total	18.3	16.8	16.3	18.6	22.3	24.3

Notes a. Household Budget Survey Data — b. ESRI Data — c: ESRI Living in Ireland Survey Data

Sources. Derived from Nolan and Callan (1996), p. 96 and Layte et al (2001), p. 24.

Additional research on poverty risk by the ESRI has shown that:

- between 1997 and 1998, the risk of falling below half average income rose for single-person households, notably where the head was aged 65 or over. In 1997, this risk was 40.1%, in 1998 it was 50.8%. By 1998, single-adult households had become the highest risk group, with a risk figure more than twice that of the next highest group;

- the poverty risk attached to households of one adult with children also increased sharply between 1997 and 1998. These households now have a 42.4% chance of experiencing poverty.

The 1998 ESRI poverty data indicate a further decrease in the number of households with children who experience poverty. In 1994, households containing children accounted for 55% of all households below the 50% relative income poverty line; in 1998, this was 28%. In general, between 1994 and 1998, there was a narrowing of the gap between the risks facing children and those facing adults. While this is clearly an improvement, the overall figure remains very high.

The 1998 ESRI poverty data clearly indicate that women in Ireland experience a greater risk of poverty than men (Table 7.10). This is particularly noticeable in the age group 65 and over, where 43.5% of women are at risk of experiencing poverty compared with 25.9% of men. The greater dependency of elderly women on social welfare payments, whose growth has lagged behind average income growth, is a central reason why the gender gap has been increasing.

Table 7.10   Risk of relative income poverty (50% poverty line), by gender and adult's age, 1994–1998

	1994%		1997 %		1998 %	
	Men	Women	Men	Women	Men	Women
All adults	14.5	16.7	15.5	21.6	16.8	22.2
Adults aged 18–64	15.6	17.9	15.3	18.3	15.3	17.6
Adults aged 65+	8.4	8.4	16.9	38.5	25.9	43.5

Source: Layte et al. (2001), p. 28

As noted earlier in table 7.9, the 1998 data record an increased risk of poverty for single-adult households and households headed by someone working full-time in the home. Both these classifications comprise primarily households headed by women and help to explain further the growth in female poverty risk.

As part of the implementation of the National Anti-Poverty Strategy (NAPS) the social partners (employers, trade unions, farmers, and the community and voluntary sector) have been involved in a dialogue led by the Department of Social, Community and Family Affairs to develop mechanisms for poverty-proofing policies of Government departments. A document was agreed that sets out how civil servants responsible for policy should assess policies for:

• impact on poverty;

• contribution to achieving the NAPS targets;

• ability to address inequalities leading to poverty.

This is an important development that has the capacity to give a new direction to policy and the distribution of resources. A recent review by the National Economic and Social Council (NESC) identified a number of areas within the existing poverty-proofing process that require improvement. It is clear that such improvements are necessary as, to date, the implementation of poverty proofing in areas such as the annual budget leaves a great deal to be desired.

The convergence of Irish incomes with the EU average has fuelled a growing expectation that Ireland should provide a EU level of services. One measure of such services is the level of social protection expenditure. Table 7.11 provides the most recently available figures for countries in the EU.

Table 7.11   Social protection expenditure in the EU between 1996 and 1998 as a % of GDP

	1996	1997	1998
Belgium	28.8	28.5	26.9
Denmark	32.5	31.4	29.1
Germany	30.6	29.9	28.2
Greece	23.1	23.6	23.7
Spain	21.9	21.4	21.0
France	31.0	30.8	28.9
Ireland	18.5	17.5	15.3
Italy	25.3	25.9	24.3
Luxembourg	25.2	24.8	23.2
Netherlands	30.8	30.3	26.8
Austria	29.6	28.8	27.5
Portugal	21.6	22.5	20.4
Finland	32.3	29.9	26.4
Sweden	34.6	33.7	32.6
United Kingdom	27.7	26.8	26.0
EU-15	28.7	28.2	26.6

Source   Eurostat, February 2000 and September 2001

The percentage of GDP spent by Ireland on social protection continues to be lower than any other country in the EU, and it is decreasing. At 15.3% of GDP, the Irish figure is more than 5 percentage points lower than the allocation in Portugal, the next lowest-spending country. Sweden, the country with the highest social-protection expenditure, spends more than twice as much as Ireland. While some of the difference may be explained by the fact that Ireland does not have as large a proportion of its population in the pension age group, the contrasts are still dramatic.

An examination by the Vincentian Partnership for Social Justice of the current social welfare and minimum wage rates underscores their inadequacy. The study concludes, "these rates do not reflect the current cost of even the most frugal standard of living. There is an urgent need to increase them to a realistic level at which people can live with some dignity and without the burden of a continuous shortfall" (Vincentian Partnership for Social Justice, 2001, p. 156).

The study was conducted during 2001 and involved 118 people in 12 community centres in seven parts of Dublin city completing a detailed questionnaire on their weekly income and expenditure. Each person represented a specific household. The study found that housekeeping and food were the most costly items for the majority of households, regardless of income. It also identified that people on social welfare experienced shortfalls because of the inadequacy of their income, rather than because of bad management. The resulting financial pressure diverted family attention away from allocating enough time, commitment or money to areas such as education. Consequently, children may leave school early to avoid further financial pressure on their parents.

Based on the survey and its findings, the Vincentian Partnership identified a number of key recommendations (pp. 159–161):

- raise the single adult social welfare rate to €184 (£145);
- lone parents with two children need €254 (£200) a week to live life with some dignity;
- increase child dependant allowance to a minimum of €25.40 (£20) a week for low-income families;
- increase the provision of state-supported, affordable, child care so that more people can avail themselves of training and work opportunities;
- encourage employers to adopt greater flexibility in working hours so that parents can work during school hours;
- increase the back-to-school clothing and footwear allowance to a more realistic level.

Many of these are sound ideas. But the sustained high rates of poverty and income inequality in Ireland require more attention. Tackling poverty effectively requires action on many fronts, ranging from healthcare to education, from accommodation to employment. However, the most important requirement is the provision of sufficient income to enable people to live a life with dignity. No anti-poverty strategy can achieve success without an effective approach to addressing low incomes.

The poorest people in Irish society were expected to live on €118.80 a week in the year 2002. This is far from adequate, and those who depend on it can expect to experience only the most frugal of living standards.

Despite the failure to address low incomes on an adequate scale, there has been progress on benchmarking social welfare payments. In its final report, published in September 2001, the Social Welfare Benchmarking and Indexation Working Group agreed that the lowest social welfare rates should be benchmarked. A majority of the Working Group also agreed that this benchmark should be index-linked to society's standard of living as it grows, and that the benchmark should be reached by a definite date.

The Working Group chose Gross Average Industrial Earnings (GAIE) as the index to which payments should be fixed. A majority agreed that the benchmark for welfare payments by 2007 should be 27% of GAIE. In 2002 terms this would mean that the lowest social welfare payment (€118.80 a week in 2002) should be €138.85.

Implementation of these recommendations would mark a breakthrough in the struggle to tackle poverty and social exclusion in Ireland. The lowest welfare payment would rise dramatically, the target would be reached within a definite time frame, and social payments would continue to increase in line with the improving living standards of the wider society.

The Community and Voluntary Pillar of Social Partners and the Trade Union Pillar both argued that the benchmark should be set at 30% of GAIE, with 27% as an interim target. In accepting the GAIE index, the Working Group was following a precedent set by the Pensions Board, which had recommended that contributory old age pensions be benchmarked at 34% of GAIE.

All members of the working group agreed that basic child income support (i.e. Child Benefit and Child Dependant Allowances combined) should be set at 33–35% of the minimum adult payment rate.

The National Anti-Poverty Strategy Review 2002 set the following as key targets:

> To achieve a rate of €150 per week in 2002 terms for the lowest rates of social welfare to be met by 2007 and the appropriate equivalence level of basic child income support (i.e. Child Benefit and Child Dependant Allowances combined) to be set at 33% — 35% of the minimum adult social welfare payment rate.

The target of €150 a week is equivalent to 30% of Gross Average Industrial Earnings (GAIE) in 2002. This means that social welfare rates will be benchmarked to increases in average industrial wages from now on. It also means that the gap between the present level of the lowest social welfare payments and 30% of GAIE will be bridged between now and 2007. If this new target is honoured there will be a substantial reduction in the numbers of people living below the poverty line. However, the issue of low pay has not been addressed.

We now move on to review the basic income debate in Ireland.

3.   The basic income debate in Ireland

In the general debate about the topic in Ireland, basic income is defined as an income paid unconditionally to everyone on an individual basis, without any means test or work requirement. In a basic income system every person would receive a weekly tax-free payment from the Exchequer and all other personal income would be taxed, usually at a single rate. For a person who is unemployed, the basic income payment would replace income from social welfare/social security. For a person who is employed, the basic income payment would replace their tax credit in the income tax system.

There has been a wide range of arguments provided to support the introduction of a basic income system. Among these are its positive impacts in areas such as:

- liberty and equality;
- efficiency and community;
- common ownership of the earth;
- equal sharing in the benefits of technical progress;
- flexibility of the labour market;
- the dignity of poor people;
- tackling poverty traps and unemployment traps;
- the fight against unemployment and inhumane working conditions;
- the need to reverse the desertification of the countryside;
- interregional inequalities;
- the viability of co-operatives;
- the promotion of adult education;
- autonomy from bosses, husbands and bureaucrats.

All of these reasons, and more, have been invoked in favour of introducing a basic income system in Ireland and beyond.[3]

In the late 1970s, the National Economic and Social Council (Ireland's Government-appointed think-tank which includes representatives of social partners, government appointees and key civil servants) commissioned a report on how personal income tax and transfers might be integrated. This report

---

[3] For a much fuller treatment of this topic see Van Parijs (1992) and Ward (1998).

(Dowling, 1977) examined three broad options, one of which was basic income. Subsequently, the report generated very little discussion about basic income. However, it did provide the basis for a wide-ranging debate on tax reform that culminated in the establishment of the Commission on Taxation.

The first report of the Commission on Taxation (1982) contained a cursory examination of basic income that it rejected, mainly on cost grounds. Similarly, the Commission on Social Welfare (1986), quoting the report of the Commission on Taxation, rejected basic income on cost grounds, but also because basic income might represent a detour from the priority objective, according to the Commission, of increasing social welfare rates to adequate levels.

Both of these major reports commissioned by Government are characterized by a marked failure to analyse basic income on any serious level. This failure is difficult to justify, even if it is understandable given the focus of both reports and the contexts in which they were produced. However, for many years afterwards these two reports were quoted, by those opposed to analysing a basic income approach, as sufficient reason for rejecting basic income. By such cursory analysis and casual dismissal is policy often made!

From 1987 onwards there have been two approaches to studying basic income in Ireland. The first approach preserved key elements of the existing tax and spending systems (Honohan, 1987; Callan et al., 1994). The second approach substituted basic income for the existing tax and welfare systems and some other government spending (Ward, 1994; CORI, 1994, 1995, 1996; Healy and Reynolds, 1995; Clark and Kavanagh, 1995; Clark and Healy, 1997).

The models developed by Honohan and Callan was similar. According to these models each adult of working age would receive an untaxed payment equivalent to that paid as unemployment assistance (in the social welfare system); this was seen as a "full basic income". Elderly people would receive somewhat higher payments and children would receive smaller amounts. All social welfare payments would be discontinued. Existing "discretionary'" tax relief (such as mortgage interest, employee pension contributions, etc.) would be retained. All government spending programmes would also be retained.

Both authors found that a very high tax rate would be required to fund this type of proposal. Tax rates in excess of 65% would be required on all personal incomes. It was suggested that such a high tax rate could act as a disincentive to people taking up employment. In addition, Callan found that the income distribution effect of this proposal was not advantageous for significant numbers of low-income households. Honohan and Callan concluded that these models of basic income should be rejected.

A series of official reports in 1996 reviewed the findings of Callan, notably the Department of Enterprise, Trade and Employment, Forfas and the expert

Working Group on the Integration of the Tax and Social Welfare Systems. These reports endorsed Callan's conclusion that this model of basic income was not viable.

4. From CORI to the Green Paper

CORI Justice Commission agreed with the Honohan and Callan assessment that this model of basic income was not viable in the Irish context. CORI, however, wanted to achieve the main benefits of basic income, while reducing the cost, so that the tax rate required (including social insurance contributions) would be no more than 50% — lower than the top combined income tax and social insurance rate in Ireland in the mid-1990s.

Sean Ward had followed this approach in his 1994 study. The main characteristics of this alternative approach were:
- a "full" basic income for older people and for children;
- a "partial" basic income for adults of working age. This would be topped up to the level of unemployment assistance for the unemployed;
- the abolition of all discretionary tax relief;
- a range of public expenditures would no longer be required;
- employers' social insurance contributions would be abolished;
- government support for industry would be reduced.

This new model had several advantages over the current systems. According to Ward it:
- provided more equity, both horizontal and vertical;
- improved incentives to recruit labour and seek work;
- provided greater simplicity and certainty.

CORI Justice Commission adapted and developed this approach in its 1994, 1995 and 1996 reports. CORI proposed some variations on how it might be implemented. A set of principles for evaluating these proposals against the *status quo* position were outlined and applied (Healy and Reynolds, 1995).

The various Government studies already referred to gave this approach little or no consideration. The Working Group on the Integration of the Tax and Social Welfare Systems considered the CORI proposal, but the methodology it used was seriously flawed (Healy, 1996).

The two major objections consistently put forward as the basis for rejecting basic income were that *(a)* it would result in tax rates that were too high and *(b)* there was no practical way of implementing such a system. The last few years have produced changed contexts on for both of these objections.

Economic growth has substantially reduced the tax rate necessary to fund a "full" basic income for everyone in Ireland. As a result of this CORI developed its original proposals further. Instead of having a substantial "partial" basic income for adults of working age it was possible to pay everyone a full basic income. From 1997 onwards all CORI proposals were for the introduction of a "full" basic income. In the interest of clarity, this is referred to here as the CORI approach, version two. It maintains all elements of version one but pays a full basic income to recipients.

At the same time CORI commissioned research to look at how its basic income proposal could be implemented. Charles Clark and John Healy (1997) came up with a recommendation on how to proceed to implementation of a full basic income system for all over a three-year period.

Of equal importance was the issue of financing a basic income system and what tax rate would be required. For years, until 1997, Government refused to study the topic or to fund an independent study.

Since 1987 the Government has negotiated with employers, trade unions and farming organizations to develop three-year national plans. In 1996 an additional pillar was added to this partnership structure, representing the voluntary and community sector. CORI Justice Commission was one of the organizations recognized as a full social partner as part of this pillar. In the course of the negotiations for a new programme called *Partnership 2000* (covering 1997–99), CORI was successful in securing agreement from the other social partners and Government to include a section on basic income which read as follows:

> Further independent appraisal of the concept of introducing a Basic Income for all citizens will be undertaken, taking into account the work of the ESRI, CORI and the Expert Group on the Integration of Tax and Social Welfare and international research. A broadly based steering group will oversee the study.

A Working Group, including CORI, was established to implement this commitment, decided to divide its work into two phases. Phase 1 examined the tax rate needed to fund basic income and the distributional implications of introducing Basic Income with this tax rate. Phase 2 looked at the dynamic effects of the proposal, including its effects on employment, economic growth, budgetary implications, and the gender dimensions of all of these. The studies were published by Government along with the Working Group's report.

The ESRI study for the Working Group found that a basic income system would have a substantial impact on the distribution of income in Ireland. Compared with the present tax and welfare system it would:

- improve the incomes of 70% of households in the bottom four deciles (i.e. the four tenths of the population with lowest incomes), and

- raise half of the individuals that would be below the 40% poverty line under "conventional" options, above this poverty line.

According to the report, these impacts would be achieved without any resources additional to those available to "conventional" options.

The Working Group's report also found that the tax rate (including Pay Related Social Insurance — PRSI — replacement) required to finance basic income, based on January 1999 estimates, would be 47%. Since then the economy has grown significantly and the revised rate, based on the most recent Revenue Commissioners' estimates of the tax base available at the time of writing, is 42.7%. It should be noted, of course, that the effective tax rate would be substantially lower than this as these calculations do not include the actual basic income payment received by the individual or household.

The final report of the Working Group on Basic Income vindicated CORI Justice Commission's claims that a basic income system would have a far more positive impact on reducing poverty than the present tax and welfare systems, and could form part of a comprehensive strategy to eliminate income poverty in the years immediately ahead.

With reference to the losers identified in the report, two issues need to be borne in mind:

- over a three-year implementation period of a basic income all the "losers" would be better off than at present. They would simply not gain as much under basic income as they would under the present system;

- the losers in the bottom four deciles identified in the report can be easily targeted and compensated through the Social Solidarity Fund that forms part of the basic income structure.

On the macro-economic aspects the report acknowledges that the findings were tentative, speculative and hard to quantify. Despite this, the report's conclusion that a basic income could encourage some people to move from the unofficial economy into regular employment was a welcome finding as it refuted some untested claims that had been made earlier.

There are many tests to check the efficiency of the tax and welfare system. The critical test of any tax and welfare system is its impact on people with lower incomes. While many poor people have benefited from developments of recent years in Ireland, especially through growth in employment, the fact remains that the gap between poor people and the rest of society has widened considerably over the past decade and a half.

The conclusion of the Working Group was that the choice between a basic income system and "conventional" tax/welfare options is a trade-off between greater equity and a risk of lower economic growth versus less equity and less risk to higher economic growth. At a time when so much concern has been expressed about Ireland's growth rate of recent years being unsustainable, the argument in favour of a basic income is further strengthened.

In the build-up to the 1997 Irish general election CORI canvassed all political parties to include a commitment on basic income in their election manifestos. The incoming Government *(Fianna Fail / Progressive Democrats coalition)* made a commitment to introduce a Green Paper on basic income within two years. This was a further breakthrough as it ensured that the work being done on basic income would be considered within the official policy making process of Government and the results of that consideration would be published for public consideration.

In Ireland, a Green Paper is a means of generating public discussion on the topic under consideration. This is followed by a White Paper outlining what Government proposes to do, which forms the basis for Government policy. It may also be followed by introduction of a Bill that goes before the *Oireachtas* (both houses of parliament).

Because of the late completion of the Working Group's studies, publication of this Green Paper was delayed until mid 2002.

5. Tax reform as "credits"

Of the changes in the Irish tax system in recent years, the most relevant to the possible introduction of a basic income system, has been the introduction of tax credits. In the tax year commencing April 6, 2001, a full tax credit system was introduced by Government to replace the existing tax-free allowance system.

Under the new system, a person is entitled to tax credits depending on his/her personal circumstances, e.g. married person's tax credit or employee (PAYE- Pay As You Earn) tax credit. The main tax credits vary, depending on marital status, widowhood age and disability.

Tax is calculated from the first cent a person earns and the credit is deducted from the total tax bill at the end. Thus the benefit is the same for all those whose tax bills are high enough to benefit from the full tax credit.

However, those whose tax bills are not large enough, and who owe the State no tax, do not benefit from an increase in tax credits in the Government's annual Budget. This produces an unfair situation, in which those on the lowest pay may not benefit from tax cuts while those with higher incomes do benefit. To counteract this, there has been a move toward making tax credits refundable.

The pressure to make tax credits refundable is growing in Ireland as more than a third of those in paid employment are outside the tax net and, consequently, do not benefit from tax reductions.

A recent national agreement, entitled *The Programme for Prosperity and Fairness* (2000-2002), contained a commitment to establish a Working Group to look at the viability of making tax credits refundable.

Most of the work in the Refundable Tax Credits Working Group has focused on the administration difficulties that could be faced by the Revenue Commissioners and employers. Many believed that it was not possible to administer a refundable tax system without putting huge burdens on employers and the Revenue Commissioners. CORI Justice Commission produced the following idea designed specifically to overcome this problem. (The Working Group is considering this proposal as we write.)

The central idea recognizes that most people with regular incomes and jobs would not receive a cash refund of their tax credit because their incomes are too high; they would simply benefit from the tax credit as a reduction in their tax bill. No change is proposed for these people and they would continue to pay tax via their employers, based on their net tax liability after their employers have deducted tax credits on behalf of the Revenue. Other people on low or irregular incomes would have the option to request that their tax credit be paid directly into their bank account by the Department of Social, Community and Family Affairs (DSCFA), which administer the social welfare system. Employers would not subtract the credit from the gross tax liability of these people. In order to qualify for direct refund of tax credits by DSCFA, a person must be 21 years of age or over, and, if under 65 have been working for at least 12 months for the equivalent of at least eight hours per week, as evidenced by tax/Pay Related Social Insurance (PRSI) returns.

Employees and self-employed, including farmers, are encompassed within the proposal. Eligibility would last for a year or for the same length of time as the Family Income Supplement. If someone loses a job, became invalided or retired, eligibility would be retained for the remainder of that year.

Other groups of people would be eligible, including spouses working in the home who could opt to receive the "married" part of the personal tax credit and the Home Working Spouse tax credit directly from DSCFA.

The merits of the CORI proposal are:

- every tax credit beneficiary can receive the full value of the tax credit;
- it would improve net income of the workers whose incomes are lowest, at modest cash cost;
- it would improve net income of the pensioners whose incomes are lowest, at modest cash cost;
- no additional administrative burden is placed on employers or the Revenue.

The administrative burden of paying tax credits to those who select this option is left with DSCFA, who have long experience of making direct payments and are experiencing a fall-off in business with a reduced Live Register.

The move to a tax credit system was completed in Ireland in 2001.

Introduction of a refundable tax credit system would take this process a step further to where every person in the country had the right to some form of payment from the State. From an age-based perspective it would mean that child benefit would be paid for every child; refundable tax credits or a social welfare payment would be available for every adult up to the age of 65; old-age pension would be paid to every adult over 65.

6. The challenges facing Government

The economies of the world are changing radically. Whether the changes are simply a continuation of the process of development experienced over the past two centuries or whether they mark a deeper transformation remains to be seen. Either way, the Irish economy has been one of the fastest changing of the past decade as it moved from being one of the poorest nations in the European Union to being one of the better off, measured in terms of per capita income.

However, there is a paradox at the heart of Irish development. Despite the unprecedented economic growth in recent years, and its accompanying prosperity, there has been a failure to address adequately the issues of social cohesion and infrastructure deficit that are still problematic throughout the country. While Ireland now has a per capita income well above the EU average, its infrastructure and social provision are far below the EU level, and Ireland's tax-take is far below the EU average, which is seen as a virtue to be protected at all costs. This combination of circumstances raises the question: how can Ireland have a EU level of infrastructure and social provision if it is not prepared to pay EU levels of taxation? Or alternatively, is Ireland satisfied to continue with levels of infrastructure and social provision below the EU average and live with a lower quality of life that accompanies such lower levels of provision?

There have been many positive developments. Despite the recent slowdown economic growth is still higher than in most EU and OECD countries. Employment has grown dramatically, unemployment has fallen substantially. The rate of long-term unemployment is much lower today than it was a decade ago.

Many argue, however, that Ireland has had prosperity without fairness. While the wealth of the nation has grown, the proportion of the population with incomes below the poverty line (set at half average income, adjusted for family size and composition) has also grown. The proportion of households below the poverty line has also grown. The gap between the better off and the poor has widened, and there is growing polarization between these two parts of society. This situation has been exacerbated by most of the recent Budgets, which saw those already better off gaining most when the resources were allocated.

There has been a growing debate about the model of society that Irish people wish to see. This has been encapsulated in the rather misleading phrase "Boston or Berlin", used to contrast the "European" model with the "American" model. It could be argued that Ireland has been moving towards the American model is characterized by low taxation, more emphasis on responsibilities of individuals, less social provision and growing inequality.

We now have a situation where the share of GNP going to wages is much lower than it was a decade ago. The share going to profits is much higher. Likewise, the share of GNP going to welfare payments is markedly lower than it was before the advent of the economic boom. While this in part is a consequence of the decline in unemployment, it is also a consequence of failure to use available resources to raise the standard of living of Ireland's poorest so as to bring them above the poverty line. Despite claims to the contrary, the reality is that Ireland's rate of poverty rose during the boom years and is one of the highest in the EU.

A reversal of recent trends in these areas is more than desirable if Ireland is to have a *fair* distribution of its resources. Addressing this issue presents a major challenge to policy makers, the social partnership process, political parties and the political process generally. If these processes do not give a much higher priority to social spending, the unfairness of the present situation will deepen, the gaps in society will widen even further and we will be left with a deeply divided two-tier society.

Fairness does not emerge spontaneously or automatically. It has to be worked for and developed in policy initiatives rooted in a strategy that acknowledges that fairness is a desired outcome. While there has been much favourable rhetoric in this area, actual initiatives and strategies have been lacking. For the most part, the strategies and policies have taken a minimalist approach, focusing on eradication of *absolute* or *consistent* poverty. Such an approach ignores core issues of equality and distributive justice and will not produce a fair society.

The substantial commitment contained in the review of the National Anti-Poverty Strategy on raising the lowest social welfare payment to 30% of average industrial income by 2007 is most welcome. However, much greater progress towards reaching such a target could have been made during the recent boom years.

Irish society is faced with substantial opportunities, challenges and choices. In these final pages we will look at a number of issues that policy makers must address in the period immediately ahead. In so doing we will reflect on whether these are best tackled by the current tax and welfare systems or by a basic income system. We will also outline the most likely politically viable pathway towards the introduction of a basic income in Ireland in the short to medium term.

We have already outlined the failure to address these related issues during the years of rapid economic growth. What we have seen is slight improvement in real terms (i.e. measured against inflation) in the standard of living of most people. At the same time the income of those in poverty has not kept pace with the growing wealth of society in general or of the better off among the population. The percentage of people and of households below the poverty line has continued to rise. That the institutions of the State that are meant to facilitate the fair distribution of resources, such as the social welfare system, have not been effective in distributing the benefits of growth to those with lowest incomes. The adjustments in the tax system have moved the benefits towards the corporate sector and to capital. Within the income tax system those on the lowest earnings find themselves in a position where they do not benefit in any way from income tax reductions in the Government's annual budgets. It could be said that the institutional changes being put in place to support the development of the new economy have cost the poorest most.

The challenge facing Irish policy makers is to ensure that the weakest are treated fairly and to move towards a society focused on securing economic development, social equity and sustainability. According to Charles Clark (2002, pp. 39–40):

> Ireland can choose to skip the pain and suffering and simultaneously adjust its social and economic institutions along with the changes brought about by globalization and technological change, to share both the costs and the benefits of the new economy. It is just this goal that Basic Income systems are designed to do.

In many ways, something like a Basic Income is inevitable if Europe is to achieve the dynamic economy that technological change and globalization offer while maintaining a commitment to social justice and a civil and humane society. Ireland can take the lead in showing how to achieve a dynamic economy that maintains its commitment to social justice and a civil and humane society.

In practical political terms the most likely next step the Irish Government could take would be to make tax credits refundable. This would have a number of very positive effects. Among these, the following would be the most important, from the perspective of addressing income distribution, equity and poverty alleviation:

- it would have a positive impact on the incomes of the lowest paid, moving them closer to the relative income poverty line;
- it would reduce the gap to be bridged by policy makers seeking to eliminate relative income poverty in Irish society;
- equally importantly, it would put in place a system that could easily be adjusted to become a straightforward basic income system.

The need to ensure competitiveness is a recurring theme in economic debate in Ireland. While how to ensure the economy is competitive is not an exact science, the issues can be analysed in a coherent manner to see what role, if any, a basic income might have in improving the competitiveness of the Irish economy. In his recent book on *The Basic Income Guarantee,* Charles Clark devotes two chapters to this aspect. He uses the criteria developed by the National Competitiveness Council (NCC) in Ireland in its Annual Competitiveness Reports. In these reports the Council has set out what it calls "critical competitiveness priorities" arranged into seven categories: social partnership; people; costs; infrastructure; telecommunications and e-business; competition and regulation; and science and technology. Clark points out that a Basic Income is relevant to the first three of these, which he analyses these in detail. We provide a short outline of some of his conclusions, as the work is too large to include in a paper of this length. We urge readers to read the full Clark text as it is, by far, the most comprehensive analysis of basic income and competitiveness in Ireland published to date.

On social partnership the NCC identified the national agreements negotiated between social partners and Government since 1987 as key elements in producing Ireland's new economy. However, the trade-off of tax reductions for moderate wage increases has run its course. The danger is that a more confrontational model will replace the negotiated approach of the past 15 years. Such an approach could be characterized by the all-or-nothing approach to worker/employer relations. Clark argues that the introduction of a basic income "would make work a much more voluntary act, based on free choice and not the condign power of material need. This would change the worker/employer relationship, making it more of a partnership and less based on the "confrontational" model of labour relations"(pp. 65–66).

In the same context Clark also addresses the focus on economic growth that has been a primary component of previous national agreements between Government and social partners. He points out that Ireland could produce more economic growth by forcing every adult to work full-time but questions if that is the type of society Ireland really wants. Given the growing pressures that have accompanied recent economic growth in Ireland it reasonable to suggest that people might prefer to work less, not more. Clark argues:

> "A Basic Income allows both men and women more freedom in making the choices of how they wish to participate in society, using the criteria of where they feel they can make a contribution and where they feel the need is greatest, and not merely avoiding destitution (p. 68)."

Education is the first aspect identified under the "people" heading. The new economy will demand greater levels of education and training and greater flexibility for people to move over and back between employment and education during their working lives. A basic income reduces the need for young people to leave school early to support their low-income families. But a Basic Income also provides greater opportunity for people to be involved in education and training at all points in their life cycle. It also allows parents to be more involved in their own children's education if they so choose.

Another part of the "people" sub-heading listed by the NCC in its approach to competitiveness concerns work incentives. A basic income would reduce the tax wedge on low and middle-income workers. It would have a minimal impact on the tax/GDP ratio. It would reduce the effective tax rate for most employees and would involve a marginal tax rate that would not act as a disincentive to taking up a job or increasing the hours a person works.

The third set of criteria identified by the NCC that has implications for basic income is "costs". There are two opposing positions taken by advocates and opponents of basic income under this heading. Some economists argue that a basic income would allow wages to fall (because it would lead to wage substitution) and this would promote full employment. They argue that this would happen because the demand for something is expected to increase as its price falls. Those on the left see this as a criticism of basic income while those on the right see it as a major point in its favour. A very different approach to the issue of Basic Income can be seen in the argument that it would lead to an increase in wages for those at the lowest end of the wage-earning spectrum because it gives people in this situation greater leverage. This is seen as leading to a reduction in income inequality.

As Ireland now has minimum wage legislation there is no danger that a basic income would produce a reduction of wages below the minimum legal level. On the other hand, there is little danger that employee as organized as those in Ireland would allow the basic income to become, in effect, a wage substitute. Given the current tight state of the labour market, there is little likelihood of a basic income having negative wage effects in Ireland.

7.   Employment, flexibility and meaningful work for all [4]

The Irish labour force and numbers employed have been growing rapidly in recent years. In 1990 the total labour force was 1,332,000 of which 1,160,000 were employed. By 2001 this had risen to 1,866,100 (Table 7.12) of which 1,786,600 were employed. This means that the employed had grown by more than 600'000 while the labour force had risen by more than 530,000. The overall labour force participation rate averaged 59.8% in 2001, up from 59.4% in 2000. Male participation averaged 71.5%, unchanged from the previous year, while female participation increased from 47.8% to 48.5%.

The year 2001 witnessed the first significant increase in Irish unemployment rates since 1993. At the end of 2000, unemployment, as measured by the Quarterly National Household Survey (QNHS), stood at 3.9% (68,800 people), and by 2001, 79,500 people were classified as unemployed, an unemployment rate of 4.3% (Table 7.12). During 2001, unemployment dropped to 3.7%, before the slowdown in the international and Irish economy began to have an impact. The QNHS unemployment data use the ILO definition of "unemployment".

A study of the profile of those who became unemployed in late 2001 showed that the newly unemployed come predominantly from the age groups 15–19 and 20–24, whose unemployment rates increased from 8.2% to 11.2%, and from 4.9% to 7.2% respectively. While some of the increase may be accounted for by seasonal factors, such student holidays, the magnitude is significant. In particular, included in the under-25s are early school-leavers who, with low skills, may find it difficult to get employment given the economic

---

[4] For a detailed analysis of these and related issues, see Standing (1999).

conditions and the greater number of competing job seekers. Unemployment continued to rise 4.6% in 2002 (McCoy et al., 2002, table 1, p. 15).

Table 7.12   Labour force changes, 2000–2001

	Sept–Nov 2000	June–Aug 2001	Change
Labour force	1 779 100	1 866 100	+87 000
In employment	1 710 300	1 786 600	+76 300
Unemployed	68 800	79 500	+10 700
of whom long term unemployed	24 200	22 100	- 2 100
Unemployment rate	3.9%	4.3%	+0.4%
Long term unemployment rate	1.4%	1.2%	- 0.2%

Source   Quarterly National Household Survey November (2001), p 14

Of the 79,500 unemployed in August 2001, 57,200 were unemployed for less than one year. Long-term unemployment fell by 2,100 between the end of 2000 and August 2001, having fallen steadily since 1988, when it stood at 10.4%, the main decline occurring after 1996. The 2001 rate was only one-third of that recorded in mid-1998. This is a substantial decrease in the level of structural unemployment, and illustrates the extent to which Irish unemployment is now dominated by frictional factors.

A major question raised by the labour-market situation concerns assumptions underpinning culture and policy-making in this area, such as the priority given to paid employment over other forms of work. Most people recognize that a person can work hard even though they do not have a job. Much of the work done in the community and in the voluntary sector is of this type, as is much of the work done in the home. The need to recognize such work has been acknowledged in the Government's 2000 White Paper, *Supporting Voluntary Activity*.

The developments of recent years present policy makers in Ireland with major challenges in the area of work. There are constant demands for increased flexibility in the labour force. Government is being pressurized to reduce the cost to employers of social insurance payments (which are well below the EU average). Likewise, there are constant demands on the State to adjust its education and training programmes to support the development of skills required by employers.

What is often ignored is that the State provides substantial subsidies to employers through, for example, adjusting the educational system to provide trained workers. Likewise, social insurance pays a large share of the protection costs of production in Ireland. In practice, these are shifts from employers' costs to State costs. A basic income could be seen as compensation for this shifting of costs. Charles Clark points out (2002, pp. 80–81):

> The benefits of flexible labour costs generally go to the firm. Part of this benefit is the ability to make adjustments to new market conditions, but part of this is merely a shift in the costs of production away from the firm and onto the worker, consumers and society as a whole, simply because they have the power to do so. This sort of labour flexibility is neither good for society nor necessary for the technological aspects of the new economy, but is brought about by the increased capital mobility of globalization and thus is a reality that must be dealt with.

Clark goes on to point out that other forms of labour market flexibility — adaptability, mobility, and work time and scheduling — have all become important ingredients in the new economy that follow from the need for flexible production to be competitive. They also lead to a shift in costs away from the corporate sector and towards the State and employees. A counter-balancing system is required to ensure that the benefits of these new developments are fairly distributed and do not go disproportionately to one sector. Increased flexibility means that people in paid employed will be required to move from job to job more frequently. But they must be supported all the time, including during these transitions.

A basic income would offer Government a mechanism to ensure that all those inside and outside the labour force can be supported in a fair and systematic way consistent with the developments in the new economy to which they must all adjust. It does this while maintaining the incentive to take up employment or to work longer hours. In a basic income system there is a guarantee that when a person takes up employment or works additional time he/she will always retain a large part of the extra pay received. It thus removes the many poverty traps and unemployment traps that have been major problems in the present tax and social welfare systems. Eliminating these traps continues to demand substantial time and effort from Government every time it seeks to adjust the present systems.

At the same time, basic income supports unpaid work that is critically important for society but which is in danger of being undermined in the transition to the new economy of the 21st century. The need to recognize unpaid work has become a major issue in Ireland. One reason for this is the tight labour market that substantially reduced the previously high levels of volunteering. Another is the growing realization of the vast amount of caring work done on an unpaid basis both in the home and in the wider community. The need to recognize the value of unpaid work has been accepted by Government and by social partners and is discussed in various policy-making arenas. Not much has been done, however, in terms of developing and/or implementing practical policies.

Basic income provides a system of support that recognizes the value of unpaid work. It does this by putting a modest floor of support under all people and allowing them the freedom to give at least a part of their time to caring, community or voluntary work, from which Irish society has always been a major beneficiary.

8. Conclusions

The idea of basic income has been around for almost 25 years in Ireland. In the 1970s it was not addressed seriously. From the mid-1980s to the mid-1990s it was dismissed in official reports as unworkable and/or too costly and/or less important than tackling tax reform or social welfare inadequacy. We have seen that these assessments were made on the basis of very little evidence.

The report of the Working Group on Basic Income, and its accompanying studies, show that basic income could be financed in the Irish context. CORI's work on implementation mechanisms has shown that a basic income system could be implemented in practice. It is clear that the model proposed by CORI Justice Commission (i.e. a full basic income for all) could be implemented and be financed without resorting to an unacceptable level of taxation.

There are many reasons why a basic income would be more appropriate to Ireland at this time than the present tax and welfare systems. A basic income would address issues of income distribution, equity, poverty alleviation, competitiveness, employment incentives and access to meaningful work, among others.

There have been positive developments in Ireland with the introduction of a tax credit. The implications of making tax credits refundable is being studied by a Government-led working group that includes the various pillars of social partnership.

We have seen that making tax credits refundable would be a major development in the present system. Taking the final step towards the introduction of a basic income would then be a question of political choice, as the basic structure of State support would have a provision for universal entitlement. In effect, it would have moved from its focus on poverty relief in the 19th and early 20th centuries to a system of universal entitlement appropriate for the 21st century.

References

Callan, T., O'Donoghue, C. and O'Neill, C. 1994. *Analysis of basic income shemes for Ireland* (Dublin, Economic and Social Research Institute).

_____ et al. 1996. *Poverty in the 1990s: Evidence from the 1994 living in Ireland surveys* (Dublin, Oak Tree Press).

Clark, C. M. A. 2002. *The basic income guarantee: Ensuring progress and prosperity in the 21st century* (Dublin, The Liffey Press).

─────── and Kavanagh, C. 1995. "Basic income and the Irish worker", in B. Reynolds and S. Healy (eds.) *An adequate income guarantee for all* (Dublin, CORI Justice Commission).

─────── and Healy, J. 1997. *Pathways to a basic income* (Dublin, Conference of Religions of Ireland).

Conference of Religions of Ireland (CORI). 1994. *Tackling poverty, unemployment and exclusion: A moment of great opportunity* (Dublin, CORI).

───────. 1995. *Ireland for all* (Dublin, CORI).

───────. 1996. *Planning for progress* (Dublin, CORI).

Department of Enterprise, Trade and Employment. 1996. *Growing and sharing our employment: Strategy paper on the labour market* (Dublin, Stationery Office).

Department of Social, Community and Family Affairs. 2000. *Statistical information on social welfare services.* (Dublin, Stationery Office).

Dowling, B. 1977. *Integrated approaches to personal income taxes and transfers* (Dublin, National Economic and Social Council).

EUROSTAT. *Expenditure on social protection* (Luxembourg).

First Report of the Commission on Taxation. 1982. (Dublin, Stationery Office).

FORFAS .1996. *Shaping our future* (Dublin, National Policy and Advisory Board for Enterprise, Trade, Science, Technology and Innovation).

Government of Ireland. 2000. *Supporting voluntary activity – White Paper on a framework for supporting voluntary activity and for developing the relationship between the State and the community and voluntary sector* (Dublin, The Stationery Office).

Healy, S. 1996. *Response to the report of the Expert Group on the Integration of the Tax and Social Welfare Systems*, Presentation to the Foundation for Fiscal Studies seminar, July.

Healy, S. and Reynolds, B. 1994. "Arguing for an adequate income guarantee", in B. Reynolds and S. Healy (eds.) *Towards an adequate income guarantee for all* (Dublin, CORI).

———. 1995. "An adequate income guarantee for all", in B. Reynolds and S. Healy (eds.) *An adequate income guarantee for all* (Dublin, CORI).

———. (eds.). 1998. *Social policy in Ireland — Principles, practice and problems* (Dublin, Oaktree Press).

Honohan, P. 1987. "A radical reform of social welfare and income tax evaluated", in *Administration*, Vol. 35, No. 1.

Layte, R. et al. 2001. *Monitoring poverty trends and exploring poverty dynamics in Ireland* (Dublin, Economic and Social Research Institute — ESRI).

McCoy, D. et al. 2002. *Quarterly Economic Commentary* (Dublin, The Economic and Research Institute — ESRI)

Partnership 2000 for inclusion, employment and competitiveness. 1996. (Dublin, Stationery Office).

Programme for prosperity and fairness. 2000. (Dublin, Stationery Office).

Report of the Working Group on Basic Income. 2001. (Dublin, Department of the Taoiseach).

Report of the Working Group on the Integration of the Tax and Social Welfare Systems. 1996. (Dublin, Stationery Office).

Standing, G. 1999. *Global labour flexibility* (Houndmills, Macmillan Press).

United Nations Development Programme (UNDP). 2001. *Human development report — 2001* (New York, United Nations Publications).

Van Parijs, P. 1992. "Competing justifications of basic income" in *Arguing for basic income* (London, Verso).

Vincentian Partnership for Social Justice. 2001. *One long struggle: A study of low income families* (Dublin).

Ward, S. 1994. "A basic income system for Ireland" in B. Reynolds and S. Healy (eds.) *Towards an adequate income for all* (Dublin, CORI).

———. 1998. "Basic income" in B. Reynolds and S. Healy (eds.) *Social policy in Ireland· Principles, practice and problems* (Dublin, Oakland Press).

MORE SELECTIVITY IN UNEMPLOYMENT COMPENSATION IN FINLAND: HAS IT LED TO ACTIVATION OR INCREASED POVERTY

8

Simo Aho and Ilka Virjo [1]

1. Introduction

This work forms part of a larger long-term project analysing the role of labour market and social policies and their reforms in the development of the unemployment problem and related poverty. Our aim here is to analyse the consequences of a 1994 reform of Finland's unemployment compensation system introducing labour market support for labour market entrants and those who had received unemployment insurance benefit for the maximum period. Other reforms relevant in this context, notably the abolition of public authorities' employment obligation in 1993, the tightening of unemployment insurance conditions in 1996, and the introduction of "combined subsidy" in 1998 are also considered.

First, we review the development of employment and unemployment as well as labour market policies in Finland since the 1980s. In Section 3, we present the background, goals and contents of the 1994 reform in detail. Section 4 presents the data for our empirical analysis. In Section 5 we analyse the general consequences of the reform and the expansion and characteristics of the recipients of the new benefit. The goal of the reform was to support labour market "activism" of the unemployed; in Section 6 we analyse how far this goal has been realized. In Section 7, we try to measure if the reform has had an impact on poverty among the unemployed. In Section 8, we draw some conclusions of our analysis.

[1] University of Tampere, Finland.

2. Employment and labour market policy in Finland

In the ideology of the Finnish welfare state, pursuit of full employment has always been a high priority. The employment law of 1971 obliged the State to promote the demand for labour and implement labour market policy measures to help balance labour supply and demand. In 1972, the Finnish constitution was amended as follows: "if needed, it is the task of the State authorities to arrange an opportunity to work for the citizens of Finland ". In spite of this, the Finnish state was not as committed to full employment as were other Nordic countries. In the 1980s, this commitment became stronger, as witnessed both in legislation and in practice.

2.1 From "right to work" towards recession

The employment law of 1987 defined full employment as the goal of the State, and made public authorities responsible for arranging training or subsidized employment (typically for six months) for the young unemployed and the long-term unemployed (this was called employment obligation). Thus, a kind of universal social right to (temporary) employment was created. As a consequence, long-term unemployment (more than 12 months) became a rarity.

Soon, however, the principles of Finnish labour market policies were revised. The background was the severe recession that hit Finland in the early 1990s. It was deeper than in any industrialized country in any period covered by OECD statistics. In 1991-93, gross domestic product (GDP) fell by 13% and total domestic demand with 25%. The employment rate decreased substantially and the unemployment rate skyrocketed.

In figure 8.1, we see the development of GDP and employment. With rapidly rising unemployment, it became impossible (both financially and practically) to fulfil the employment obligation; it was relaxed in 1992 and abolished in 1993. The opportunity to participate in active labour market policy measures (APM) was no longer offered to all those experiencing prolonged unemployment, and long-term unemployment started to grow rapidly. This had far-reaching consequences for the income security of the unemployed.

Finland has traditionally had a dual unemployment compensation system, consisting of an earnings-related benefit (with an average replacement rate of about 60% of previous earnings) and a low means-tested flat-rate benefit paid by the State. The conditions of entitlement to insurance benefit are membership in an unemployment fund (typically associated with labour unions) and prior to

1996, at least six months' employment during the past 12 months. Those who do not qualify are entitled to a state allowance.

Figure 8.1   Gross domestic product (in 1995 prices) and number of employed aged 15–64, annual average), Finland, 1989–2001

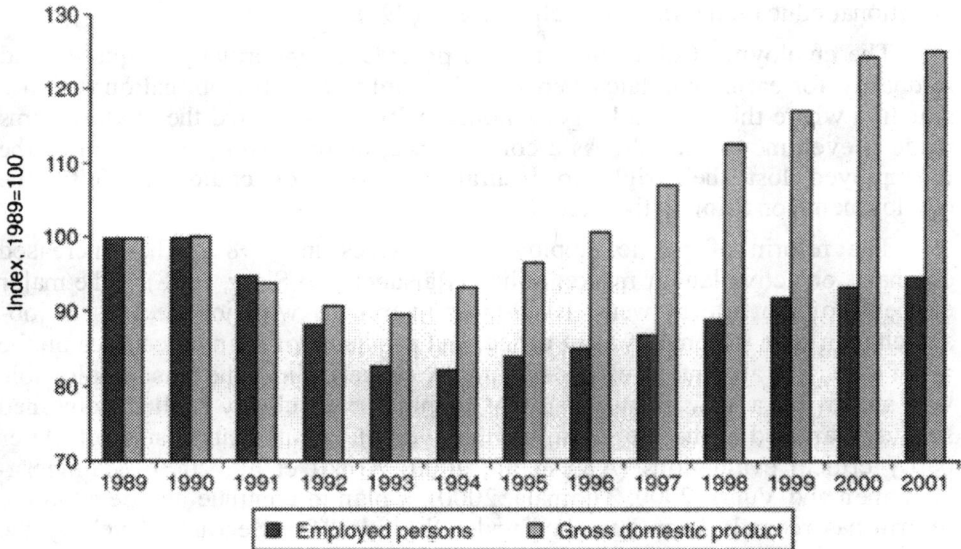

Source   Statistics Finland — Internet service (<www.stat.fi>)

In 1994, a new benefit, called a "labour market support", was introduced for those who did not fulfil the employment conditions for unemployment insurance or had received unemployment benefit for the maximum period allowed. The benefit has similar characteristics to the traditional state allowance and has largely replaced it.

While high unemployment remained persistent in spite of strong economic growth from 1994 onwards, "benefit dependency" and "incentive traps" soon became big political issues. In 1996, the Government implemented a programme of small reforms in social security systems, social assistance norms, income taxation, and children's day-care fees in order to make employment — even temporary or low-income employment — more profitable than social security.

The employment condition of unemployment insurance was also tightened and raised to ten months' employment during the previous two years. This was motivated by the fact that subsidized employment in the public sector was not effective in facilitating subsequent employment on the open labour market, but was used as a means to gain or renew the right to the earnings-related unemployment benefit. Since the reform, a single period of subsidized employment alone has not been sufficient to fulfil the employment condition. From 1994 on, offering subsidized jobs for the young was increasingly replaced by "labour market training with labour market support" (i.e. without wages or a formal employment relationship). Since the reforms of 1996–97, the right to labour market support for under 25-year-olds can be gained only through vocational education (Aho and Vehviläinen, 1997).

The employment obligation used to provide an opportunity to qualify and re-qualify for earnings-related benefit. The abolition of the obligation led to a situation where this was no longer automatically possible, and the 1996 reforms made it even more difficult. As a consequence, an increasing proportion of the unemployed lost their right to insurance benefit, or could not fulfil the employment condition in the first place.

The reform of public employment services in 1998 further increased emphasis on active labour market policy (Räisänen and Skog, 1998).[2] The major elements of the reform were: fixed-term interviews with job seekers; a job-search plan with the employment office; and provision of training courses on the art of extensive and intensive job seeking. A concern about the least employable was shown by a new, higher form of employment subsidy (called combined subsidy) targeted at the long-term unemployed on labour market support. After partly critical evaluations (Aho et al., 2000; Arnkil et al., 2000; Malmberg-Heinonen and Vuori, 2000; Tuomala, 2000), a plan to continue and develop the reform has recently been launched under the title "The Second Wave" by the Ministry of Labour (Työministeriö, 2001).

In general, what were the effects of labour market policies and their reforms during the 1990s? Extensive subsidized employment and labour market training have no doubt decreased open unemployment; in the 1990s, the

---

[2] There has been one exception to the emphasis on active labour market policy: the older unemployed have been given an opportunity for early retirement through a generous unemployment pension. Since 1990, unemployment (with some other conditions) at the age of 60 has given the right to retirement with an unemployment pension (previously, the age limit was lower). However, conditions were also tightened after the recession. In 1994, those not qualified for unemployment insurance benefit (who did not fill the employment condition or whose entitlement had expired) lost their right to unemployment pension at age 55; in 1997, the age limit was raised to 57. Recently, in order to make the unemployment pension less attractive, employers' contributions were increased when employees retired on unemployment pension, and that pension was also cut. The implication is that active labour market measures should be re-targeted to older workers, who previously might have taken early retirement — but this seems not to have taken place (Hytti, 1998; Aho and Österman, 1999; Virjo and Aho, 2002).

unemployment rate was 3 to 4 percentage points lower than it otherwise would have been (see table 8.1, below). Evaluation studies have shown, however, that participation in these schemes has not notably promoted subsequent employment on the open labour market (Aho et al., 1999; Aho et al. 2001). According to the evaluations, the 1998 service reform did not have any significant impacts on employment, either (Aho et al., 2000; Malmberg-Heinonen and Vuori, 2000; Tuomala, 2000).

Evaluations of the 1996 reforms conclude that they were in fact successful in removing "incentive traps" and had a positive, albeit quite small, impact on employment (Niinivaara, 1999; Laine and Uusitalo, 2001).

The commitment in the 1980s to provide a universal employment opportunity (in the form of a subsidized job after a certain length of unemployment) was replaced during the recession by emphasis on improving "the functioning of the labour market" (Räisänen and Skog, 1998; Työministeriö, 2001) and on promoting labour market activity of the unemployed. In this respect, the Finnish welfare state has changed qualitatively. "Benefit dependence" has been discouraged through tightened entitlement conditions and sanctions, and removal of "incentive traps" so as to promote casual employment. In 1995, the paragraph in the Constitution obliging the state to arrange employment opportunities for its citizens was somewhat relaxed. It is no longer "the task" but "a pursuit" of the public authorities "to secure everyone the right to work".

Nevertheless, extensive investment in active labour market policies has not significantly reduced persistent long-term unemployment stemming from the recession. There is no reason to expect that these policies will have a greater impact in future. If demand for low-skilled labour is structurally low, as is the case in Finland, temporary subsidized employment and generally rather short vocational courses cannot provide the remedy for persistent unemployment.

Several years ago, it seemed that the Government had surrendered in the face of structural unemployment. An indication of this was the revision of the Ministry of Labour's strategy, which gave priority to "fulfilling the demand for labour". It states that attempts will be made "to shorten the average duration of unemployment" and "to reduce the flow to long-term unemployment" – not ambitious goals when nearly 10% of the labour force is suffering long-term unemployment (Työministeriö, 2001). However, more resources have been targeted at the least employable. Also, structural unemployment has been put back on the agenda.

2.2 The labour market context of the 1990s

Although the 1994–2000 economic recovery was remarkable in comparison to other countries, it was not sufficient to repair the employment losses of the recession, especially in view of the parallel increase in labour supply. To understand the context of the 1994 reform, it is essential to consider that, in addition to the increase in unemployment, the recession was followed by a change in the structure of unemployment, with long-term and repetitive unemployment becoming more common. Conventional unemployment statistics do not provide clear information on the extent of the problem, because subsidized employment masks the duration of open unemployment. Figure 8.2 is based on Aho's calculations, where the annual flow of the unemployed (those having at least some experience of unemployment during the current year) has been categorized on the basis of four previous years' work and unemployment history (see Appendix for the data and classification criteria).

In 1990, unemployment affected 14% of the labour force (the combined proportion of the unemployed and those on unemployment pension). The rate peaked at 33% in 1994 and fell to 24% in 2000, still about 10 percentage points above the level of 1990. Short- and medium-term unemployment increased during the recession, but by 2000 had fallen back to levels only a little higher than in 1990.

Figure 8.2   Unemployment by category (annual flow), Finland, 1990–98

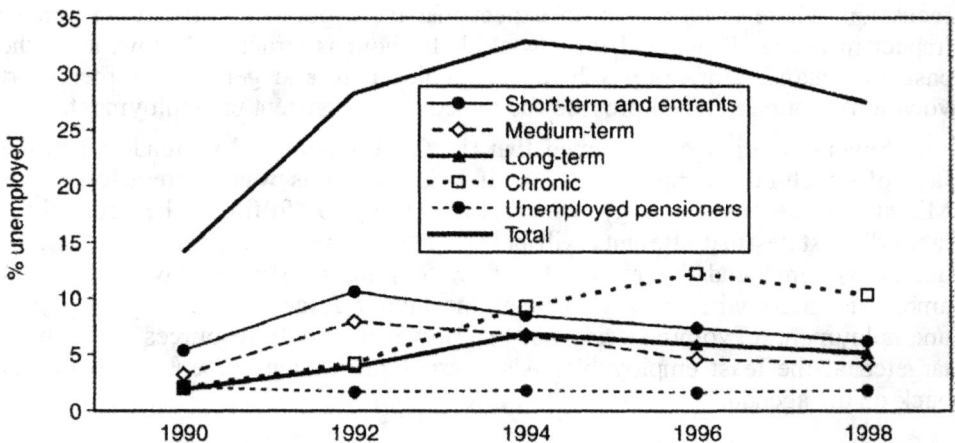

Source: Aho's calculations. Typology is based on employment histories during previous four years (see Appendix).

However, some victims of the recession were unable to re-establish their position on the labour market and became persistently unemployed. Even since the recession, the flow to long-term unemployment has been high among elderly employees. A question is whether long-term unemployment is mainly a "shadow of the recession" or if there is a constant new flow into chronic unemployment. We can already say that this flow has continued among the elderly workforce. But a considerable proportion of the long-term unemployed are not elderly (Virjo and Aho, 2002).

The combined proportion of the long-term and chronically unemployed reached its peak in 1996 – 18% of the labour force -, and has decreased slowly since; in 2000 it was still about 13%, almost four times higher than in 1990. When the proportion of unemployed pensioners (about 2% through the period) is added to these figures, we get an estimate of structural unemployment in Finland.

Thus, not only are there more unemployed in Finland now than before the recession, but also the majority of them are more or less permanently excluded from the open labour market. The problem does not seem to be disappearing despite the improved employment situation.

It is also important to consider that, in dealing with the unemployment problem, the role of active labour market policy has traditionally been quite strong in Finland. The measures include labour market training and subsidized jobs in the public and private sectors, and start-up grants for unemployed people starting their own business. During 1990–1997, the annual volume of active labour market policy measures approximately doubled and reached its peak; it has been slowly decreasing since. Table 8.1 shows how significant the role of these measures has been.

Table 8.1   Participation in active labour market policy measures (APM), Finland, 1990–1998

	1990	1992	1994	1996	1998	2000
Percentage of the labour force						
- at the end of the year	2.0	3.1	3.6	4.2	4.1	2.9
- during the same year	5.0	7.9	10.0	10.8	10.1	7.8
- during the previous four years	9 0	12.6	17.4	20.9	21.1	19.4
Percentage of the unemployed						
- during the same year	32.0	33.8	35.9	39.6	42.0	38.2
- during the previous four years	44.0	44.5	53.8	59.4	62.3	60.1

Source Aho's calculations based on register data (see Appendix 8.1).

3. The 1994 reform

The main focus of this paper is the 1994 reform, even though it is obvious that, when evaluating Finnish labour market developments as a whole, we have to take into account the other reforms mentioned above. In this section, the Government's quite radical Bill is discussed in detail, together with the actual outcome of the legislative process.

In 1993, the Finnish Government proposed a major reform to unemployment security and labour market policy. According to the Bill 235/1993, the basic flat-rate unemployment benefit would only be paid to those fulfilling the six-month employment condition. The benefit would also have a maximum length of 500 working days rather than unlimited duration. On the other hand, the benefit would no longer be reduced by the spouse's income. The main arguments for the proposal were as follows:

- *employment condition*: People from other countries of the European Economic Area would not instantly qualify for Finnish unemployment security. It was the Government's idea that unemployment security should only apply to people who had been employed. Thus, unemployment benefits would not be an incentive for young people to remain unemployed instead of studying;
- *maximum duration*: This was supposed to push the unemployed to seek work. It was considered wrong in principle if unemployment security was a permanent alternative to paid labour;
- *no means-testing*: Before the reform, many people who had been employed for long periods but who did not have a voluntary unemployment insurance (or belong to a trade union), did not receive any benefit at all because of their spouse's income. This resulted in increased inequality between the sexes and undermined the right to an individual income. Because the benefit would be for a limited duration and demand fulfilment of stricter conditions, it was considered financially possible to abolish means-testing.

For those failing to meet the stricter conditions of the basic benefit, a new "labour market support" was suggested. In monetary terms, it would be as high as the basic flat-rate benefit, but without additions for children. It would be means-tested (though not for those who had received basic benefit for 500 days) and limited to 300 working days.

The Bill stated that support would be an activation benefit for young people entering the labour market. They would be entitled only after a four-month wait (less for those who had vocational training), and those living with their parents would receive a lower benefit. Means-testing, the four-month wait, and the reduction for those living with parents would be lifted for the duration of labour market training. The main point of labour market support was to push the unemployed on benefit into training without increasing the benefit. The main objective was to make the young unemployed targets of a diligent active and labour market policy. The fact that even those who had received 500 working days of basic benefit would receive labour market support was considered almost as a curiosity.

The argument for limiting the duration of support was that it should not be an alternative to paid labour; other countries did not pay unemployment benefits to people who had been out of work for a long time. Instead, this group should receive municipal social assistance. The Government's proposal stated that those whose entitlement to labour market support had expired and who were not employed should become welfare cases.

After a long discussion, the Bill was accepted but with major changes. These were due less to parliamentary opposition — even though opposition parties were strongly against the reform the Government had a clear majority — than to the fact that parts of the bill were considered constitution-level legislation. The right to a basic income is guaranteed by the constitution, and any changes that would decrease it "substantially" would demand a very large majority in parliament. Consequently, these parts of the bill were changed to reduce the waiting time from four to three months, and increase provisions for children in labour market support. Most importantly, labour market support was to be paid for an unlimited time.

Because these changes had to be made out of Constitutional concerns, they were compensated for in monetary terms by extending means-testing of the benefit to everyone except:

- during the first 180 working days for those previously on regular unemployment benefit;
- for those over 55 years old who had been employed previously; and
- during labour market training.

Because of these changes, the supposedly radical reform was more ideological and rhetorical in nature than practical. The name and nature of the new benefit emphasized labour market activation: but for most people it was similar to the old basic flat-rate benefit. The major practical changes concerned the young and the introduction of labour market training with the support.

In conclusion, the reform was tailored for young people coming into the labour market. They should not be able to access benefits easily; instead, they should have incentives to choose employment, labour market training or vocational training. Even though the above-mentioned changes to the bill mostly concerned long-term unemployed who were previously employed, they were made for constitutional reasons. It was not considered likely that the support would become a major benefit for anyone other than entrants to the labour market. For example, citing statistics from 1993, the Government stated that it was "highly unlikely" that anyone would be unemployed for more than 800 days. Furthermore, the Government was optimistic about the new support, since it stressed activation, and therefore periods on labour market support would probably be shorter than on basic flat-rate benefit. It was predicted that more than 60% of the beneficiaries of labour market support would be less than 25 years old.

4. Data

Statistics Finland has created data from various administrative registers. The data include large representative samples of the population from the years 1990 (5%), 1994 (5%), and 1997 (8.6%). At present, the data covers the years 1987–2001. All individuals in each sample can be followed throughout the period.

Information on employment has been taken from the registers of employment pension funds (this insurance is compulsory and all employment relationships as well as entrepreneurial activity are registered). Information about unemployment and participation in active labour market measures comes from the register of labour administration (public employment services). In addition, various registers concerning education have been used. If the source of figures in a table or graph is not presented, the calculations are based on the above-mentioned data.

Our data contains information about entitlement to labour market support (LMS) on a day-to-day-basis up to 2000. In addition, we have information from the Social Insurance Institution on the amount of benefit actually paid, up to 1998. Many who had the right to receive LMS may not have received any benefit for many reasons, most importantly the three-month waiting period and means-testing. In a small number of cases, a person might have been on support for such a short time that s/he received less than FIM 500, which is registered as zero because the statistical unit is FIM 1,000 (= approximately 168 €).

In the following section, there is a comparison between the labour market policy right to receive LMS and actual payment. The support can be paid either because the person has never qualified for the employment condition (DNQ), or because s/he has exhausted the maximum duration for regular (earnings-related or basic flat-rate) benefit (MAX).

Table 8.2 shows the proportion of people who do not receive any benefit even though they are in a labour market situation that entitles them to it. The reason to this can be means-testing or the long wait period. Those who were unemployed or in active measures at the end of the year should have received labour market support the following year, because it is paid retrospectively. In 1995, about 15% of both groups with the right to LMS did not receive any benefit. In 1997, there is a difference between the groups: over 20% of those who never qualified for regular benefit did not receive any LMS, whereas the share in the other group was only half as high.

In the group that received the maximum regular benefit, means-testing is the most likely explanation for not receiving LMS. In the other (DNQ) group, most non-receivers are likely to have left unemployment during the three-month waiting period, and the share of those who did not receive benefit because of means-testing will have been much smaller. In a small number of cases, refusing to take a job or enter an APM can also be the reason for not receiving a benefit. After 1996, people less than 25 years of age without vocational education, who refuse to apply for such training, make up a (probably small) group of non-receivers.

Table 8.2   Recipients of labour market support as a percentage of those entitled before means-testing and other conditions (including those in APM), 1995 and 1997

Year, basis for entitlement to LMS	Receive LMS the following year (%)
1995, DNQ	84.0
1995, MAX	85.0
1997, DNQ	78.0
1997, MAX	89.0

DNQ= has never qualified for regular benefit;

MAX= has received maximum amount of regular benefit

See Appendix 8 1

5.   General developments

Figure 8.3 shows what has happened to unemployment in Finland over the past 15 years. From 1994 to 1996, the number of people on labour market support increased rapidly to about 200,000. Since then, the number has remained quite stable even though unemployment has fallen considerably. This means that even though LMS at first seemed merely to replace basic flat-rate unemployment benefit, its share has subsequently grown at the expense of earnings-related benefit as well. This can be seen even more clearly in Appendix 8.2. In 2001, almost half of all unemployed were on LMS. The "no benefit" group almost disappeared after 1994, probably because they were instead registered in the

LMS group, despite receiving little or no benefit because of means-testing. The Government intended labour market support as a temporary activation benefit for the young. In figure 8.4, we see the number of people on LMS by age. The totals are higher than in figure 8.3 because they also include people in active labour market measures.

At first, most people on LMS came from the youngest working-age groups. As seen in Appendix 8.3, about 64% of the people on LMS in 1994 were under 35 years and 43% were under 25 years old. Even this is less than the Government's estimate that 60% would be under 25.

As the number of people on LMS rapidly increased, the share of the youngest age groups fell; in 1995, 52% were under 35 and only 30% were less than 25 years of age. After 1995, the trend continued, but more slowly. In 1999, more than half of all on LMS were at least 35 years old. Logically, the share of the younger age groups is larger in the group that has never qualified for regular unemployment benefit. In 1994, this group was much larger than the other, mainly because people who had received basic flat-rate benefit at the beginning of 1994 had a transition period entitlement for 300 working days. Since 1995, those on LMS have been divided roughly equally between the two reasons for entitlement.

The only way to explain this development is that Government heavily miscalculated the effects of the reform. Its calculations were based on the bill and not on the law that was passed, but it remains a the fact that what was meant to be a springboard into the labour market for the young became the dominant benefit form for the majority of all unemployed. Many older long-term unemployed have been on LMS for years. One explanation for the miscalculation is that, in arguments for the Bill, the calculations were based on the lengths of unemployment spells at the beginning of 1990s. At that time, the "employment obligation" was still in effect, which meant that unemployment spells were automatically cut by subsidized employment after a given period. In short, one could say that when making the calculations, the Government forgot that it had just abolished the employment obligation.

Figure 8.3   Unemployment in Finland by benefit type, 1986–2001 (annual averages)

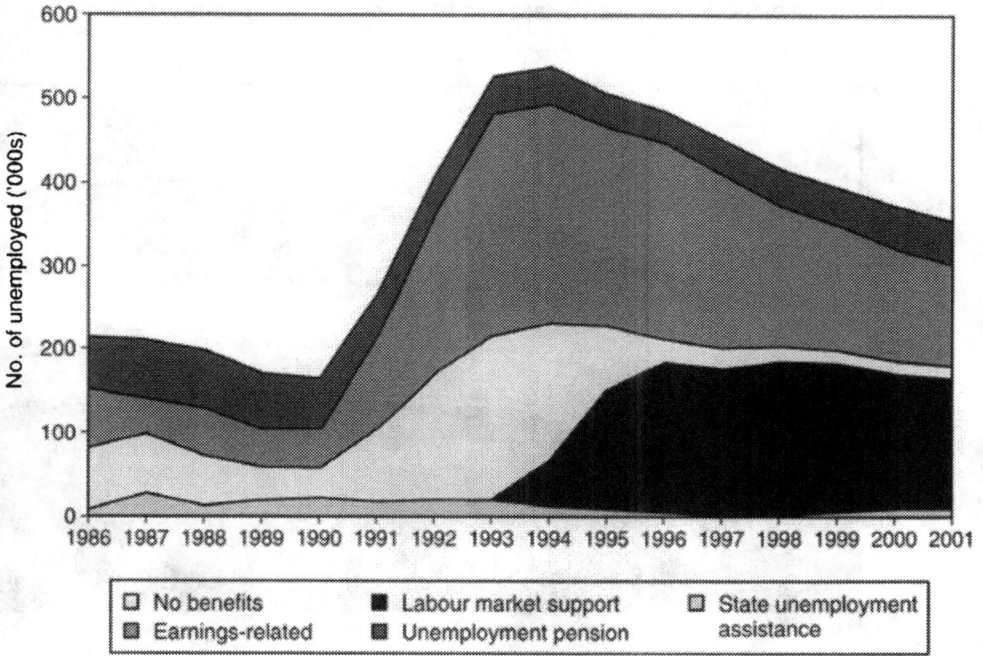

Source: Finnish Labour Review, 2002, p 2.

Figure 8.4   People on labour market support (unemployed or in active measures
             at the end of the year) by age and labour market policy status, 1994–98

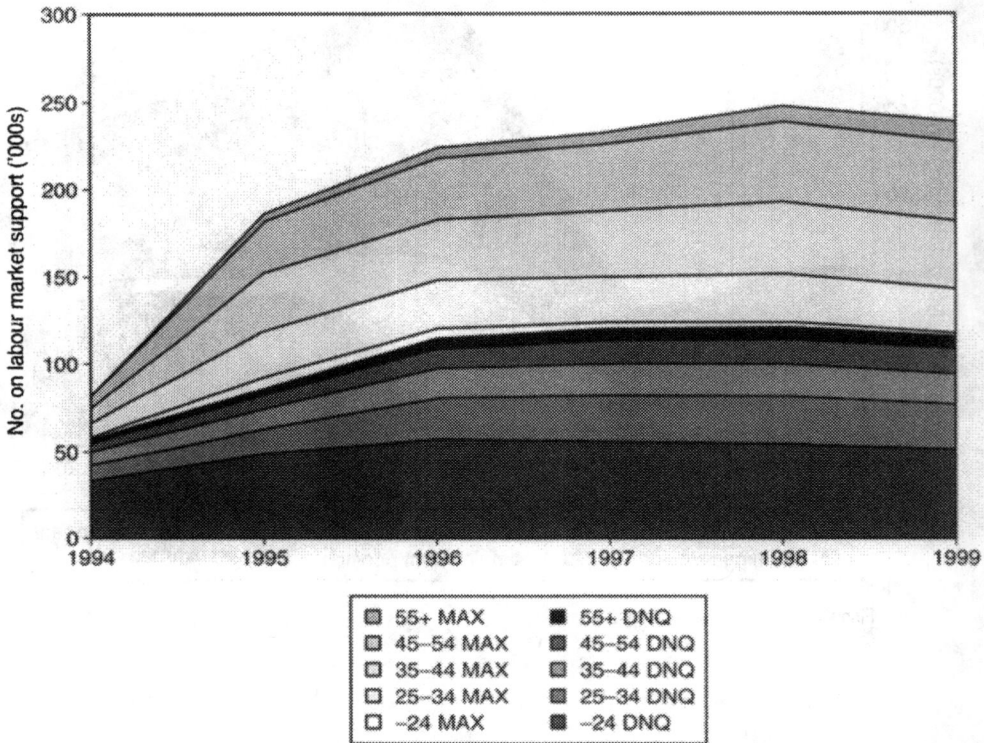

Note: DNQ = has never qualified for regular benefit.
        MAX = has received maximum amount of regular benefit.
Source: Authors' calculation.

6.   Activation

A major argument for the reform was that it would activate the unemployed. A new measure, labour market training with LMS, and thus without pay or an official employment contract, was introduced. We will now see to what extent this goal was achieved.

Figure 8.5 shows the share of people who were in active labour market measures at a given time. Because of the special arrangement for older unemployed entitled to regular unemployment benefit ("the unemployment pension tube") and its policy implications, those at least 55 years of age are distinguished from other unemployed. People on LMS do not have the right to enter the "tube", so the distinction is not relevant for them.

Figure 8.5   Share of people in active labour market policy measures (APM) of those unemployed or in APM at the end of the year, 1991–99

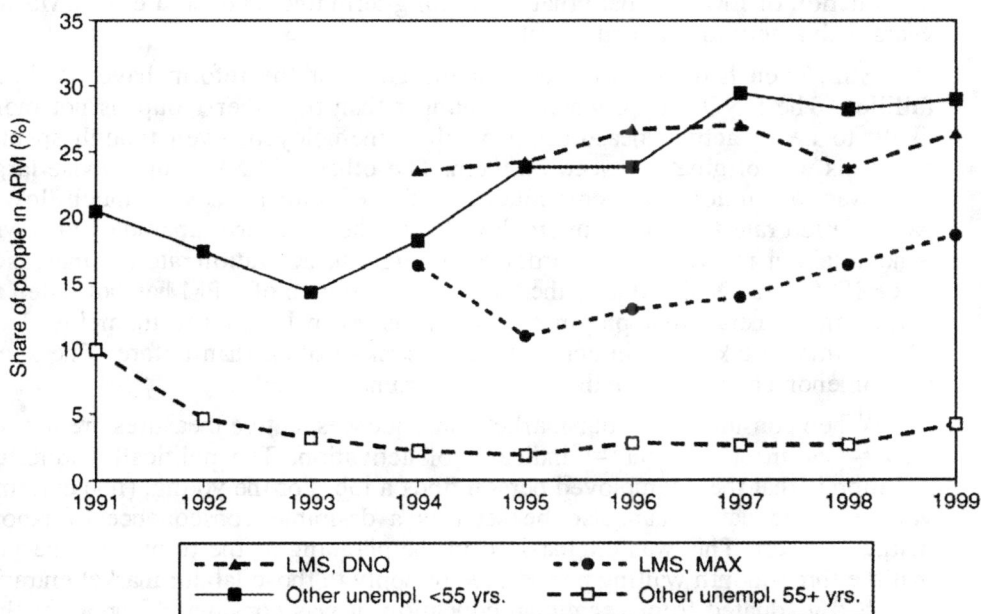

Note: DNQ= has never qualified for regular benefit
        LMS = labour market support
        MAX = has received maximum amount of regular benefit.

As can be seen, the distinction by age is relevant: active measures are seldom targeted at older unemployed. When comparing the participation rate in active measures by benefit type we see that for those on LMS who have never qualified for regular benefit, the rate does not differ very much from other unemployed. In 1994, their participation rate was slightly higher, but it was lower than that of the other unemployed in 1998–99. In the year 2000, the activation rate of other unemployed has decreased. This is due to the improved employment situation: as unemployment decreases, more resources are targeted at the least employable people.

The group that has received the maximum amount of regular benefit has a considerably lower participation rate than other unemployed, even though the rate has steadily increased from the rock bottom figure of 1995. The increase is even more rapid from 1998. This is probably partly due to the introduction of "combined subsidy", which is more favourable to the employer in monetary terms than LMS — in "combined subsidy", both LMS and regular employment subsidy are paid to the employer. The new subsidy employs people in public or third sector jobs, and is largely directed to the long-term unemployed on LMS. In a way, the subsidy is a reaction to the unintended consequence of the introduction of LMS, namely that many long-term unemployed are on LMS for years with a very low activation rate.

Still, even here, we can see that the goals of the reform have not been fulfilled. The DNQ group, which is younger than the other group, is not more likely to be in active measures than other unemployed, even though special emphasis was originally placed on them. The other (MAX) group, whose large size was an unforeseen consequence of the reform, has a much lower participation rate than other unemployed. For the long-term unemployed, LMS is not a labour market springboard, even though the activation rate has increased since 1995. This is also due to the fact that the volume of APM has not fallen as fast as the general unemployment rate. Thus, even long-term unemployed on LMS come to take part in active measures more often than before. The same phenomenon can be seen in the case of older unemployed.

When considering labour market consequences, active measures are not the only — or most relevant — indicator of activation. The politically preferred situation is that the unemployed person finds a job. For the young, (re-) entering vocational education can also be seen as a desirable consequence of labour market support. This was emphasized in the planning of the reform by the fact that the three-month waiting period did not apply to those labour market entrants who had graduated from vocational education. It was considered important that those without secondary education would get one. In 1996, this goal was enforced so that those under the age of 25 without vocational training had to apply for training in order to receive LMS.

Figure 8.6 shows the share of all who were in one sense or the other "active" at the end of the following year. The DNQ group has the highest activation rates, mostly due to the fact that many of them have entered education. In this sense, LMS seems to have some activating effect — even though it is quite clear that many people are in this group merely while waiting for the start of their education and so it cannot be seen as an "activation" consequence. On the other hand, re-employment rates for those in the DNQ group are consistently lower than those of other unemployed, and they are lowest of all for the MAX group. As only a very small proportion of the MAX group entered education during the year, their activation rates differ even more conspicuously from others than when judged solely on the basis of their participation in active measures. The slow rise in activation rates can be seen for the MAX group as well until 1999, but it does not depend on an increased re-employment probability. On the contrary, the total activation rate of the group diminished in 2000, even though their participation in active labour market policy measures increased.

Figure 8.6   Percentage of the unemployed or those in APM who were active at the end of the following year

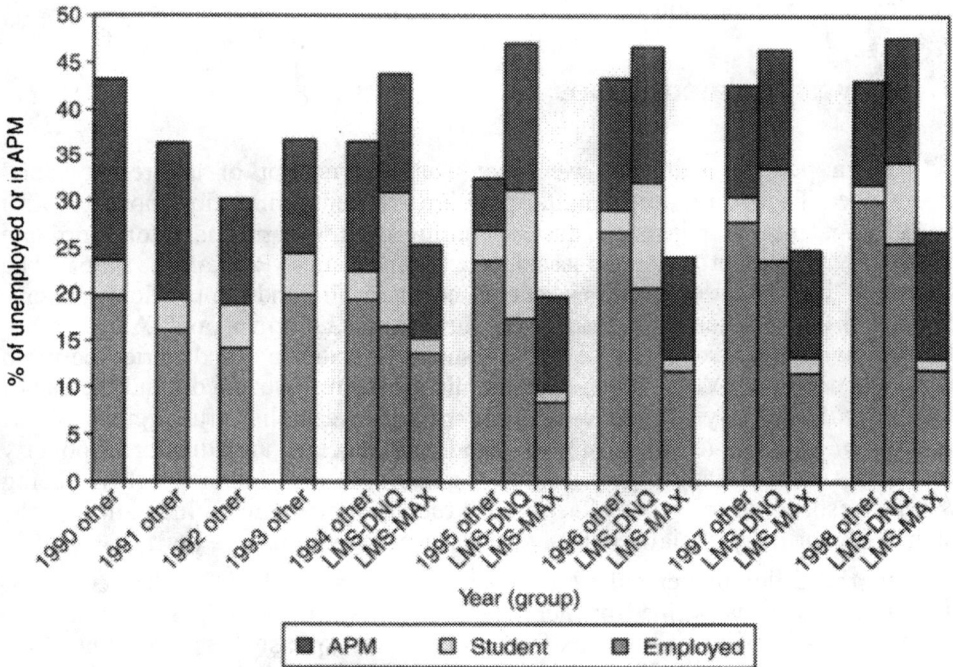

Note.   DNQ= has never qualified for regular benefit;
          LMS = labour market support;
          MAX = has received maximum amount of regular benefit

The differences in re-employment probability between the three groups are dramatic. In particular, the MAX group's re-employment probability is in a class of its own. While it remained very low, the two other groups' re-employment probability steadily increased in 1994–1999. Because of an unfavourable economic trend, the re-employment rates have decreased again in 2000.

Even though there has been an increase in the re-employment probability of the DNQ group, their total activation rate has remained quite stable, as the share of those entering education fell. This is probably due to two reasons: first, many people prefer employment to education, and more employment chances were created during the period. Second, in more favourable economic times, fewer people have unemployment spells between stages of education.

Even from an optimistic viewpoint, it can be concluded that the activation effects of LMS are limited. Even in the best year more than half of the DNQ group was not active at the end of the following year. In the other group, only about one-fourth was active at the end of the year — and more than half of this was due to participation in active labour market measures, rather than employment or education.

7. Poverty-related issues

As a poverty indicator, we have used the receipt of last-resort social assistance. There are considerable problems when connecting poverty with social assistance. For instance, the commonly used poverty indicators correlate weakly with receipt of social assistance (Kangas and Ritakallio, 1996). The relatively high level of social assistance norms in Finland kept official poverty figures from skyrocketing during the recession (Lehtonen and Aho, 2000). Furthermore, non-take-up of social assistance is extensive and varies between population groups (Virjo, 2000). Despite the problems, we can defend the use of this indicator by saying that we are not trying to establish true figures of the number of poor but to use receipt of social assistance as an indicator of poverty trends. As such, it should give reliable figures. It is also important that – being the last-resort system — social assistance receipt figures are an indication of the shortfall in primary social security, such as unemployment benefits.

In the following calculations (Figure 8.7 and Table 8.3), the receipt of social assistance is defined by household. That is, an individual is deemed to have received social assistance if s/he or his/her spouse has a register entry showing receipt. This definition is rather crude, since it does not tell us about the level of benefit dependency, but the trends should still become clear.

The number of unemployed social assistance recipients grew rapidly at the beginning of the 1990s and did not start to decline until 1997. Even then, the share of unemployed people receiving assistance did not significantly fall. There is an indication that the 1994 reform increased poverty among the unemployed: from 1993 to 1994, the share of unemployed receiving social assistance leaped by five percentage points. This is a remarkable change-taking place simultaneously with the reform: the share of social assistance recipients is fairly stable before and after this point. Moreover, we see that those on LMS had a much higher need of social assistance than other unemployed. Against this interpretation, however, even among unemployed other than those on LMS, the share increased temporarily in 1994.

Figure 8.7 Number and share of social assistance recipients in different groups of unemployed or in APM at the end of the year, 1990–98

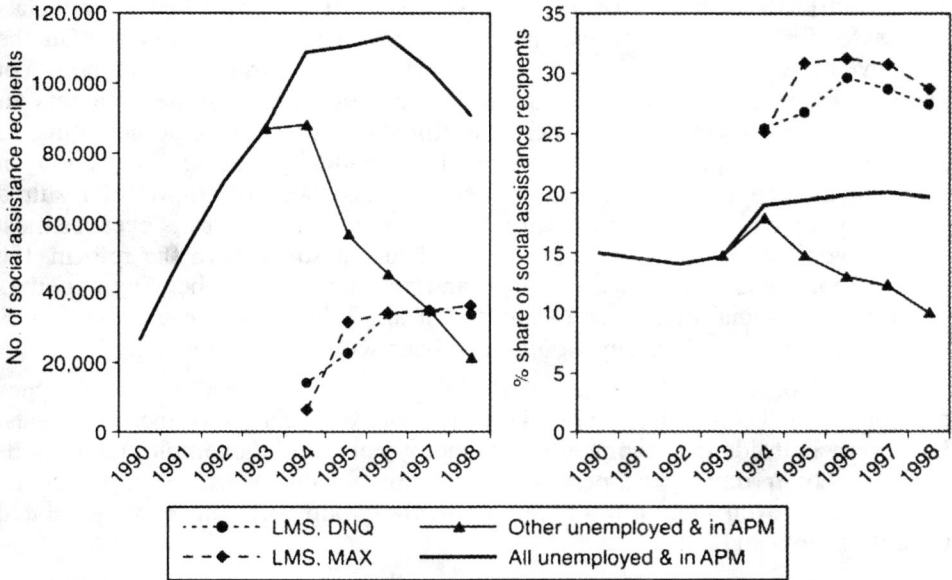

Note: DNQ= has never qualified for regular benefit.
LMS = labour market support
MAX = has received maximum amount of regular benefit
APM = active labour market policy measures

Table 8.3 shows the development of benefit types within groups of unemployed. The share of people on labour market support has increased markedly in almost every group. The share of people on earnings-related benefit has remained stable or even increased in many groups. The explanation is that as the proportion of people on LMS grows, the proportion of those on basic flat-rate benefit decreases. Still, a strong decrease in the share of people on earnings-related benefit can also be seen in some groups. LMS has largely replaced the basic flat-rate benefit, but to some extent even earnings-related benefit.

When it comes to the poverty indicator, the most striking finding is that, in most groups, there seems to be no correlation between unemployment benefit types and the receipt of social assistance. This is especially true if we look at only the LMS figures. In two groups, namely "chronic" and "unemployment pension tube", the poverty indicator seems correlated with the share of people on earnings-related benefit. In most groups, the share of social assistance recipients has been rather stable.

So, even though we found that people on LMS rely on social assistance much more often than people on earnings-related benefit, this effect seems to disappear after controlling for the type of unemployment. In other words, it seems that LMS itself does not produce poverty — it is the fact that a person has drifted to, for example, chronic unemployment that explains poverty. On the other hand, we cannot deduce from this that labour market support does not increase poverty. First, the system may affect the unemployment careers of people, and thus their unemployment classification. As we have pointed out, the structure of unemployment has changed dramatically during the period in question. Second, there was a reform of social assistance in 1998, which resulted in fewer people on LMS being entitled to social assistance. This is because most unemployed on low incomes also receive housing support; in the reform, the level of housing support was increased and an allowance for housing expenses was added to social assistance (Keskitalo et al., 2000). As a result, the figures from 1998 are lower than they would have been without the reform.

It is also clear that the structural changes inside the unemployment types categorized in Table 8.3 correlate with the share of social assistance recipients. For instance, inside the "short-term" unemployment group, unemployment spells became shorter during the period in question, which affects need for social assistance — even though fewer people in the group were on earnings-related benefit in 1996 and 1998.

One interesting finding derived from the table is the large difference between the "chronic unemployment" and "recycling" groups in terms of assistance receipt. Both groups have been without open-market employment, but the latter has frequently participated in active labour market measures. It seems that even though the net effect of such measures on employment probability is virtually non-existent, they have a social function in preventing poverty. To a large extent, this is made possible because people have managed to renew their right to earnings-related benefit with the help of APM. Another explanation is that their income during APM is, in all other cases except labour market training with LMS, substantially higher than during unemployment.

Table 8.3   Receipt of social assistance by unemployment type

Unemployment type	Year	% of total unemployment (including in APMS)	% of earnings-related benefit	% of LMS, DNQ	% of LMS, MAX	% living in households who received social assistance
Short-term	1994	4.7	61	7	0	11
	1996	4.5	52	7	0	8
	1998	4.7	52	14	0	8

Unemployment type	Year	% of total unemployment (including in APMS)	% of earnings-related benefit	% of LMS, DNQ	% of LMS, MAX	% living in households who received social assistance
Students and entrants from education	1994	9.8	24	39	1	17
	1996	8.2	21	56	5	20
	1998	7.6	15	72	5	18
From outside the labour force (child care and others)	1994	4.0	22	41	1	29
	1996	5.1	19	59	2	31
	1998	3.6	17	68	7	30
Medium-term	1994	18.2	61	4	1	14
	1996	11.7	62	13	1	13
	1998	12.0	63	18	2	12
Long-term	1994	23.5	42	4	10	19
	1996	18.1	48	15	15	18
	1998	17.7	46	22	22	18
Chronic	1994	14.2	12	9	5	30
	1996	20.1	9	24	53	32
	1998	20.1	4	32	59	33
Recycling	1994	14.5	31	6	7	25
	1996	19.7	38	13	23	22
	1998	22.8	26	22	45	23
'Unemployment pension tube	1994	11.1	70	0	0	7
	1996	11.9	87	0	0	4
	1998	11.5	91	0	0	3
Total unemployed and in active labour market policy measures	1994	100.0	41	10	4	19
	1996	100.0	41	20	19	20
	1998	100.0	37	26	27	20

Note: See Appendix 8.1

8. Conclusion

The 1994 reform was less radical than originally intended and the difference between the regular flat-rate benefit and LMS for most population groups was more ideological than practical. Without the parliamentary amendments, the impact of the reform would have been more dramatic. Since the amendments were made because of constitutional requirements, we can conclude that the constitution protected the weakest of society.

Despite this, the consequences have been breathtakingly large and unforeseen. This is mostly due to the fact that LMS was introduced shortly after the abolition of the employment obligation.

A steadily rising share of the unemployed has been on LMS since its introduction. Only a small share of them has been young. The activation levels are at best the same as those of the other unemployed, and then only for half of those on LMS, namely the group that has never qualified for regular benefit.

The large group on LMS that has received the maximum amount of regular benefit has much lower activation rates than other unemployed, and their re-employment chances are weak. Although the activation rate of this group seems to have increased in recent years, it is not due to the 1994 LMS reform. Many people have been on the benefit for years, and there is reason to fear that older unemployed will remain on LMS for very long periods. This will cause poverty during and even after unemployment, since fragmentary employment history affects the level of old-age pension.

So, when it comes to the first part of the question in this paper's title, we can say that the reform has not resulted in increased activation of the unemployed. How about the other question: Did the 1994 reform increase poverty? The dramatic effects seen in figure 8.7 are largely a consequence of the abolition of the employment obligation and the tightening of employment conditions to qualify for earnings-related benefit. In other words, without the 1994 reform but with the two above-mentioned reforms, the poverty consequences would probably have been similar.

That said, elements in the 1994 reform seem to have increased poverty. These include stricter means-testing for some groups, lower benefit for those living with their parents, the fact that people on LMS do not qualify for the "unemployment pension tube", and the fact that labour market training with LMS — which in most cases does not increase income — has partly replaced other active labour market measures. Our results and other studies indicate that participation in active labour market measures reduces poverty. The LMS reform has probably weakened this effect. Labour market training with LMS has become the main active labour market policy measure for young unemployed.

While analyses of the poverty effects of the reform are by no means complete, we deduce that the 1994 reform did increase poverty, even though other reforms were more important in this respect.

On the basis of these analyses the answer to question posed in the title is as follows: No, more selectivity in unemployment security has not increased activation of the unemployed; Yes, more selectivity (especially in the form of

While analyses of the poverty effects of the reform are by no means complete, we deduce that the 1994 reform did increase poverty, even though other reforms were more important in this respect.

On the basis of these analyses the answer to question posed in the title is as follows: No, more selectivity in unemployment security has not increased activation of the unemployed; Yes, more selectivity (especially in the form of abolishing the employment obligation) has led to increased poverty, even though the 1994 reform had only a limited role in this. In any case, the reform did not have the desired consequences. The intended "activation springboard for the young" became a "permanent livelihood for a majority of the long-term unemployed".

References

Aho, S.and Österman, P. 1999. *Ikääntyvien työssäkäynti, työttömyys ja varhainen eläkkeelle siirtyminen 1987-1996* (Helsinki, Ministry of Social Affairs and Health), Publication No. 7.

_____ and Vehviläinen, J. 1997. *Keppi ja porkkana. Tutkimus alle 20-vuotiaita aktivoivan työvoimapoliittisen uudistuksen vaikutuksista ja koulutuksen ulkopuolelle jäävistä nuorista* (Helsinki, European Social Fund), Publication No. 3.

_____, Halme, J. and Nätti, J. 1999. "Tukityöllistämisen ja työvoimakoulutuksen kohdentuminen ja vaikuttavuus 1990–96" in *Työpoliittinen tutkimus 207* (Helsinki, Ministry of Labour).

_____, Susanna, K and Nätti, J. 2001. "Evaluating active labour market policies with matched control groups: Employment impact of labour market training and subsidized employment in Finland in 1994 and 1997", in A. Holm and T. Pilegaard-Nielsen (eds.) *Labour market research with register data in Nordic countries* (Copenhagen, Nordic Council).

_____ et al. 2000. "Vuoden 1998 työvoimapoliittisen uudistuksen arviointia", in *Työpoliittinen tutkimus 224* (Helsinki, Ministry of Labour).

Arnkil, R., Nieminen, J. and Spangar, T. 2000. "Suomen työvoimapoliittisen uudistuksen uudistuksen arviointi palveluprosessin ja paikallistoimistojen näkökulmasta. Evaluoinnin loppuraportti", in *Työpoliittinen tutkimus 219* (Helsinki, Ministry of Labour).

Hytti, H. 1998. *Varhainen eläkkeelle siirtyminen — Suomen malli"* (Helsinki, Social Insurance Institution), Publication No. 32.

Kangas, O. and Ritakallio, V-M. 1996. "Eri menetelmät — eri tulokset. Köyhyyden monimuotoisuus", in O. Kangas and V-M. Ritakallio (eds.) *Kuka on köyhä?*

Köyhyys 1990-luvun puolivälin Suomessa (Helsinki, National Research and Development Centre for Welfare and Health Studies 65).

Keskitalo, E., Heikkilä, M. and Laaksonen, S. 2000. *Toimeentulotuen muutokset. Vuoden 1998 perusturvamuutosten arviointitutkimuksen loppuraportti* (Helsinki, Ministry of Social Affairs and Health), Publication No. 16.

Laine, V. and Uusitalo, R. 2001. *Kannustinloukku-uudistuksen vaikutukset työvoiman tarjontaan* (Helsinki, Government Institute for Economic Research Studies 74).

Lehtonen, H. and Aho, S. 2000. "Hyvinvointivaltion leikkausten uudelleenarviointia", *in Janus*, Vol. 8, No. 2, pp. 97–113.

Malmberg-Heinonen, I. And Vuori, J. 2000. "Työnhakuryhmätoiminnan vaikutukset työmarkkina-asemaan ja koettuun terveyteen", in *Työpoliittisia tutkimuksia 221* (Helsinki, Ministry of Labour).

Niinivaara, R. 1999. *Kannustinloukkutyöryhmän ehdotusten toteutumisen arviointia* (Helsinki, Ministry of Finance).

Räisänen, H. and Skog, H. 1998. *Towards a better functioning labour market. Senior government advisor's report for the labour market policy system* (Helsinki, Ministry of Labour).

Tuomala, J. 2000. "Työnhakukoulutuksen vaikutusten arviointi", in *Työvoimapoliittinen tutkimus 222* (Helsinki, Ministry of Labour).

Työministeriö. 2001. "Toinen aalto. Työvoimapolitiikan uudistuksen jatkaminen", in *Työhallinnon julkaisu 269* (Helsinki, Ministry of Labour).

Virjo, I. 2000. "Toimeentulotuen alikäytön laajuus ja syyt", in *Janus 8*, No. 1, pp. 28–44.

_____ and Aho, S. 2002. "Ikääntyvien työllisyys 1990-luvulla. Rekisteritutkimus yli 50-vuotiaiden erityisongelmista työmarkinoilla", in *Studies in Labour Policy 242* (Helsinki: Ministry of Labour).

APPENDICES

Data and variables in figure 8.2 and table 8.3

The annual flow of the unemployed consists of individuals who have at least some unemployment or participation in labour market measures during the given year. The labour force in table 8.1 includes all individuals who have been in gainful employment during the given year, or belonged to the flow of the unemployed, or are retired with unemployment pension.

The variable in figures 8.5 and 8.6, describing the type of unemployment, is based on the employment and unemployment history of the past four years (e.g. for the year 1990, the variable is based on the labour market career in the years 1987–90). The categories are based on the time spent in the labour force (later TLF) during the four-year period, the proportion of open-market employment of TLF, and information on eventual student status in secondary or tertiary education. The categories are exclusive and based on the following criteria:

1. short-term unemployment in employment 86–99% of TLF;

2. students or entrants from education who studied during the last year of the period;

3. other labour market entrants, not belonging to the labour force during the previous year (e.g. concerning 1990, not in the labour force in 1989);

4. medium-term unemployment, in employment 50–85% of TLF;

5. long-term unemployment, in employment 15–49% of TLF;

6. chronic unemployment, in employment 0–14% of TLF; or

7. recycling: equally chronic but participated in active labour market measure (ALP) at least twice during past four years;

8. pension tube: entitled to earnings-related unemployment benefit until retirement with unemployment pension;

9. unemployment pension, retired with unemployment pension during the last year of the period.

In table 8.2, categories 1–3 and 6–8 are combined.

Figure 8.A2   Unemployment benefit types in Finland, 1986–2001 (shares counted from annual averages)

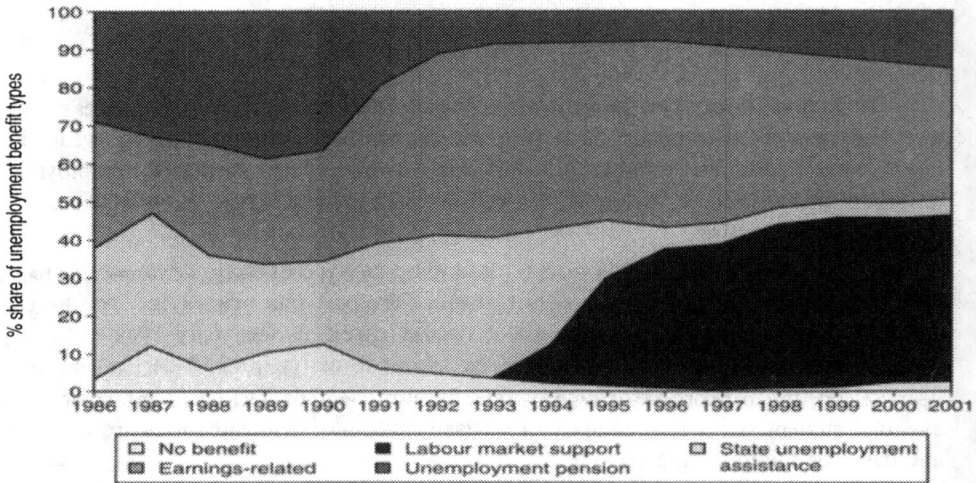

Source· Finnish Labour Review, 2002, p 2

Table 8.A3   People on labour market support in Finland, 1994–99 (as percentage of those unemployed or in active measures at the end of the year), by age and labour market policy status

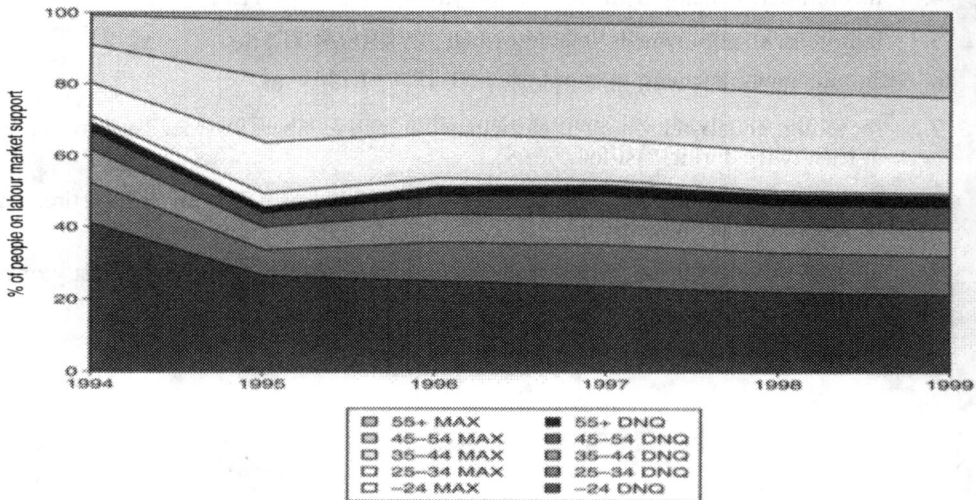

Note·   DNQ = has never qualified for regular benefit
        MAX = has received maximum amount of regular benefit

Mass joblessness, the Bismarckian model and the limits to gradual adaptation: The case of Belgium

9

Ive Marx[1]

1. Introduction

Belgium seems to epitomize just about everything that is wrong with continental European labour markets. For more than two decades, it has been confronted with high unemployment and holds the dubious honour of having one of the highest long-term unemployment rates in Europe. Yet it has maintained a comparatively low relative poverty rate, including among the unemployed. This may come as surprise to those who have argued that structural unemployment has led to "new poverty" in the Bismarckian income protection systems in continental Europe.

This article seeks to shed light on Belgium's apparent success in containing poverty under conditions of mass unemployment. It will be shown that gradual but fundamental changes to the original Bismarckian income protection system have helped to keep down poverty levels. Belgium's social insurance-based benefit system has been transformed into a minimum income protection system, in which benefits are a function of assumed need rather than past contributions. However, these changes have come at the expense of the fairness and legitimacy of the system. It will be argued that, although reforms of recent decades have gone a long way in countering the potential poverty consequences of chronic unemployment, there appear to be limits on further progress through gradual adaptation. These limits are in part economic in nature, in part political.

[1] University of Antwerp, Belgium.

2. The new poverty thesis

It is a familiar claim that Europe's chronic mass unemployment has given rise to "new poverty" (e.g., Lawson and Wilson, 1995; Funken and Cooper, 1995). The argument runs roughly as follows. In Europe, where the Bismarckian model prevails, income protection has been principally provided through social insurance. In a social insurance system, the level of support given to an unemployed person is generally dependent on past contributions, previous wages and work history. This has several implications. First, new labour market entrants are, at least in principle, not entitled to unemployment insurance benefits. As we know, Europe's unemployment, as it has emerged over the past few decades, is largely a problem of labour market entrants failing to gain access to jobs. Youth unemployment rates have, for the past two decades, and depending on the state of the business cycle, topped 20% or 30% in many European countries. Female unemployment rates have also been high. Many unemployed women are new entrants or re-entrants after a period of voluntary withdrawal from the labour market. It is reasonable to assume that many of these entrants or re-entrants, with no or insufficient contribution records, are not entitled to unemployment benefits and so lack adequate income protection. Furthermore, in a social insurance system, even a person with a good contribution record will eventually deplete his or her entitlement after prolonged unemployment. Again, it is well established that unemployment in much of Europe is long-term in nature. In the European Union as a whole, about 30% of the unemployed at any given time have been out of work for more than a year.

It seems plausible that many unemployed are inadequately protected within the framework of Europe's social insurance-based systems. Over the past few decades, dependence on social assistance among the working-age population has surged in most European countries, not least among the unemployed (Gough et al., 1997). This is often presented as evidence that the social insurance-based model fails to deal with rising need among the working-age population. Many also see the rise in social assistance dependence as evidence that poverty has risen. Proponents of the new poverty thesis argue that levels of income support provided under social assistance fall well short of widely used poverty thresholds, a claim supported by some studies (Andries, 1996; Gough et al., 1997). In short, it is reasonable to suspect that the Bismarckian model, which remains dominant in much of Europe, fails to deal with the poverty consequences of chronic mass unemployment.

3. Unemployment and poverty in Belgium

Belgium, like most other European countries, experienced a dramatic increase in unemployment after 1973. The actual extent of the increase depends on the measure of unemployment used. The most widely used measure for cross-country and cross-temporal comparisons are the standardized unemployment rate, as defined by the ILO and calculated on the basis of labour force survey data.

By this measure (as by any commonly used measure), Belgian unemployment soared dramatically after the energy price shocks of the early 1970s following much the same pattern as in the rest of Europe. During much of the 1980s and 1990s, Belgium's standardized unemployment rate hovered around the EU average. In 1997 Belgium's ILO unemployment rate stood at 7% (OECD, 1998).

However, Belgium stands out in that unemployment has been exceptionally persistent for the past few decades (Table 9.1). Throughout the 1980s and 1990s, Belgium had just about the highest long-term unemployment share in the OECD area, with more than 65% of the unemployed out of work for more than one year at some stages of the business cycle. In the late 1990s, the share of long-term unemployed in total unemployment had dropped but was still above 60%. Hence, although Belgium's standardized unemployment rate is not particularly high compared to the European average, a comparatively large share of the workforce is structurally excluded from the labour market. Moreover, unemployment (including long-term unemployment) is particularly high among the groups widely perceived as inadequately protected under social insurance: youngsters and women, many of whom are new entrants without contribution records. In 1997, Belgium's youth unemployment rate stood at well over 20% and its female unemployment rate at almost 12%.

Table 9.1   Labour market performance of Belgium in a European perspective, 1997

	ILO unemployment rate %	Long-term unemployment share %	Labour slack* %	Non-employment %
Belgium	7.1	60.5	14.0	32.9
Denmark	4.6	27.2	8.8	18.7
France	14.2	41.2	15.0	33.3
Germany	9.0	47.8*	9.9	26.7
Ireland	10.6	57.0	14.5	32.4
Italy	9.8	66.3	17.3	35.0
Netherlands	4.4	49.1	9.5	22.1
Portugal	6.2	55.6	7.3	28.1
Spain	16.2	55.5	23.6	36.3
United Kingdom	8.2	38.6	10.3	22.6
OECD Europe	8.9	47.6	-	29.4

Sources: OECD (1998) *Employment Outlook*; * Standing, 1999 (Figures for 1996)

The standardized unemployment rate, while one of the more appropriate measures for international and cross-temporal comparisons, is also a strict measure of involuntary labour market exclusion. It is based on the number of people who report they are unemployed, available for work and actively making efforts to find a job. Discouraged workers - jobless persons who want a job but are no longer actively looking for one - are not counted as unemployed under the ILO definition.

One alternative, albeit equally flawed measure is the official unemployment rate (Table 9.2). This includes all those officially registered as full-time unemployed and entitled to unemployment benefits. The official unemployment rate in Belgium has normally been to be higher than the standardized rate because it includes people who are officially registered as unemployed but not actively looking for work. Hence, this measure also includes, to some extent, what one might label "discouraged workers", provided that they are (still) entitled to unemployment insurance benefits. That the number of people receiving unemployment benefits is higher than the number of the ILO unemployed indicates the peculiar nature of Belgium's "social insurance" system, as we will see. For much of the 1990s, the official unemployment rate hovered between 10% and 12%, while the ILO unemployment rate was in the 7% to 9% range. It is important to emphasize, once again, that the vast majority of the officially unemployed are long term unemployed. In 1999, more than 60% had been registered as full-time unemployed for over a year, and 40% for over two years (RVA, 2000).

Table 9.2   Evolution of the number of people entitled to unemployment insurance benefits for full-time unemployment, Belgium 1970-2000

Year	Full-time unemployed (No)	Full-time unemployment as a % of the labour force
1970	70 753	1.9
1975	174 480	4.4
1980	322 310	7.9
1985	505 944	12.3
1990	364 696	8.7
1995	555 252	12.9
2000	439 149	10.1

Source. Deleeck (2001)

An even wider measure of unemployment is the broad unemployment rate as calculated by the OECD (1997a). This measure includes not only people claiming benefits for full-time unemployment, but also those claiming benefits for part-time and temporary unemployment, those in the main early retirement scheme (officially an unemployment scheme) and those in special employment programmes. According to the OECD, broad unemployment as a percentage of the broad labour force was around 25% for much of the 1990s. The broad unemployment estimate for Belgium arguably overstates the extent of unemployment. For instance, people who receive career interruption benefits are counted as unemployed (excluding this category would reduce the broad unemployment rate by about a percentage point or so). Similarly, those in direct job creation schemes also count as unemployed, although this is appropriate since most of these job schemes do not offer permanent employment and participants have to accept a suitable regular job if offered one. In other respects, the broad unemployment rate understates the true extent of involuntary labour market exclusion. For instance, people on social assistance are not included. Neither are people who want a job but who are not entitled to unemployment benefits or who have lost or depleted their rights. So even the OECD broad unemployment rate largely excludes discouraged workers - a group that ought to be included in proper measure of involuntary labour market exclusion.

Another alternative measure of unemployment is Standing's (1999) index of labour market slack. This index, calculated on the basis of labour force data, does include discouraged workers – that is it includes those who say that they want work and are available for work but are not actively looking for employment. Standing's measure of labour market slack also includes involuntary part-time workers, employed persons who are laid-off or not working for economic reasons, and people on "short time", that is, working fewer than their normal or contractual hours for economic reasons beyond their immediate control. This measure of labour market slack almost doubles Belgium's ILO unemployment rate for 1997 to around 14% (Table 9.1). It is striking that the difference between Belgium's standardized rate and its "adjusted" rate is substantially bigger than for most of the other OECD countries included in Standing's analysis.

Perhaps the broadest indicator of labour market exclusion - though not necessarily involuntary exclusion - is the non-employment rate, the share of the working-age population not in work. It is in this respect that Belgium is the true outlier in the northern European context (Table 9.1). Belgium's non-employment rate (33% in 1997) exceeds the EU average (30%) and the OECD average (24%). The gap between Belgium's non-employment rate and the OECD average has also widened over the past few decades. Belgium's exceptionally high non-employment rate reinforces the point that chronic labour market exclusion is a far bigger problem than suggested by the conventional ILO unemployment rate.

What are the poverty consequences of mass joblessness in Belgium? In keeping with common practice in current poverty research, I use a relative poverty threshold. Analyses of the Luxembourg Income Study (LIS) datasets have consistently shown Belgium to have one of the lowest relative poverty rates in the OECD area (Atkinson, 1997; Gottschalk and Smeeding, 1997). This is certainly the case for the working-age population. Poverty estimates on the basis of the European Community Household Panel (ECHP) present a somewhat different picture: ECHP poverty rates for Belgium tend to be higher than the LIS-based estimates (Eurostat, 2001). This discrepancy exists for many OECD countries, and country rankings on the basis of LIS and ECHP are quite similar, but it is bigger for Belgium than for most other countries. The reasons remain unclear, but all the available evidence points to the relatively small but apparently significant differences in measurement methodology (Cantillon et al., 2002).

We are most interested in the poverty exposure of the unemployed. Gallie et al. (2000) have estimated that, in 1994, about 22% of Belgium's unemployed lived in relative financial poverty, a proportion that is the second lowest among the 11 EU countries included in their study (Table 9.3). Their estimate is based on ECHP data and is roughly consistent with the figure we find using our main data source, the Belgian Socio-Economic Household Survey for 1997 (Table 9.4).

In both instances, the poverty estimates are for the self-reported unemployed, i.e. people who say that their labour market status is "unemployed". In Belgium this is commonly understood as being jobless and looking for work, though not necessarily very actively. It is also useful to point out that in the Belgian Socio-Economic Panel, poverty status is measured on the basis of income received during the month prior to the interview. Hence, it is quite reasonable to assume that the reported labour force status at the time of the interview is representative of the labour force status during the reference month for the income measures. In the ECHP, by contrast, an individual's poverty status is measured on the basis of income received during the year prior to the interview, while his or her measured labour market status reflects the status at the time of the interview.

Table 9.3   Relative poverty among the unemployed, 1994, based on ECHP

	Percentage below 50% of mean equivalent household income
Belgium	22.7
Denmark	8.1
France	28.1
Germany	26.8
Greece	25.7
Ireland	31.3
Italy	37.2
Netherlands	25.1
Portugal	29.6
Spain	33.2
United Kingdom	48.5
Source: Gallie et al. (2000)	

Table 9.4   Poverty incidence by labour market status, Belgium, 1985-1997

Labour market status	Relative poverty incidence (%)			Share in working age population (%)		
	1985	1992	1997	1985	1992	1997
Non-employed	6.4	9.0	11.2	44.5	40.6	41.2
Unemployed	10.4	13.4	22.2	7.6	7.4	8.7
- with UE benefit	10.0	12.2	19.3	6.6	6.6	6.6
- no UE benefit	13.3	22.6	31.4	0.9	0.8	2.1
Working age population	3.9	4.4	5.1	100.0 (n=6 598)	100.0 (n=3 528)	100.0 (n=4 228)

Source Own calculations on the basis of the Belgian Socio-Economic Panel

Note: UE benefits = unemployment benefit

4.   Belgium's low poverty rate among the unemployed explained

I now want to shed light on the relatively weak relationship between unemployment and poverty in Belgium. First, I focus on the composition of the unemployed, demonstrating that unemployment in Belgium is a breadwinner phenomenon only to a limited extent. This accounts for the weak link between unemployment and poverty and is not accidental. Labour market policy in the past has put overwhelming emphasis on maintaining "full employment" in the traditional sense and hence on safeguarding the Bismarckian model. Then I focus on benefit policies that affect living standards of the unemployed, arguing that gradual but fundamental changes to the original, Bismarckian social insurance system have helped to keep down poverty among the unemployed.

4.1 The robust labour market position of the male breadwinner

The most important explanation for the limited overlap between unemployment and poverty lies in the fact that unemployment in Belgium is only to a limited extent a breadwinner problem. Unemployment rates for men, particularly for prime-age men - those most likely to be the principal breadwinner - have remained quite low, even for men with low educational attainment. In 1997, 7% of the male workforce and 6% of the prime-aged male workforce was registered as ILO unemployed (Table 9.5). The European Union averages were 9% and 8% respectively. Employment rates have also remained high. In 1997, over 86% of Belgian prime-aged men had a job. The EU average stood slightly lower at 85%.

The vast majority of prime-age men have a job and usually a stable one. Data on job tenure indicate comparatively high job stability in Belgium, with average job tenure among the highest in the OECD area (OECD, 1997a). Furthermore, few work for a low-wage. Low-wage work is less prevalent among Belgian men than in most other OECD countries (OECD, 1995). The last column of Table 9.5 shows the share of the male workforce receiving less than 66% of the median gross wage. About 4% of men in full-time employment work for a low wage, compared to around 10% in Germany and France and 13% in the UK. This is relevant to Belgium's comparatively low poverty rate. Research has established a strong cross-country correlation between the incidence of low pay (which is reflective of both minimum wage levels and minimum benefit levels, since these set wage floors) and the incidence of relative poverty at working age (Marx and Verbist, 1998).

Table 9.5   Labour market position of prime-aged men in a European perspective, 1997

	Unemployment rate (%)	Employment rate (%)	Low pay incidence* (%)
Belgium	6.2	86.4	3.9
Denmark	4.1	88.7	-
France	12.9	86.3	10.6
Germany	8.0	85.1	7.6
Ireland	9.7	81.7	-
Italy	7.5	83.0	9 3
Netherlands	3.6	90.1	8.1
Portugal	5.0	88.0	-
Spain	13.6	79.9	-
United Kingdom	6.7	85.4	12.8
OECD Europe	7.4	85.2	-

Source: OECD (1995 and 1998) *Employment Outlook*; * figures for mid 1990s

The fact that the labour market position of the male breadwinner has remained so robust in Belgium is in many respects remarkable. After all, Belgium, an early industrializer (Cassiers, De Villé and Solar, 1996), suffered massive job losses in manufacturing during the 1970s and 1980s. The industrial sector, being rather old and energy intensive, was hard hit by the oil shocks and the economic downturns of the 1970s and 1980s. The share of industrial employment (including mining and construction) in total employment, which was still around 40% in 1975, fell rapidly thereafter, reflecting major structural adjustments in steel, coal and textile industries. During the 1980s, Belgium recorded the fourth largest job loss percentage in manufacturing in the OECD area. By 1992, employment in industry represented less than 28% of total employment (OECD, 1997b).

Like most continental European countries, Belgium expanded early retirement schemes to alleviate the social consequences of structural economic adjustment and massive job shedding in industry. Kohli et al. (1993) and Esping-Andersen (1996, 1999) have even argued that in Continental Europe early retirement policies "became the main -if not exclusive- means to facilitate industrial restructuring" (Esping-Andersen, 1999, p.130). Whether this is true or not remains questionable, but it is certainly the case that Belgium went further than any other Continental European country in the expansion of early retirement. Labour force participation among men over the age of 55 dropped rapidly and massively during the late 1970s and 1980s. At 37%, it is now one of the lowest in the OECD area (Table 9.6). To put this figure into context, the OECD average is 65% and the EU average is 53%.

Table 9.6   Labour market position of older men (55-64) in a European perspective, 1997

	Unemployment rate (%)	Employment rate (%)
Belgium	4.8	32.2
Denmark	4.4	61.0
France	8.5	38.9
Germany	13.4	47.3
Ireland	6.4	57.8
Italy	4.6	41.5
Netherlands	3.2	43.0
Portugal	6.4	58.2
Spain	10.8	50.5
United Kingdom	7.8	58.6
OECD Europe	7.8	48.4

Source: OECD (1998) Employment Outlook

The main early retirement scheme consists of a social security benefit, which has the formal status of an unemployment benefit because it is paid by the unemployment insurance administration, topped up by a "pension" paid by the industry fund of the former employer. In many cases, early-retired workers also receive an additional benefit from their old firm, enabling them to accumulate a net income only marginally below their last wage.

The massive expansion of early retirement arguably had two major effects on unemployment and poverty. First, it seems reasonable to suspect that it averted a serious rise in "real" unemployment among older workers. With the huge job losses in Belgium's industrial sector after the oil shocks of the 1970s and 1980s, many of the workers who lost jobs were sole breadwinners with few formal qualifications or with specific technical skills. Many lived in industrial regions and would have found it hard to find employment elsewhere. There can be little doubt that the poverty consequences of high unemployment among traditional breadwinners would have been grave, "real" unemployment benefits being insufficient for households needs.

It is difficult to ascertain to what extent early retirement prevented a rise of open unemployment among older men. The unemployment rate for men between the ages of 55 and 64 has remained comparatively low in Belgium, during much of the 1990s remaining 5%, compared to a EU average of about 8%. This is not to suggest that all those who took early retirement would have otherwise become unemployed. It is fair to say that job shedding was encouraged by the availability of financially attractive early retirement schemes, co-funded by Government and employers (at the industry level and often also at the firm level). The co-funded nature of early retirement allows employers to externalize much of the cost of laying off redundant older workers. There is typically little resistance from trade unions because laid-off workers tend to suffer minimal income loss. On the contrary, many workers have developed a strong preference for early retirement (Schokkaert et al., 2000). The fact that early retirement remains widespread even in today's improved economic context is almost wholly due to the fact that trade unions have insisted on its continuation. So far, they have been successful, despite growing resistance from employers complaining of labour shortages. The Government too has proclaimed its intention to scale back early retirement but, wary of trade union and public reaction, has so far taken few steps to do so.

It is possible that the labour supply reduction effect of mass early retirement has also helped to support the robust labour market position of prime-age men and others, by reducing competition for less skilled jobs. In fact, the original reason for government paying a major part of the early retirement bill was that it helped combat youth unemployment. Indeed, employers were, and in theory still are, required to hire a young person to replace the person taking early retirement. In practice, the replacement rule has never been respected.

4.2 Adapting the Bismarckian system: Departure from the equivalence principle

Belgium's unemployment insurance system is Bismarckian in that the level of support given to an unemployed person is related to previous wages and work history. It seems odd, therefore, that despite the high levels of unemployment, especially among youngsters and women, who tend to be labour market entrants or re-entrants without contribution records, poverty is not rampant among the unemployed in Belgium. Moreover, in a social insurance system, even someone with a good contribution record will eventually exhaust his or her entitlement.

Despite the fact that Belgium has one of the highest long-term unemployment rates in Europe, poverty among the unemployed is relatively low. So too is social assistance dependence, one of the most readily available indicators of social insurance failure. The share of the working-age population receiving means-tested income support has risen only moderately over the past 25 years, relative to the rises recorded in other European countries. The proportion of the non-elderly population on means-tested income support has never exceeded 1% of the population, which is a much lower share than in most other European countries (Gough et al., 1997).

The explanation is that Belgium's social insurance model has evolved into something approaching a basic protection model (see also Andries, 1996b).

First, the duration of unemployment benefits now depends more on assumed need than on of work history and past contributions, as is theoretically the case in Bismarckian systems. Contrary to most other countries, unemployment insurance benefits are not time-limited in Belgium. However, in the early 1980s, when the number of benefit claimants was rising rapidly, a distinction was introduced between three categories of claimants: heads of households (those providing for dependent persons such as children or non-working spouses; single persons; and so-called "cohabitants". The last category consists of unemployed persons who live with a person with an income above a certain threshold (possibly another unemployed person). They are the only categories liable to have their benefit terminated after an "abnormally" long spell of unemployment and then only if total household income is far above the social assistance level.

Until 1993, the general rule was that benefit termination proceedings were initiated if a cohabitant's spell of unemployment was more than twice the total average, taking also into account the sex and age of the person. After 1993, this period was shortened to 1.5 times the average spell. In practice this means that termination proceedings are not initiated until a spell of unemployment exceeds three or four years. In regions with unfavourable labour market conditions, this can be eight years or more. Even then, benefit termination is not automatic. Local unemployment officials have considerable discretion in granting exemptions. For example, they can judge that a claimant has made "extraordinary" efforts to find work. Yet since the early 1990s there have been considerably fewer exemptions for this reason. Despite a tightening of rules on benefit termination, the Belgian system remains atypical in terms of average duration. This helps to explain why only a relatively small proportion of the unemployed end up on social assistance. Single persons, heads of household and cohabitants only risk suspension of unemployment benefit in the event of proven fraud. This is the main reason why some of the unemployed resort to social assistance, at least for the duration of the suspension, which is usually temporary.

The levels of benefits, like their duration, have become a function of assumed need. Belgium's unemployment benefit system, as it exists today, is characterized by a particularly strong emphasis on minimum income protection. In theory, in a social insurance system, benefits are a function of past contributions and earnings. In Belgium, this equivalence principle has been gradually weakened, if not abandoned over the past two decades. The inflation-adjusted value of maximum benefit levels has been allowed to erode. The real value of guaranteed minimum benefit levels, by contrast, increased substantially during the 1970s, the early 1980s and the early 1990s. As a result, only a very small gap remains between maximum and minimum benefits. Thus in 1975, the difference between the minimum and maximum benefit for an unemployed head of household was almost 25%; by 1995 this had shrunk to less than 13%.

Moreover, unemployment benefits frequently exceed individual entitlements under the equivalence principle. The period during which an unemployed person was in full-time education counts as time worked. Of the unemployed in the "head of household" category, almost half receive the guaranteed minimum benefit (RVA, 2000).

The level of (minimum) benefit also distinguishes between "heads of household", "single persons" and "cohabitants". Benefits are highest for the first two categories of claimant, because they are assumed to be most needy. Heads of household are entitled to supplementary child benefits if they have dependent children. For cohabitants, benefits are still linked to previous wages during the first period of unemployment, albeit within narrow margins. However, after roughly the first 18 months of unemployment (depending on work history) they all receive a relatively low flat-rate amount.

Table 9.7   Minimum benefits for the main benefit categories in unemployment insurance, 1970-2000 (Belgium francs, 2000 prices)

	1970	1975	1980	1985	1990	1995	2000
Head	20 709	29 413	30 301	31 017	30 244	32 483	31 130
Single	19 039	22 610	23 282	22 176	21 631	23 243	22 277
Cohabitant	19 039	22 610	23 282	14 520	13 600	13 831	13 530

Source. Cantillon et al. (2001)

Table 9.8   Distribution across benefit categories in unemployment insurance, Belgium 2000

	%
Head of household	**36.4**
Men	17.5
Women	18.8
Single persons	**18.0**
Men	10.9
Women	7.1
Cohabitants	**45.4**
Men	13.8
Women	31.7
Others	0.2
	100.0

Source: RVA (2000).

During the past two decades, policy was not only guided by a concern to improve minimum protection for the most needy among the unemployed. Cost containment was also a major concern. Introduction of the relatively cheap "cohabitant" category in the early 1980s dramatically contained the cost of the system. Despite the immense increase in the number of claimants, especially between the mid 1970s and mid 1980s (Table 9.2), the cost of the unemployment insurance system remained stable as a share of GDP.

5.   Deficiencies, inequities and the limits to gradual reform

Contrary to what is often argued or implied in the international literature, there is, at least in the case of Belgium, not much evidence that mass unemployment has given rise to large-scale "new poverty". Labour supply reduction policies (early retirement) and gradual adaptations of the Bismarckian social protection model have helped to mitigate the poverty consequences of job shedding and mass unemployment. But the relatively favourable picture from the poverty perspective obscures some serious problems and fundamental inequities. Moreover, there are clear signs that the limits of gradual adaptation have been reached.

5.1 Inadequate minimum income protection for unemployed breadwinners

Poverty among the unemployed is low in Belgium basically because many live in a household with at least one wage earner. Almost eight out of ten households on unemployment benefit have other financial means (Table 9.9). For them, unemployment benefit is only one component of household income and frequently not even the principal one. So, the majority of the unemployed would not be poor even without unemployment benefit, as is evident from the pre-transfer poverty rate for households on unemployment benefit in Table 9.9.

However, the fact that the majority of the unemployed do not live in poverty obscures the problem of severe hardship among a minority of households who have to subsist on unemployment benefit. In 1997, an astonishing 60% of households surviving on unemployment benefit (plus possible child benefits) lived below the poverty threshold (Table 9.10). Note also that poverty rates for this category have dramatically increased since the mid-1980s. The rise in poverty among the unemployed is due to this factor and to the rise in the proportion of household heads in the unemployed population. The composition component is largely related to the wave of benefit suspensions following the tightening of rules and practices regarding benefit duration for unemployed cohabitant.

Table 9.9   Profile of households receiving unemployment benefits (UEB), Belgium, 1997

	Households with UEB	Households that have to make ends meet on UEB	Households receiving UEB and other income
Share in the population of households receiving UEB (%)	100.0	22.9	77.1
Share in the total population (%)	13.0	3.0	10.0
Pre-transfer poor (%)	55.7	0.0	72.3
Lifted from poverty thanks to UEB (%)	29.1	42.1	25.2
Poor despite UEB (%)	15.2	57.9	2.5

Source. Cantillon et al. (1999)

Table 9.10   Poverty rates for households with unemployment benefits (UEB), Belgium, 1985-1997

	1985	1988	1992	1997
Households with UE benefit (%)	8.6	9.7	8.9	15.2
Households that have to make ends meet on UEB (%)	30.0	38.7	46.0	57.8
Households receiving UEB and other income (%)	2.2	2.5	2.7	2.5

Source: Cantillon et al. (1999)

The reason for the high poverty incidence among unemployed breadwinners is that the benefit package for sole providers is often well below the relative poverty threshold. This is especially the case for households with dependent children and for single persons. For example, the maximum unemployment benefit for an unemployed household head amounted in 1997 to 36,400 Belgian francs (BEF) and the minimum to almost 32,000 BEF. At that time, the poverty threshold for a couple with one child stood at 42,500 BEF and the threshold for a two-adult household with two dependent children at 49,600 BEF. Universal child benefits and supplementary child benefits for unemployed heads would have helped to close the gap substantially, but not enough to lift such households out of poverty.

Moreover, the value of unemployment benefits relative to the average living standards and hence the relative poverty threshold, deteriorated substantially during the 1980s and 1990s. The inflation-adjusted value of unemployment benefits remained more or less stable (Table 9.7), but the gap between unemployment benefits and average living standards increased (Cantillon et al., 2001).

Why, one might ask, are unemployment benefits for sole providers not higher and why have they dropped relative to general living standards? Their inadequacy seems manifestly at odds with my assertion that minimum income protection has been a prime policy concern.

The major obstacle is the gap between benefits and minimum wages. De Lathouwer (2001) has calculated that an unemployed person with a non-working spouse and two dependent children on maximum unemployment benefit gains only 9% by moving from unemployment to a minimum wage job. A single parent with two children, including one below the age of three, would actually suffer a net income loss of 6%, taking into account the additional cost of child care.

As Cantillon (1994) argued, the fundamental problem seems to be that both minimum wages and benefits have become increasingly inadequate to provide a decent standard of living for a single income household. After all, we live in an era in which the average living standard and hence the relative poverty standard is determined by the double income household. Neither minimum wages, nor real wages have matched the rise in real living standards, which has been driven by the proliferation of double earnership, not by wage growth.

In theory, there is no reason why social insurance benefits should not exceed (net) minimum wages. But in reality there is the concern about dependency traps. This is particularly pertinent in the Belgian context, where unemployment benefits for household heads and single persons are, for all practical purposes, of unlimited duration.

Increasing maximum benefits substantially enough to make a real impact on poverty among unemployed breadwinners would necessarily require a simultaneous increase in the minimum wage. The perceived obstacle is, however, that higher minimum wages would lead to even higher unemployment. Belgian minimum wages, some point out, are already among the highest in the OECD area (OECD, 1998; Dolado et al., 1996).

The validity of this approach depends on whether a higher minimum wage would induce higher unemployment. Effective wage floors are already much higher than the national minimum wage. In reality, very few jobs actually pay the national minimum wage. Collective wage agreements at the industry level (where most wage setting occurs) tend to set minimum wages substantially above the nationally agreed minimum.

Moreover, recent research has shown the link between minimum wages and employment outcomes to be all but linear (Dolado et al., 1996; OECD, 1998). A significant number of recent empirical studies have rejected the conventional wisdom that there is a simple and inescapable trade-off between low wages and unemployment. Even the OECD has come to the conclusion that "there is considerably more flexibility across OECD countries than is often recognized in the setting of minimum wages and, hence, they can be tailored to limit some of their negative features" (OECD, 1998, p. 57).

It is the principle that seems to matter most in current policy discourse. The current consensus is that a wedge between net minimum wages and unemployment benefits should remain, that if anything should be increased, and that there is no scope for substantially increasing the minimum wage.

There is, however, a way out of the dilemma of benefit inadequacy and the (perceived) limits to minimum wage increases. The solution is to increase take-home pay for low-wage workers by reducing their social security contributions. This would create substantial scope for increasing maximum unemployment benefits, while maintaining a gap with in-work income. The gross minimum wage is, after all, still substantially higher than for example, the maximum unemployment benefit package for a head of household. What make the gap between a benefit package and net in-work income so narrow are the social security contributions and personal income taxes that a wage earner has to pay. Recently, measures have been taken to reduce the social security burden on the lowest wages. Employer social security contributions on the lowest wages have been substantially reduced, though without compensating reductions in benefits.

However, the route of shifting social security and fiscal contributions from the low-paid, who are most prone to fall into dependency traps, to the better paid, also seems to have limits. One perceived obstacle to reducing payroll taxes on the lowest paid and shifting more of the social security bill towards the better paid is that the social security system is already regarded as disadvantageous to the better paid (Schokkaert and Sweeney, 1999). As already pointed out, the real value of maximum unemployment benefits has eroded substantially over the past two decades and a gap barely remains between maximum and minimum benefits. Previously, one only paid contributions up to a certain maximum, which seemed a compensation for the fact that benefits were also constrained. These contribution ceilings were abolished in the mid-1980s to help fill the deficits in the social security budget resulting from the massive rise in benefit dependency. So, while maximum benefit levels have declined, the better paid have been obliged to pay increased contributions. In addition, the better paid already face marginal income-tax rates among the highest in the OECD area. There is, therefore, a reluctance to place even more of the social security and tax burden on the higher paid. It is argued, especially from the Right, that enough "solidarity" has been requested from higher-income groups.

To what extent these economic and political obstacles to improving benefit adequacy are real or perceived remains open to debate. Nevertheless, it is the case that a marked policy shift occurred during the 1990s, away from income protection towards activation. During much of the 1990s, the real value of unemployment insurance compensation did not keep up with living standards, and the generosity in duration of unemployment benefits declined too, though Belgium's unemployment insurance system remains atypically generous. It is difficult to ascertain how much this has increased employment and labour participation. The fact remains that unemployment has remained high in Belgium despite the *de facto* cuts in benefit generosity. It is also an established fact that poverty among the unemployed has increased.

5.2 Unequal treatment

As we have seen, the unemployed population is not a homogenous group. There is considerable inequality between those who subsist on unemployment benefit and those for whom the benefit acts as a supplementary household income. In fact, many of those people claiming unemployment benefits - and they can do so for many years - enjoy a comparatively high standard of living. This is illustrated in Table 9.11, which shows the distribution of unemployment benefits across income deciles in 1997. Almost 40% of the benefit payout flows to the top half of the income distribution.

The issue here is fairness. In a social insurance system, it is normal for benefits to flow to the higher-income groups. But the present distribution of unemployment benefits is neither consistent with the Bismarckian insurance rationale of the system nor with its basic income protection rationale. Although people claim unemployment benefits for long periods, contrary to Bismarckian logic, there is no link between the duration of benefits and the contribution record. There are no duration limits for unemployed household heads and single persons. Even cohabitants whose household income exceeds the (relatively high) threshold, continue to receive benefits for several years.

Table 9.11   Distribution of unemployment insurance benefits across household income deciles, Belgium, 1997

Decile	% share of unemployment benefits
1	11.4
2	16.4
3	10.3
4	11.9
5	11.6
6	9.9
7	8.5
8	6.8
9	7.6
10	5.6
Total	100.0

Source. Cantillon et al (1999)

The fairness problem here is that, especially among those in the cohabitant category, job search intensity is low. This largely explains why the official unemployment rate, based on the number of benefit claimants, is much higher than the standardized rate, based on the number of people who are not employed, available for work and actively looking for a job. In addition, reports from local employment agencies suggest that job offers are often turned down, especially by women with a working partner. Benefit claimants have the right to refuse a job offer if it does not match their educational qualifications. A recent interview-based survey of the long-term unemployed also revealed low search intensity and limited willingness to accept low-paid jobs (De Lathouwer and Bogaerts, 2000). Low search intensity is especially prevalent among women with young children.

Availability for the labour market is thus low among a considerable proportion of benefit claimants. The vast majority of unemployed in the cohabitant category are women, who voluntarily stay at home, often to care for children. This situation is unfair *vis-à-vis* those who do the same but are not entitled to a social income. It is true, of course, that one typically needs to have a contribution record to become eligible. But a short work career can entitle a person to a disproportionately lengthy spell on unemployment benefit. This is arguably unfair if the unemployment is, to some extent, voluntary, which is frequently the case.

It is not only a question of fairness. Many of the non-employed without a social income could benefit from either an earned or a social income. Non-employment rates in Belgium are especially high for women with low levels of formal education. As a consequence, single earnership remains comparatively widespread. Single-earner households without unemployment benefit in their income package often have substantially lower living standards than those with unemployment benefit. In fact, working-age poverty, such as it exists in Belgium, is largely concentrated among such single-earner households (Cantillon, 1994; Marx and Verbist, 1998).

Moreover, many of the unemployed entitled to unemployment benefits probably have better employment chances than many of the non-employed who are not officially unemployed. To gain entitlement to an unemployment benefit a person generally needs to accumulate a sufficient contribution record. There is anecdotal evidence of strategic behaviour in this respect, i.e. unemployed persons (mostly women) who have lost their entitlement re-entering the labour market for just long enough to become eligible again.

The inequity between women staying more or less voluntarily at home with unemployment benefit and those without is a subject of debate. Some advocate a time-limited benefit for all those who stay voluntarily at home to take care of children or other needy persons, regardless of their past or present labour market attachment. Non-employed persons would, in other words, also be entitled. Such a scheme could take the form of an extension of the present system of career interruption that provides a flat-rate benefit to workers withdrawing from their jobs for up to five years, albeit at the discretion of their employer.

There are many kinds of objection against such an extension of the career-interruption scheme. Those who object on ideological grounds argue, plausibly, that this would represent a setback to the economic emancipation of women and amount to a subsidy for the traditional breadwinner household. Others argue that Belgium already has one of the highest benefit dependency rates in the OECD area and that there is little scope for increasing this. The high taxes and social security contributions necessary to finance existing social expenditure are already seen as inhibiting job growth and causing unemployment. In short, since the present "model" is already regarded as self-reinforcing, there is little willingness to facilitate further access to social income.

6. Beyond gradual adaptation: the paradigm shift towards the active welfare state

In Belgium, the unemployment insurance system has been transformed from its Bismarckian origins into a minimum income protection system. The link between previous wages, work history and benefits has been all but abandoned. Benefit generosity has become largely a function of assumed need, rather than an unemployed person's contribution record. This gradual transformation from a social insurance system to a basic protection system has helped to contain poverty under conditions of mass unemployment, as well as the budgetary cost of mass dependency.

However, the limits of gradual adaptation appear to have been reached. At least, this has become the dominant perception. First, there is the problem of high and rising poverty among the unemployed subsisting solely on their benefit. It is widely recognized that benefit increases would help lift unemployed sole breadwinners out of poverty but the perception remains that this would further erode work incentives and reinforce the present situation of "welfare without work". Second, there is the problem that working-age poverty is frequently associated with (female) non-employment rather than registered unemployment. Here, too, the current consensus is that widening access to benefits is not the way to proceed.

In policy discourse, emphasis is now put on the need to move towards a new paradigm called the "active welfare state", where poverty is reduced through high levels of (sometimes subsidized) employment rather than through generous benefits. Specifically, the consensus is that the female employment rate, which remains among the lowest in northern Europe, should be boosted. This, it is argued, would help reduce poverty among households with an unemployed breadwinner. It would also improve living standards of single-earner households and reduce dependence on unemployment benefits as secondary household income.

However, Esping-Andersen (1996) has claimed that the labour market position of women, particularly less educated women, will remain peripheral as long as high minimum wages and high non-wage costs make less-skilled work expensive, and as long as tax/benefit policies effectively discourage second-earner participation. He claims that continental Europe is caught in deadlock because of the inherent difficulties in pushing through reforms. Trade unions forcefully defend the existing rights of insiders - high wages, job security, early retirement - because many families depend on the male breadwinner's wage. The dilemma, it seems, is that welfare of families depends largely on precisely those elements of the model that harm the employment prospects of less educated women and youngsters.

Belgium seems a case in point. Early retirement - originally introduced to combat youth unemployment – is proving very difficult to scale back, even though economic conditions have improved and employers complain of labour shortages. Initiatives to reduce benefit generosity, especially the duration of unemployment benefits, have encountered stiff and effective opposition from trade unions and from the Left. Despite benefit terminations, Belgium's unemployment insurance system remains atypical in terms of duration generosity. The erosion of the real value of unemployment benefits and the rise in poverty among the unemployed, documented has become a political issue.

The Government reacted to widespread criticism of its social policy failure by increasing minimum unemployment benefits; thereby effectively departing from the "active welfare state" line adopted when it took office. Measures to enhance labour market and wage flexibility prove difficult even to discuss. For example, proposals to make wages less rigid, which were discussed and, to some measure, implemented in the Netherlands, have never even reached the negotiating table in Belgium. It is questionable whether greater labour market flexibility, benefit cuts and so on, would effectively boost employment growth and reduce benefit dependence. But reform proposals generally encounter extraordinary resistance. This indicates that it may well prove difficult to achieve any paradigmatic shift that would offer a way out of the present dilemmas.

References

Andries, M. 1996. "Minimum-inkomensbescherming van uitkeringstrekkers in drie continentaal-Europese welvaartsstaten", in *Belgisch Tijdschrift voor Sociale Zekerheid*, 4, pp. 785-808.

_____. 1996b. "The politics of targeting: The Belgian case", in *Journal of European Social Policy*, Vol. 6, No. 3, pp. 209-233.

Atkinson, A. 1997. *Poverty in Europe* (Oxford, Blackwell).

Cantillon, B. 1994. "Family, work and social security", in S. Baldwin and J. Falkingham (eds.) *Social security and social change: New challenges to the Beveridge model* (London, Harvester Wheatsheaf).

_____, De Maesschalck, V. and Van Dam, R. 2001. *Welvaartsvastheid en adequaatheid van de sociale minima 1970-2001* (Antwerpen, CSB-Berichten).

_____ et al. 1999. "Sociale indicatoren 1976-1997", in *Belgisch Tijdschrift voor Sociale Zekerheid*, Vol.41, No.4, pp. 747-800.

_____ et al. 2002. "Child poverty *a la carte*? The effects of measurement period for income and poverty estimates", in J. Bradshaw (ed.) *Children and social security* (Aldershot, Ashgate).

Cassiers, I., de Villé, P and Solar, P. 1996. "Economic growth in postwar Belgium", in N. Crafts and G. Tonioli (eds.) *Economic growth in Europe since 1945* (Cambridge, Cambridge University Press).

Deleeck, H. 2001. *De architectuur van de welvaartsstaat opnieuw bekeken* (Leuven, Acco).

De Lathouwer, L. 2001. "Les pièges à l'emploi en Belgique: diagnostic et options politique", in *Cahiers Economiques de Bruxelles*, No. 171, pp. 41-70.

_____ and Bogaerts, K. 2000. "Schorsingen, een negatieve prikkel voor herintrede op de arbeidsmarkt?", in *Nieuwsbrief van het steunpunt WAV*, jrg. 10, Nos. 1-2, pp. 128-134.

Dolado, J. et al. 1996. "The economic impact of minimum wages in Europe", in *Economic Policy*, August, pp. 319-372.

Esping-Andersen, G. 1996. "Welfare states without work: The impasse of labour shedding and familialism in continental European social policy", in G. Esping-Andersen (ed.) *Welfares states in transition: National adaptations in global economies* (London, Sage).

Eurostat. 2001. *European social statistics: Income, poverty and social exclusion* (Luxembourg, Eurostat).

Funken, K. and Cooper, P. (eds.). 1995. *Old and new poverty: The challenge for reform* (London, Rivers Oram Press).

Gallie, D., Jacobs, S. and Paugam, S. 2000. "Poverty and financial hardship among the unemployed", in D. Gallie and S. Paugam (eds.) *Welfare regimes and the experience of unemployment in Europe* (Oxford, Oxford University Press).

Gottschalk, P. and Smeeding, T. 1997. "Cross-national comparisons of earnings and income inequality", in *Journal of Economic Literature*, Vol. 35, No. 2, pp. 633-687.

Gough, I. et al. 1997. "Social assistance in OECD countries", in *Journal of European Social Policy*, Vol. 7, No.1, pp. 17-44.

Kohli, M., Rein, M. and Guillemard, A. 1993. *Time for retirement* (Cambridge, Cambridge University Press).

Lawson, R. and Wilson, W.J. 1995. "Poverty, social rights and the quality of citizenship", in K. Mcfate, R. Lawson and W. Wilson (eds.) *Poverty, inequality, and the future of social policy: Western states in the new World order* (New York, Russell Sage).

Marx, I. and Verbist, G. 1998. "Low-paid work and poverty: a cross-country perspective", in S. Bazen, M. Gregory and W. Salverda (eds.) *Low-wage employment in Europe* (Cheltenham, Edward Elgar).

Orgnaization for Economic Cooperation and Development (OECD). 1995. *Employment Outlook* (Paris, OECD).

_____. 1997a. *Employment Outlook* (Paris, OECD).

_____. 1997b. *OECD Economic Survey: Belgium* (Paris, OECD).

_____. 1998. *Employment Outlook* (Paris, OECD).

Rijksdienst voor Arbeidsvoorziening (RVA). 2000. *Jaarboekverslag* (Brussels, RVA).

Schokkaert, E. and Sweeney, J. 1999. "Social exclusion and ethical responsibility: Solidarity with the least skilled", in *Journal of Business Ethics,* Vol. 21, No. 2, pp. 251-268.

_____, Verhue, M. and Pepermans, G. 2000. "Vlamingen over het pensioensysteem", in P. Pestiau et al. (eds.) *De toekomst van onze pensioenen* (Garant, Leuven), pp. 55-75.

Standing, G. 1999. *Global labour market flexibility* (Houndmills, Macmillan).

10

Assessing Unemployment Traps in Belgium Using Panel Data Sample Selection Models

Anna Cristina D'Addio[1], Isabelle de Greef[2] and Michael Rosholm[3]

1. Introduction

The combination of unemployment benefits, high taxes on labour income, social contributions, and conditional transfers such as additional child benefits, may reduce the willingness of unemployed workers - especially the low skilled - to find and/or to accept a job (OECD, 1996, 1999). Low returns associated with being employed rather than unemployed may affect the decision to move into employment and thereby contribute to the persistence of unemployment. The situation in which households or individuals have no (financial and/or non-financial) incentives to leave unemployment for employment is termed an "unemployment trap". To assess whether unemployment traps exist and affect the transition into employment is important for policy, because increasing the participation rate in the labour market is a priority of most European countries.

The computation of replacement rates - i.e. the ratios between household/individual disposable income when employed and the equivalent disposable income when unemployed - is crucial for insights on the presence or absence of the unemployment traps. In computing this ratio, the assumptions made on the wages of individuals who are out of work are obviously critical.

[1] CIM, Aarhus School of Business, Department of Economics, University of Aarhus, Denmark and CERI-SIS, Catholic University of Louvain, Belgium.

[2] IRES, Catholic University of Louvain, Belgium.

[3] Department of Economics, University of Aarhus, Denmark.

Two main approaches have been adopted in the study of financial unemployment traps. The first is based on representative households/individuals and computes replacement rates using specific assumptions (e.g. OECD, 1996, 1997), while the second exploits real data using econometric techniques (e.g. OECD, 2002; Pedersen and Smith, 2001; Kyyrä, 1999; Gurgand and Margolis, 2001; Gregg et al., 1999; Holm et al., 1999). Various studies have also focused on whether unemployment experience has a scarring effect on subsequent earnings, a phenomenon that would help explain the existence of unemployment traps for individuals, some of whom have been successful in the labour market (e.g., OECD, 2002; Arulampalam, 2000; Nickell et al., 1999; Jacobson et al., 1993; Ruhm, 1991; Stevens, 1997).

For Belgium, most of the evidence on unemployment traps has been provided by the approach based on representative households (De Lathouwer and Bogaerts, 2001; De Lathouwer, 2000; Defeyt, 1998; Valenduc, 2001; De Greef, 2000). Although this approach in identifying those households/individuals that are more likely to be trapped, it is based on possibly unrealistic *ad hoc* assumptions not necessarily satisfied in reality. For this reason, among others, in our analysis we have adopted the approach based on real data.

In this article we investigate whether unemployment traps exist in the transition into employment in Belgium, exploiting data extracted from waves 3 to 7 (covering the years 1993-97) of the Panel Study of Belgian Households (PSBH) on individuals who have experienced at least one spell of unemployment during the survey period. In our analysis, we specify and estimate by maximum likelihood techniques a parametric panel-data random effects model composed of a wage equation and a selection equation. The correction for sample selection is to avoid a potential bias caused by unobserved differences that affect both the probability of being employed and the wage level. If the decision to work is affected by expected earnings, it is likely that individuals who are currently working have higher wages than those that would be earned by unemployed individuals. In that sense, the correction for potential selection bias (Heckman, 1979) accounts for non-randomness of the selection process into employment since wages are observed only for those who are employed, i.e. those who have received job offers and for whom the offered wage exceeds the reservation wage.

Most empirical analyses on unemployment traps assume that the sample selection process is constant over time. The argument crucial to this assumption is that fixed effect-type estimators eliminate sample selection bias since they difference out both the unobserved individual-specific effect and the sample selection effect (e.g., Jensen et al., 2002). Since there is no reason to believe the sample selection process is time-invariant (unobservable variables may occur in both the selection equation and the equation of interest, and may exhibit a complex correlation structure) we have used panel-data estimation techniques, explicitly accounting for the sample selection problem.

Based on the wage equations corrected for sample selectivity, we have computed expected wages and used them to calculate replacement rates for all individuals in the sample (including those that have not moved out of unemployment during the survey period). This allows us to compute both an observed and an estimated income ratio, as in Kyyrä (1999). While the observed income ratio is based on the observed wage earned by workers who move into work, the estimated one is based on the expected wage for workers who have not moved into employment.

Section 2 surveys the previous evidence on unemployment traps. Section 3 briefly outlines the Belgian tax system and its unemployment insurance scheme. Section 4 presents the econometric model. Section 5 describes the dataset, Section 6 reports and discusses the results, Section 7 draws conclusions.

2.   Previous evidence on unemployment traps

Most evidence on unemployment traps has been provided within the approach using representative households/individuals (e.g., OECD, 1997). Assuming the level of (potential) wages, this approach computes the change in the household/individual's disposable income associated with the transition from unemployment into employment, with the aim of identifying family/individual types with high probabilities of being financially trapped. This way of proceeding is relevant and rich on details. However, it is based on specific and arbitrary assumptions concerning, for example, the hourly wage rate and the previous length of unemployment. The unemployed are assumed to have fully rational behaviour, although this does not always correspond to reality (e.g. due to lack of knowledge of the rules of the tax and benefits system), and their unobserved differences are not taken into account. Furthermore, commuting costs and additional costs of health care and social housing, which are likely to intensify financial traps, are frequently ignored in this literature.

Fewer studies have adopted the approach exploiting real data and econometric techniques, owing mainly to lack of appropriate data on earnings and methodological problems. A majority of those studies have focused on earnings losses associated with the experience of unemployment (e.g.

Arulampalam, 2000);[4] only a few authors have investigated how the transition into employment is affected by unemployment compensation schemes (e.g. Gurgand and Margolis, 2001; Pedersen and Smith, 2001; Kyyrä, 1999). Much of this literature has assumed that the wages of workers who have experienced unemployment are equal to those earned by employed individuals with otherwise similar observable characteristics (Layard et al., 1991). In this approach, expected wages of individuals who are out of work are either estimated or derived from the survey questionnaires and therefore are not "arbitrarily" assumed. Some studies have used the wage earned in the last job prior to unemployment. Others have used unemployed workers' own expectations about the wages they would get in a future job (Pedersen and Smith, 2001), or the average wage obtained by people who are employed. Some are based on the expected wage adjusted for selectivity, the wage obtained by workers after an unemployment experience (post-unemployment wages), and some are based on post-unemployment wages corrected for sample selection bias in a cross-sectional framework (Kyyrä, 1999; Holm et al., 1999).

Three important results should be emphasized from such studies. First, some transitions from unemployment to employment are associated with a decrease or only a modest increase in disposable income. Second, unemployed workers are re-employed at lower wages than in their previous job. Third, wage losses suffered by workers who have experienced a period of unemployment are persistent; the average wage rate tends to remain below the expected average wage rate without job loss for several years after the unemployment spell.

For Belgium, more particularly, the main results can be summarized as follows: single-parent families and households with only one source of income are more exposed to unemployment traps than other types of household (De Lathouwer and Bogaerts, 2001; De Lathouwer, 2000; Defeyt, 1998; Valenduc, 2001; De Greef, 2000).

There are several ways to explain why it may be meaningful to accept a job associated with negative short-term financial returns. The unemployed may assign high importance to inter-temporal perspectives: they may expect higher wages in the future (promising career prospects) or anticipate falling unemployment benefits simultaneously with depressing effect of long unemployment on the post-unemployment wage. Some may even be willing to

---

[4] See also Laurent (2001); Pedersen and Westergard-Nielsen (1993). On displaced workers, see e.g. Fallick (1996); Kletzer (1998).

accept a job associated with long-term income losses if they enjoy working or if they simply feel "ashamed" about being unemployed.

Furthermore, theory suggests several reasons why a period of unemployment may be followed by wage losses. Jobs associated with post-unemployment wages are by definition short-tenure at the time at which one observes them (no tenure effect). Lower post-unemployment wages may also result from a deterioration of skills or a loss of firm-specific (or sector-specific) human capital, which is not transferable to a new job. A lower quality job match between the worker and the firm may also cause a reduction in post-unemployment wages. Further, a decline in the reservation wage over time can lead to acceptance of a job with a lower wage. That decline may be justified, for instance, by an (expected) fall in the level of unemployment benefits, (e.g., Van den Berg, 1990). Finally employers may rank workers on the grounds of their employment/unemployment experience.

3.   Unemployment insurance and tax systems in Belgium during the 1990s

Studies have shown how important and persistent unemployment is in Belgium. Besides arguments about the structural nature of the problem, the existing tax system is likely to make people less willing to accept jobs. Furthermore, the sudden removal of conditional transfers (such as additional child benefits) on moving into employment reduces work incentives, especially for temporary jobs.

Since January 2000, some measures have been taken to make-work more attractive. However, since the data used in this study cover the years 1993-97, we describe the unemployment insurance and tax systems prevailing in that period. All the amounts reported in this section relate to 1997.

3.1 Unemployment insurance scheme

The Belgian unemployment insurance scheme is characterized by a generous level of benefits (De Lathouwer and Bogaerts, 2001; De Lathouwer, 2000), especially for persons with low incomes, and by an indefinite entitlement period. The payment of unemployment benefits may, however, be suspended for unemployed people who live with a working partner or their parents (referred to as "cohabitants") depending on various conditions (De Greef, 2000). Moreover, all unemployed may be sanctioned for various reasons, such as unavailability to take a job (Grubb and Martin, 2001; OECD, 1997).

To be eligible for unemployment benefits, a worker must have been employed for a long period. The length of required employment depends on age of the worker; on the first day of unemployment, individuals aged less than 36 must have been employed for 312 days during the previous 18 months. Unemployment should be involuntary and the worker should be available for and actively seeking, employment, and entitlement depends on school curricula and on past receipt of unemployment benefits.

The level of benefit depends on household composition, length of unemployment, age and previous wage. Since 1987, the unemployed have been able to top up benefits by working for an *Agence locale pour l'emploi* (Local Agency for Employment) for a maximum of 45 hours per month at an hourly rate of €3.72. With some exceptions, people working for these agencies are registered as unemployed.

Concerning household composition, three categories are identified - head of household, single, and cohabitants – with heads of household receiving the highest level of benefit, cohabitants the lowest. The amount of benefit is constant for heads of household (60% of previous wage), while it declines for single persons (from 60% the first year to 42% the second year) and for cohabitants (from 55% the first year to 35% the first quarter of the second year and to a lump sum the second quarter of the second year). However, if a cohabitant has been employed for more than 20 years, he/she benefits indefinitely from the second-period compensation (35% of previous wage).

The amount of unemployment benefit depends on previous earnings but has upper and lower limits, set at a maximum €864.9 and a minimum €759.3 for heads of households. Finally, the level depends on age. Unemployed individuals over 50 receive an additional amount. This supplement, conditional on having worked more than 20 years, varies with household type and the age of the individual. In short, the system is complex and not really generous and indefinite.

3.2 The tax system

The tax system consists mainly of social security contributions and a progressive income tax. Social security contributions paid by employees correspond to 13.07% of gross earnings. Spouses are taxed separately. However, if a spouse has no earnings or earns less than 30% of total household earnings, 30% of net household earnings is attributed to the partner. The amount that may be transferred to the spouse with low or no earnings is limited to a maximum of €7,362.4.

Several tax allowances exist. Each individual is granted a personal income exemption, which depends on household composition. The other main tax allowances are related to number of children, childcare costs and work-related expenses. The tax exemption is higher for replacement incomes such as pensions, unemployment benefits, than for earnings. Tax schedule prevailing in Belgium in 1997 meant that the marginal income tax rate rose from 25% for those earning up to the equivalent of just over 6,000 Euros, to 55% for those earning over about 60,000 Euros annually. An additional local income tax is levied on taxable income at an average rate of 7%.

4. Methodology and data

The following reports the results of estimated wages, which is tested by use of panel data requiring contents for possible sample selectivity bias. The model is described briefly in the Appendix. The empirical analysis is based on the Panel Study of Belgian Households (PSBH). This survey was carried out for the first time in the spring of 1992 (wave 1). Since the questions about incomes and employment status have been modified from 1994 onwards, we considered the waves 3 to 7 (spring 1994 to spring 1998) that contain information about 9,398 individuals aged at least 16. The information we use is retrospective; therefore the analysis covers the years 1993 to 1997.

At each survey date, individuals report their labour market status at that time and for each of the preceding 12 months. They also declare (if they work) their annual income for the previous year, net of taxes and social security contributions.

The sample used in this study consists of individuals who experienced at least one unemployment spell. They are followed from that moment until the end of the observation period. The sample thus consists of both unemployed individuals who have moved towards employment, and unemployed persons who remain unemployed throughout the observation period. Individuals who moved from unemployment into self-employment have been excluded from the analysis, mainly because it is difficult to distinguish their wages from profits. This leaves 1,338 persons who have been unemployed at least once during the observation period, experiencing 1,948 unemployment spells. We focus only on those spells involving payment of unemployment benefits (1,661).

Half of the unemployment spells end in employment (paid work and self-employment); 35% of the unemployment spells are ongoing. The 12% that end in non-participation (retirement, housekeeping or students) and the 3% ending in so-called "other activity" have been discarded. After that, the sample consists of 1,341 spells of unemployment, experienced by 959 individuals. We will use separate samples for men (601 spells) and women (740 spells). The sample is unbalanced and individuals are observed from one to five times.

The dependent variables are an employment indicator and the individual's monthly net (log)-wage. The employment indicator takes a value of 1 if the individual moves from compensated unemployment into paid work in a given year, and it is 0 if the individual remains unemployed in that year. To be considered as employed in the PSBH, people have to work at least 15 hours per week. To determine this status, we have used hours actually worked, since earnings also cover extra hours worked.

The dependent variable of the wage equation is the (log) monthly net wage including tips, commissions, bonus and holiday earnings deflated by the consumer price index (base 1997), justified of labour supply theory (see D'Addio and De Greef, 2001).

At each survey date, the interviewed individuals report wages net of taxes and social contributions. However, for a quarter of the unemployment spell, which ended with transition into employment, information concerning wages is missing. This is allowed for in the estimation procedure (see Section 4).

For each of the five waves, the number of months in which the person is unemployed or employed to compute the monthly in-work and out-of-work income. Monthly wages are computed by dividing annual salaries by the number of months of work.[5] This does not allow us to separate wages associated with different jobs when the person has been employed in more than one job during a year.

Broadly speaking, only human capital and work-related variables (i.e. experience and its square, educational attainments, a part-time indicator, a supervision-tasks indicator, an indicator of previous professional experience) have been used in the wage equation. In order to capture the effects of financial (and to some extent non-financial) incentives, many other variables appear in the selection equation.

Tables 10.1 and 10.2 present descriptive statistics for the available samples of men and women.

We start with the description of the variables used in the wage equation. Experience refers to "potential" work experience and is computed as the difference between the age at the survey date and the age when the individual

---

[5] The same methodology is applied for unemployment benefits.

left school. We also introduced its quadratic form to capture concavity in the experience-wage profiles as postulated by human capital theory. Another variable indicates whether the individual had actual work experience in the past. Further, to capture level of responsibility associated with previous job experience, a dummy variable is introduced taking the value 1 if the individual had never supervised other workers.

To see whether experience of previous long unemployment spells has a "scarring" effect on subsequent earnings, we have included an indicator taking the value of 1 if the individual had been unemployed for more than 12 months at the start of the year t.

We have used an indicator for part-time employment, which is a striking feature in female labour market participation. For women, 31.5% of transitions from unemployment into employment are made in the form of part-time jobs; for men, the equivalent figure is only 7%.

Education is introduced through a set of indicators for the highest level of formal education attained primary school or without education (the reference), lowers secondary school (three years after primary), upper secondary school (six years after primary), high school (two to four years after secondary school), and university.

Table 10.1   Descriptive statistics – men

	Spells 'E'		Spells 'U'		Spells 'E'+'U'	
Number of observations	363		238		601	
Continuous variables	Mean	St. Dev.	Mean	St. Dev.	Mean	St. Dev.
Age	31 7	8.8	39.1	12 9	34.6	11 2
Experience	16 0	12 5	21 3	13.9	16 0	12.5
Children	0 5	0.9	0.7	1 2	0.6	1 0
Dummies	*Frequency*		*Frequency*		*Frequency*	
Educational dummies						
Primary school or no education	9.4		25 6		15.8	
Lower secondary school	27.8		32.4		29 6	
Upper secondary school	36 6		25.2		32 1	
High school	16 3		10.1		13.8	
University	9 9		6 7		8.7	
Household dummies						
Children under 3 years	10.7		8.8		10.0	
Not head of household	48 5		76 0		59.4	
Married	40.2		48 5		43 5	
Not married	52.3		37.6		46 5	
Divorced, separated or widowed	7 5		13 9		10.0	
Single	9.1		15.1		11 5	
Couple	82.1		81.9		82 0	
Single-parent	8 8		3.0		6 5	
Additional child benefits	2 7		5 0		3 7	

Regional membership dummies			
Brussels	11.8	12.2	12.0
Wallonia	55.1	54.6	54.9
Flanders	33.1	33.2	33.1
Job attributes dummies			
Part-time	5.5		
No responsibility	83.7	94.1	87.9
Previous work	92.8	91.6	92.3
Time dummies			
1993	20.7	11.3	17.0
1994	22.6	7.6	16.6
1995	18.2	10.9	15.3
1996	20.9	10.1	16.6
1997	17.6	60.1	34.5
Other dummies			
Bad health	9.1	27.3	16.3
High mental distress	10.2	15.1	12.1
Financial support from State	11.6	17.2	13.8
Long-term unemployment	29.8	78.1	48.9
In debt	38.0	31.1	35.3
Financial difficulties	35.0	41.2	37.4
Worse financial situation	29.7	41.2	34.3
Householder	62.5	54.2	59.2
Belgian	88.7	84.4	87.0
Social activity	48.5	44.5	46.9

Note: 'E' = employment; 'U' = unemployment, St.Dev = standard deviation

Table 10.2   Descriptive statistics – women

	Spells 'E'		Spells 'U'		Spells 'E'+'U'	
Number of observations	398		342		740	
Continuous variables	**Mean**	**St. Dev.**	**Mean**	**St. Dev.**	**Mean**	**St. Dev.**
Age	30.1	7.7	36.5	10.7	33.1	9.7
Experience	10.6	8.5	18.2	11.9	14.4	11.0
Children	0.8	0.9	0.8	1.0	0.8	1.0
Dummies	*Frequency*		*Frequency*		*Frequency*	
Educational dummies						
Primary school or no education	5.3		17.5		10.9	
Lower secondary school	18.3		31.6		24.5	
Upper secondary school	38.7		37.4		38.1	
High school	29.7		11.7		21.4	
University	8.0		1.8		5.1	
Household dummies						
Children under 3 years	18.8		16.7		17.8	
Not head of household	84.2		93.3		88.4	
Married	47.5		47.2		47.4	
Non married	42.7		24.4		34.2	
Divorced, separated or widowed	9.8		28.4		18.4	
Single	8.3		7.6		8.0	
Couple	75.6		70.2		73.1	

Single-parent	16.1	22.2	18.9
Additional child benefits	4.0	18.1	10.5
Regional membership dummies			
Brussels	11.1	10.8	11.0
Wallonia	47.7	48.8	48.2
Flanders	41.2	40.4	40.8
Job attributes dummies			
Part-time	22.86		
No responsibility	93.5	96.2	94.7
Previous work	91.5	85.7	88.8
Time dummies			
1993	21.6	8.2	15.4
1994	20.3	5.6	13.5
1995	19.1	8.2	14.1
1996	18.6	6.4	13.0
1997	20.4	71.6	44.0
Other dummies			
Bad health	8.0	13.2	11.4
High mental distress	20.4	25.2	22.6
Financial support from State	9.1	20.2	14.2
Long-term unemployment	32.7	86.0	57.3
In debt	30.7	33.3	31.9
Financial difficulties	24.1	41.5	32.2
Worse financial situation	21.1	36.3	28.1
Householder	53.3	51.5	52.4
Belgian	94.2	91.2	92.8
Social activity	48.2	46.5	47.4

Note. 'E' = employment; 'U' = unemployment; St.Dev = standard deviation

Other variables commonly thought to have an effect on wages, such as type of job, sector, industrial, firm size and union coverage, have not been introduced, mainly owing to lack of information about them in the available data set.

Besides the individual's age, its square, educational attainment and the long-term unemployment indicator, the following variables are also included in the selection equation.

Two variables allow for health, one reflecting physical health and the other, mental distress (De Greef, 2000). A measure of social involvement (Sweeney, 1998) is used to differentiate socially active people from others. Individuals are ranked as socially active if they belong to an association (e.g., a sports club, cultural or humanitarian association) or if they have a very active network of friends.

To measure the effect of additional public financial support received when unemployed, a dummy variable has been introduced, taking the value of 1 if the unemployed person or his/her household has social housing with low rent or food stamps, for example.

Three dummy variables relate to financial difficulties. A dummy indicates if the individual, or another member of his/her household, is in debt (excluding mortgage loans). A second takes the value 1 if the person has financial difficulties in paying bills related to rent, heating, etc. A third is equal to 1 if the person is dissatisfied with his financial situation.

A home ownership dummy indicates whether the individual owns the accommodation he/she is living in. Some variables are included to account for household composition. These are the number of children, the presence of children aged less than three, being married, being a single parent, not being head of the household, and being entitled to additional child benefits. The variable for nationality indicates Belgian nationality. Finally, a dummy is included for whether or not the individual lives in Flanders.

5. Estimation results

The estimation of (1) and (2) simultaneously by maximum likelihood on the samples of men and women gives the results reported in Tables 10.3 to 10.5. In order to test their robustness, we also estimated an ordinary random effects probit model of the selection equation and a random effects (GLS) wage equation. These results are available on request, and they show that most of the parameter estimates are very robust across the two different specifications. The main gain from the panel data sample selection model thus consists in the modelling of the correlation structures in the error components, which are used in the calculation of expected wages.

Considering the selection equation results, previous long-term unemployment status dramatically reduces the transition probability into employment for both men and women. Not being the household head is also associated with a much lower transition probability into employment for both samples, while being married leads to a higher transition probability for women.

For women, eligibility for additional child benefits strongly reduces the transition probability. Male homeowners have a higher transition probability, but it is reduced the more children they have. Bad health is also an important hindrance to men finding employment, but apparently not for women. University education is associated with better employment prospects for women, while for men this is true for education beyond primary school.

In summary, variables associated with financial incentives were important in the transition from unemployment to employment, particularly for women.

Turning to the wage equation results, for both sub-samples, past experience of long-term unemployment has a significant negative effect on earnings prospects, through lowering the post-unemployment (log) wage. Similar results were found by Gregory and Jukes (1997) and Nickell et al. (1999), who pointed to the fact that in the UK, long unemployment spells are associated with larger wage losses (see also for converse evidence, Arulampalam, 2000).

For women, the best earnings prospects are associated with the highest educational attainment, while for men educational level does not seem to affect the wage very much. Women who have held some supervision tasks in the past have also a comparative advantage.

Potential work experience considerably improves the unemployed earnings prospects. As suggested by human capital theory, the significance of the quadratic term of work experience confirms concave experience-wage profiles for both samples.

Turning to the issue of sample selection, we notice from Table 10.5 that the correlation coefficient of the idiosyncratic error terms is significantly different from 0 (and positive) only for women. Moreover, for women the probabilities associated with the support points of the random effects are significant, while for men they are not (only one of them is). This suggests that the sample selection issue is particularly important for women. The significant correlation coefficient and its positive sign are consistent with economic sense: those who find wage offers relatively high with respect to their characteristics are also more likely to be hired.

Table 10.3   Estimation results of (1) and (2) by maximum likelihood – selection equation

Coefficients	Men		Women	
η_1	-0.2788	(1.3838)	0.0823	(1.6746)
η_2	1.1511	(1.4816)	1.7633	(1.6985)
Age	0.1167	(0.0717)	0.1064	(0.1026)
Age^2	-0.0023**	(0.0098)	-0.0025	(0.0015)
Social activity	0.2228	(0.1891)	-0.2309	(0.1875)
Housing allowances	0.2699	(0.2862)	-0.3152	(0.2644)
Long-term unemployment	-1.1699**	(0.1959)	-1.6434**	(0.2341)
In debt	0.1643	(0.1911)	-0.0748	(0.1791)
Financial difficulties	0.0574	(0.1931)	-0.1669	(0.2127)
Mental distress	-0.1872	(0.278)	0.1327	(0.1816)
Children under 3 years	-0.0508**	(0.354)	-0.2112	(0.2351)
Bad health	-0.5948	(0.2533)	-0.1199	(0.3285)
Financial satisfaction	-0.2678	(0.1959)	-0.1577	(0.1855)
Not head of the household	-1.2931**	(0.2588)	-1.1742**	(0.3105)
Householder	0.4449*	(0.2178)	0.1728	(0.1978)
Number of children	-0.2786**	(0.121)	-0.0139	(0.1093)
Belgian nationality	-0.1561	(0.277)	0.2182	(0.3253)
Lower secondary school	0.2217	(0.2887)	0.2058	(0.323)
Upper secondary school	0.6405*	(0.3191)	0.3797	(0.319)
High school	0.5419	(0.3951)	0.4605	(0.3641)
University	0.7112	(0.4126)	0.9875*	(0.4851)
Married	-0.3341	(0.2359)	0.5058**	(0.2196)
Lone parenthood	-0.0819	(0.2317)	0.328	(0.287)
Additional child benefits	0.2158	(0.4509)	-0.9416**	(0.3814)
Living in Flanders	0.2761	(0.2185)	-0.0975	(0.1855)

Standard errors in parenthesis. *: 5%, **: 2%

Table 10.4   Estimation results of (1) and (2) by maximum likelihood – wage equation

Coefficients	Men		Women	
α_1	10.0082**	(0.132)	9.7449**	(0.1855)
α_2	10.6209**	(0.1255)	10.2367**	(0.1798)
Experience (# years)	0.0254**	(0.007)	0.0355**	(0.0095)
Squared experience	-0.0051**	(0.0022)	-0.0095**	(0.0037)
Long-term unemployed	-0.1407**	(0.0485)	-0.1772**	(0.0563)
Part-time worker	0.0251	(0.0538)	-0.0485	(0.0742)
No responsibility	-0.0481	(0.0742)	-0.1497**	(0.0409)
Previous professional experience	-0.002	(0.0741)	-0.0217	(0.074)
Lower secondary school	-0.1821*	(0.0881)	0.1143	(0.1404)
Upper secondary school	-0.0706	(0.0955)	0.0862	(0.138)
High school	0.1359	(0.0993)	0.3574**	(0.1427)
University	0.1175	(0.1041)	0.4632**	(0.1489)

Standard errors in parenthesis. *: 5%; **: 2%

Table 10.5   Estimation results of (1) and (2) by maximum likelihood – other parameters

	Men	Women	Men	Women
	FB	FB	€	€
Mean wage for individuals moving into work				
a) Observed wage	43 345.97	33 966.95	1 074.52	842.02
b) Expected wage as predicted using (4)	43 031.76	32 622 26	1 066.73	808.68
c) Expected wage imputed when wage missing	42 207.88	30 173.39	1 046.31	747.98
Mean wage for individuals not moving into work				
d) Expected wage as predicted using (4)	39 668.18	26 801.66	983.35	664.40

Note: 1€ = 40 3399 FB

To summarize the results, previous long-term unemployment experience has a negative and significant impact for the two samples: it reduces individuals' probability of moving into employment and it lowers earnings prospects. The hypothesis concerning the depreciation of human capital during unemployment is thus supported; long-term unemployment is likely to have a scarring effect on subsequent earnings.

The results also suggest that more experienced workers earn higher wages and that workers with higher qualification levels earn more than those with only a basic educational level.

Let us now turn to the discussion of unemployment traps.

In order to evaluate whether unemployment traps affect the transition into employment for the available sample, we have computed three income ratios, in the spirit of Kyyrä (1999). The key in computing them is the wage that is, however, observed only for those who move into work.

To be able to compute the income ratios for individuals who either have been unemployed for the entire survey period (i.e. those we term "fictionally" employed) or have not reported the wage at the date of the interview, we have used the expected wage calculated on the basis of (8) in Section 4. For individuals moving into work, we used both the observed (OW) and the expected (EW) wage.

Table 10.6 shows the mean of the different wages used in the computation of the income ratios. Three mean wages have been calculated for those who find jobs. These are (a) the mean observed wage; (b) the mean expected wage; (c) and the mean expected wage for those with a missing wage observation. For those who do not move into work, we could only compute the mean expected wage.

The mean predicted wage is very similar to the mean observed one. However, those who do not have an observed wage have a considerably lower mean expected wage than the overall mean. This holds for both men and women, but the difference is larger for women. Furthermore, men who do not find jobs have expected wages that are, on average, 9% below the expected wages of those that do find employment. For women this difference is 21%. Another remarkable difference is that the wages earned by women who manage to obtain jobs are 22% lower than those of men.

Table 10.6 Mean observed and expected wages

	Men		Women	
ρ	-0.2051	(0.3310)	0.6500**	(0.1465)
σ^2_ε	0.0617**	(0.005)	0.0600**	(0.0081)
P11	0.1104	(0.0733)	0.1462	(0.0945)
P12	0.5771**	(0.1835)	0.3491**	(0.1124)
P21	0.0672	(0.0522)	0.1978**	(0.0616)
P22	0.2453	(0.1836)	0.3069**	(0.0939)
Log-likelihood	-330.8721		-394.7893	
Number of cases	601		740	

In computing the three income ratios, the numerator is the individual's disposable income when employed (obtained by adding the wages and other non-related work incomes, NWI); the denominator is the individual's disposable income when unemployed (derived by adding the unemployment benefits, UB, and other non-work related incomes, NWI). For observations with missing unemployment benefits, we estimated their amount (251 spells).

Since we do not know the wage earned in the last job prior to employment, this estimation is based only on three components out of four, i.e. age, unemployment duration and household composition. In the ratios below we imputed the maximum and minimum unemployment benefit. As the results are very similar we report those obtained with the maximum imputation; the other is available on request.

The income ratios computed are (1) an observed income ratio (OIR) that can only be computed for the individuals who move into jobs during the observation period and who have an observed wage,

$$\text{OIR} = (\text{NWI} + \text{OW}) / (\text{NWI} + \text{UB}) \qquad (14)$$

(2) an estimated income ratio (EIR_1) calculated imputing the expected wage to the entire sample

$$\text{EIR\_1} = (\text{NWI} + \text{EW}) / (\text{NWI} + \text{UB}) \qquad (15)$$

and (3) a combination of both (EIR_2): for those who find employment and have an observed wage we used the observed wage and for the remainder of the sample we used the expected wage. It writes as

$$\text{EIR\_2} = (\text{NWI} + \text{OW} \cdot \text{I\{found job and wage is observed\}} + \text{EW} \cdot \text{I\{did not find job or no observed wage\}}) / (\text{NWI} + \text{UB}) \qquad (16)$$

Since disposable income is likely to vary with household composition, we have classified households in categories, distinguishing between (1) singles; (2) couples, i.e. those living with a partner and without children under 6; (3) couples with young children, i.e. those living with a partner with at least one child under 6; (4) single parents with older children, i.e. individuals living alone with children 6 or above; (5) single parents with young children, i.e. individuals living without a partner and having at least one child under 6.

Presence of unemployment traps is revealed by an income ratio smaller than 1. When it equals 1, individuals are likely to choose between working and not working on the basis of their preference for leisure, the social network associated with employment, etc. When the ratio is above 1, individuals have a financial incentive to move into work. Obviously, according to the value a person gives to having a job, different scenarios may appear. We have summarized results obtained when each of the previous ratios is smaller or equal to 1 in Tables 10.7 to 10.9.

From Table 10.7, reporting the ratio lower or equal to 1 for those who move into employment (i.e. the OIR), we learn that 4.17% of men and 12.95% of women who accepted employment experienced a cut in disposable income. There is not much variation in the ratio across household types, but 19% of women having experienced long-term unemployment in the past accepted a cut in disposable income when moving to employment, compared to only 4% of men. It is also interesting to notice from Table 10.10 (reporting the CDF of estimated and observed income ratios for the different samples), that 24% of employed women accepted either a reduction or a less than a 20% increase in disposable income. For men, the figure was less than 13%.

Table 10.7 Observed income ratio

Observed income ratio: OIR (workers with observed wage)						
	Men		Women		Men	Women
	N° of cases		N° of cases		%	%
	Total	OIR<1	Total	OIR<1		
All	288	12	278	36	4.17	12.95
Singles	27	1	33	3	3.7	12.0
Couples without children under 6	70	4	50	7	5.71	14.0
Couples with children under 6	164	5	163	22	3.05	13.5
Single parents without children under 6	3	0	2	0	0.0	0.0
Single parents with children under 6	24	2	38	4	8.33	10.53
Long-term unemployment	81	4	90	17	4.94	18.89

Table 10.8, reporting EIR_1, shows that for almost 3% of men, and for more than 22% of women, finding employment is or will be associated with a financial loss. This situation is even worse for single women with children under 6 (49%) and for those having experienced a long unemployment spell in the past (30%).

From Table 10.10, we observe that 14% of all men and 37% of all women in the sample would gain less than 20% in disposable income, should they find employment. The numbers for the combined income ratio EIR_2 in Table 10.10 are close to those in Table 10.9.

Table 10.8   Estimated income ratio – EIR_1

Estimated income ratio: EIR_1 (whole sample)	Men		Women		Men	Women
	N° of cases		N° of cases		%	%
	Total	EIR<1	Total	EIR<1		
All	601	16	740	164	2.66	22.16
Singles	69	1	59	16	1.45	27.12
Couples without children under 6	164	11	151	26	6.71	17.22
Couples with children under 6	329	3	390	56	0.91	14.36
Single parents without children under 6	5	0	4	0	0.0	0.0
Single parents with children under 6	34	1	136	66	2.94	48.53
Long-term unemployment	294	14	424	126	4.76	29.72

Table 10.9   Estimated income ratio – EIR_2

Estimated income ratio: EIR_2 (whole sample)	Men		Women		Men	Women
	N° of cases		N° of cases		%	%
	Total	EIR<1	Total	EIR<1		
All	601	27	740	160	4.49	21.62
Singles	69	2	59	13	2.9	22.03
Couples without children under 6	164	15	151	29	9.15	19.21
Couples with children under 6	329	8	390	57	2.43	14.62
Single parents without children under 6	5	4	4	0	80.0	0.0
Single parents with children under 6	34	2	136	61	5.88	44.85
Long-term unemployment	294	18	424	121	6.12	28.54

Table 10.10   CDF of observed and estimated income ratios

CDF	0.8	0.9	1.0	1.1	1.2
OIR					
Men	1.7	2.4	4.2	8.0	12.5
Women	5.8	9.4	12.9	16.2	24.1
EIR_1					
Men	0.2	0.7	2.7	7.0	14.1
Women	5.7	13.2	22.2	29.3	36.5
EIR_2					
Men	1.0	1.8	4.5	10.0	16.8
Women	6.6	13.6	21.6	27.0	33.1
EIR for those who do not find jobs					
Men	0.4	0.8	5.5	13.4	23.1
Women	8.5	18.1	27.8	33.9	38.0

In Table 10.11 we summarize the results for those who have been unemployed throughout the survey period.

Table 10.11 Estimated income ratio for the "fictionally" employed – ({EIR_2 = EIR_1}<1)

	Men		Women		Men	Women
	N° of cases		N° of cases		%	%
	Total	EIR<1	Total	EIR<1		
Everybody	238	13	342	95	5.46	27.78
Singles	36	3	126	3	8.33	2.38
Couples without children under 6	82	1	77	7	1.22	9.09
Couples with children under 6	113	9	163	22	7.96	13.5
Single parents without children under 6	2	3	2	0	150.0	0.0
Single parents with children under 6	5	0	74	4	0	5.41
Long-term unemployment	186	12	294	90	6.45	30.61

Note that 5.5% of men and 28% of women would have no immediate financial incentive to move into work since this transition would be associated with a considerable reduction in disposable income. Single men (8%) and couples with children under 6 (13%) are more exposed to risk of these traps. Women who have experienced long-term unemployment are very likely to have no incentive to accept jobs since the wages they would earn will be lowered by the negative influence of their previous career, confirming once again the importance of previous history on the labour market for this group. Note also from Table 10.10 that 38% of the women who do not find jobs would gain less than 20% should they accept one.

Finally, in Table 10.12 we report the mean estimated and observed income ratios for those individuals having moved into employment (and having reported the wage) during the observation period.

Table 10.12 Mean observed and estimated income ratios for workers

Variable	Men		Women	
	N°	Mean	N°	Mean
Mean (OIR)	288	2.2693	278	1.8158
Mean (EIR_1)	288	2.2763	278	1.6721
Mean (EIR_2)	288	2.2693	278	1.8158

6.   Conclusions

This paper has investigated whether unemployment traps affect the transition into employment of individuals interviewed in waves 3 to 7 of the Panel Study of Belgian Households. To this end, we have estimated their post-unemployment wage and a selection equation (for finding employment) using a panel data sample selection model.

Although significant differences appear between men and women, a common factor affecting wage levels and participation decisions is experience of long periods of unemployment. The long-term unemployed have more difficulty (re-) integrating into the labour market and obtain lower salaries when they do find jobs. More experienced workers have the best earning prospects. Nevertheless for better educated women, who participate more and earn more compared to those with only a basic education, the wages offered are lower than those offered to men, *ceteris paribus*. The problem of sample selection seems particularly important for women, suggesting that their transition back into work is highly selective.

A high proportion of women's transitions into work are associated with financial loss, while for men the problem is of little importance. This is confirmed by the estimated income ratio computed for all individuals present in the sample and for those "fictionally" employed. For the latter, 6% of men and 28% of women are "trapped" financially in unemployment since their transition into work would be accompanied by a substantial reduction in disposable income. This is particularly true for single women with children under 6. Long-term unemployment experience worsens the picture: almost 31% of women and 7% of men who did not find jobs and who had experienced previous long-term unemployment are unlikely to have incentives to accept jobs.

The results of our analysis lead to several considerations. First, since long-term unemployment significantly and negatively affects both earnings and participation decisions, policies oriented to preventing people from becoming long-term unemployed could have, as a consequence, an improvement in the incentives these people have to enter the labour market and eventually to lower unemployment itself. Second, since experience matters, it would be possible to increase the propensity of people to participate in the labour market by making them more experienced, even through temporary jobs that interrupt unemployment and allow them to accumulate general human capital. Third, as the transition into work is frequently associated with a loss or very small increase in disposable income, especially for women, the value given to having a job seems to be high for this group. Finally, the fact that women receive lower wages and are more at risk of being "trapped" in the unemployment state is an important consideration for policy concerns. Increasing employment of women through the design of incentives schemes (such as those linked to child care) could alleviate their labour market problems and lower the overall unemployment rate.

Abandonment of the right to eternal unemployment benefits, or a more dramatic time-variation in unemployment benefits, could help in providing the right incentives to take employment, as could the abandonment of the right to "unemployment-state-specific" additional support.

References

Arulampalam, W. 2000. *Is unemployment really scarring? Effects of unemployment experience on wages*, Discussion Paper No. 189 (Bonn, *Institute for the Study of Labor - IZA*).

D'Addio, A. C. and De Greef, I. 2001. *"Un modèle d'offre de travail pour l'étude des incitants financiers liés à la transition chômage-emploi pour la Belgique"*, miméo (Louvain,Université catholique de Louvain).

Defeyt, P. 1998. *Lutter contre les pièges financiers: Analyse et propositions* (Ottignies, Belgium, Institut pour un Développement durable).

De Greef, I. 2000. "Les pièges financiers en Belgique. Aperçu de la législation du chômage, des spécificités institutionnelles et études de cas types", in *Revue Belge de Sécurité Sociale*, No. 3.

De Lathouwer, L. 2000.*Les pièges à l'emploi en Belgique* (Antwerp, Center for Social Policy (CSB)- Berichten).

———— and Bogaerts, K. 2001. *Financiële incentieven en laagbetaald werk. De impact van hervormingen in de sociale zekerheid en de fiscaliteit op de werkloosheidsval in België* (Antwerp, Center for Social Policy (CSB)- Berichten).

Fallick, B. 1996. "A review of the recent empirical literature on displaced workers", in *Industrial and Labour Relations Review,* October, pp. 142-155.

Gregg, P., Johnson, P. and Reed, H. 1999. "Entering work and the British tax and benefit system", in *Institute for Fiscal Studies* (London).

Gregory, M. and Jukes, R. 1997. *The effects of unemployment on subsequent earnings: A study of British men 1984-1994*, Discussion Paper No. 21 (London, Centre for Economic Policy Research).

Grubb, D. and Martin, J. P. 2001. *What works and for whom: A review of OECD countries experiences with active labour market policies*, Working Paper No.

2001-14, Institutet för Arbetsmarknadpolitisk Utvärdering (Uppsala, Sweden, IFAU-Office of Labour Market Policy Evaluation).

Gurgand, M. and Margolis, D. 2001. "RMI et revenus du travail: une évaluation des gains financiers à l'emploi", in *Economie et Statistique*, Nos. 6/7, pp. 346-347.

Heckman, J. 1979. "Sample selection bias as a specification error", in *Econometrica*, Vol. 47, pp. 153-161.

Holm, P., Kyyrä, T. and Rantala, J. 1999. "Household economic incentives, the unemployment trap and the probability of finding a job", in *International Tax and Public Finance*, Vol. 6(3), pp. 361—378.

Husted, L. et al. 2001a. *Qualifications, discrimination, or assimilation? An extended framework for analysing immigrant wage gaps*, Discussion Paper No. 365, Bonn, Institute for the Study of Labor (IZA).

_____. 2001b. "Employment and wage assimilation of male first-generation immigrants in Denmark", in *International Journal of Manpower*, Vol. 22(1/2), pp. 39-68.

Jacobson, L. S., Lalonde, R. J. and Sullivan, D. G. 1993. "Earnings losses of displaced workers", in *American Economic Review*, Vol. 83, pp. 685-709.

Jensen, P., Rosholm, M. and Verner, M. 2002. *A comparison of different estimators for panel data sample selection models*, Working Paper 2002-1, (Denmark, University of Aarhus).

Kletzer, L. 1998. "Job displacement", in *The Journal of Economic Perspectives*, Vol. 12, pp. 115-136.

Kyriazidou, E. 1997. "Estimation of a panel data sample selection model", in *Econometrica* Vol. 65, pp. 1335-1364.

Kyyrä, T. 1999. *Post-unemployment wages and economic incentives to exit from unemployment*, Research Report No.56 (Helsinki, Valtion Taloudellinen Tuktimuskeskus).

Laurent, S. 2001. *Capital humain, emploi et salaire en Belgique et ses régions* (Liége, Quatorzième Congrès des Economistes Belges de Langue Française).

Layard, R., Nickell, S. and Jackman, R. 1991. *Unemployment, Macroeconomic Performance and the Labour Market* (Oxford, Oxford University Press).

Nickell, S., Jones, T. and Quintini, G. 1999. "A picture of the job insecurity facing British men", in *The labour market consequence of technical and structural change*, Discussion Paper No. 42 (London, Centre for Economic Policy Research).

Organization for Economic Cooperation and Development (OECD). 1996. *Employment Outlook* (Paris, OECD).

_____. 1997. *Employment Outlook* (Paris, OECD).

_____. 1999. *Benefit systems and work incentives* (Paris, OECD).

_____. 2002. *Income changes when moving in and out of work* (Paris, Social Policy Division, OECD).

Pedersen, P. and Smith, N. 2001. *Unemployment traps: Do financial disincentives matter?*, Discussion Paper No. 274 (Bonn, *IZA*).

_____. and Westergard-Nielsen, N. 1993. "Unemployment: A review of the evidence from panel data", in *OECD Economic Studies* 20, pp. 65-95.

Ruhm, C. 1991. "Are workers permanently scarred by job displacements?", in *American Economic Review*, Vol. 81, pp. 319-324.

Stevens, A. 1997. "Persistent effects of job displacement: The importance of multiple job losses", in *Journal of Labour Economics*, Vol.15, pp. 165-188.

Sweeney, J. 1998. *Why hold a job? The labour market choice of the low skilled* (Leuven, Katholique Universiteit Leuven), p. 263.

Valenduc, Ch. 2002. "La réforme de l'impôt des personnes physiques : ses effets sur l'imposition des salaires, l'incitation à l'emploi et sur la distribution des revenus", in *Bulletin de Documentation - Federal Public Service Finance*, No. 3, pp.145-203, May-June

Van den Berg, G. J. 1990. "Search behaviour, transitions to non-participation and the duration of unemployment", in *Economic Journal*, Vol. 100(402), pp. 842-865.

Vella, F. and Verbeek, M. 1999. "Two-step estimation of panel data models with censored endogenous variables and selection bias", in *Journal of Econometrics*, Vol. 90, pp. 239-263.

Verbeek, M. and Nijman, T. 1996. "Incomplete panels and selection bias", in L. Mátyás and P. Sevestre (eds.) *The econometrics of panel data*, 1st edition (New York, Kluwer Academic Publishers).

Wooldridge, J. 1995. "Selection corrections for panel data models under conditional mean independence assumptions", in *Journal of Econometrics*, Vol. 68, pp. 115-132.

Appendix

As the employment selection process may be non-random. Sample selectivity may bias the parameters of interest, if not adequately controlled for.

Despite the greater complexity of the methodology to be applied, allowance must be made for the data structure when dealing with sample selection. In general, two approaches have been followed - two-step estimators, following Heckman (1979),[6] or maximum likelihood estimators. We chose the latter. Further, although one can choose between a random and a fixed approach, this study uses the random effects approach. In the fixed effect approach, time-invariant covariates are absorbed in the fixed effects and so cannot be used to gather insights into the factors determining wages.

The model for wages we consider can be formulated as follows:

$$y_{it}^* = x_{it}^{'}\beta + \alpha_i + \varepsilon_{it} \qquad (1)$$

$$d_{it}^* = z_{it}^{'}\gamma + \eta_i + \upsilon_{it} \qquad (2)$$

$$d_{it} = 1 \text{ if } d_{it}^* > 0, \ 0 \text{ otherwise} \quad (3)$$

$$y_{it} = y_{it}^* \cdot d_{it} \qquad (4)$$

where i ($i=1,...,N$) denotes the individual and t ($t = 1, ..., T$) denotes the time period; d_{it} is an indicator for an observed wage, y_{it} denotes the log of the observed wage, x_{it} and z_{it} are vectors of explanatory variables, possibly with common elements, and with an exclusion restriction. The equation of interest is (1) and the selection process is described by (2). β and γ are the unknown parameter vectors to estimate. The α_i and η_i are unobservable time invariant individual-specific components, which may be correlated with each other. Finally, ε_{it} and υ_{it} are unobserved disturbances, possibly correlated. The variable y_{it}^* is observed only if $d_{it} = 1$, that is, if the person i is employed in period t.

---

[6] Two-step estimators are not quite suited to our purposes; either they are of the fixed effect type (e.g. Kyriazidou, 1997), or the correlation structure of the error components is specified *ad hoc* (e.g. Wooldridge, 1995; Verbeek and Nijman, 1996; Vella and Verbeek, 1999). Jensen et al. (2002) contains a survey of available panel data sample selection estimators.

Since (1) and (2) are estimated simultaneously by maximum likelihood, we had to specify the joint distribution of the error components ε_{it} and υ_{it}. We assumed that the idiosyncratic error terms follow a bivariate normal distribution

$$(\varepsilon_{it}, \upsilon_{it}) \sim N(0,0,\Sigma), \text{ where } \Sigma = \begin{bmatrix} \sigma_\varepsilon^2 & \rho\sigma_\varepsilon \\ \rho\sigma_\varepsilon & 1 \end{bmatrix} \qquad (5)$$

Let $\theta = [\beta, \gamma, \sigma_\varepsilon, \rho, p, \alpha, \eta]$ denote the parameter vector. The likelihood of a single observation, conditional on the random effects, is then

$$L_{it}(\theta) = f(\varepsilon_{it}, \upsilon_{it} \mid \alpha_i, \eta_i, x_{it}, z_{it}) \qquad (6)$$
$$= \left[\left(1 - \phi_{\upsilon\varepsilon}\left(-z'_{it}\gamma - \eta_i \mid y_{it} - x'_{it}\beta - \alpha_i\right)\right) \cdot \phi_\varepsilon\left(y_{it} - x'_{it}\beta - \alpha_i\right)\right]^{c_{it} d_{it}}$$
$$= \left[\Phi_\upsilon(z'_{it}\gamma + \eta_i)\right]^{(1-c_{it}) d_{it}} \cdot \left[\Phi_\upsilon(-z'_{it}\gamma - \eta_i)\right]^{(1-d_{it})}$$

where the conditional distribution $\upsilon \mid \varepsilon \sim N\left(\dfrac{\rho_\varepsilon}{\sigma_\varepsilon}, (1-\rho^2)\right)$; Φ and ϕ are respectively the standard normal distribution and probability density functions for the variables referred by subscripts.

The random effects are assumed to follow a bivariate discrete distribution with 2×2 points of support, and we assume independence between idiosyncratic errors and random effects. c_{it} is an indicator taking the value 1 if the wage is observed for an individual who finds employment (in some cases, it is not, see Section 5).

Let $\alpha = \{\alpha_1, \alpha_2\}$, $\eta = \{\eta_1, \eta_2\}$, $p = \{p_{11}, p_{12}, p_{21}, p_{22}\}$, where $p_{kj} = \Pr[\eta_k, \alpha_j]$. For a single individual, the likelihood contribution is then

$$L_i(\theta) = \int_{-\infty}^{\infty} \int_{-\infty}^{\infty} \left[\prod_{t=1}^{T_i} f(\varepsilon_{it}, \upsilon_{it} \mid x_{it}, z_{it}, \alpha_i, \eta_i)\right] dG(\eta_i, \alpha_i) \qquad (7)$$
$$= \sum_{j=1}^{2}\sum_{j=1}^{2} p_{kj} \prod_{t=1}^{T_i} f(\varepsilon_{it}, \upsilon_{it} \mid x_{it}, z_{it}, \alpha_i, \eta_i)$$

where $G(\cdot)$ is the joint CDF of the random effects.

To be able to compute the income ratio for each individual in the sample, (including those who never find employment, the expected log wages is computed as in Husted et al. (2001a, 2001b).

Conditional on the entire path of participation indicators, the expected log wage for an individual is

$$E\left[y_{it} \mid d_{i1},...,d_{iT_i},x_{it},z_{i1},...,z_{iT_i}\right] \tag{8}$$
$$= x_{it}\beta + E\left[\alpha_i \mid d_{i1},...,d_{iT_i},z_{i1},...,z_{iT_i}\right] + E\left[\varepsilon_{it} \mid d_{it} \cdot z_{it}\right]$$

where T_i is the maximum number of periods over which an individual is observed. The expected values of the error components of the wage equation are

$$E\left[\alpha_i \mid d_{i1},...,d_{iT_i},z_{i1},...,z_{iT_i}\right] = \sum_{j=1}^{2}\alpha_j q_{ji}^{\alpha} \tag{9}$$

$$E\left[\varepsilon_{it} \mid d_{it}=1,z_{it}\right] = \rho\sigma_\varepsilon \sum_{k=1}^{2} q_{kit}^{\eta} \frac{\phi(z_{it}\gamma+\eta_k)}{\Phi(z_{it}\gamma+\eta_k)} \tag{10}$$

$$E\left[\varepsilon_{it} \mid d_{it}=0,z_{it}\right] = -\rho\sigma_\varepsilon \sum_{k=1}^{2} q_{kit}^{\eta} \frac{\phi(z_{it}\gamma+\eta_k)}{1-\Phi(z_{it}\gamma+\eta_k)} \tag{11}$$

The term q_{ji}^{α} denotes the parameters of the individual-specific probabilities of α_i. Its expression is

$$q_{ji}^{\alpha} = \frac{\sum_{k=1}^{2} p_{kj} \prod_{t=1}^{T_i}\left[\Phi_\upsilon(z_{it}\gamma+\eta_i)\right]^{(1-c_{it})d_{it}} \cdot \left[\Phi_\upsilon(-z_{it}\gamma-\eta_i)\right]^{(1-d_{it})}}{\sum_{l=1}^{2}\left[(p_{l1}+p_{l2})\prod_{t=1}^{T_i}\left[\Phi_\upsilon(z_{it}\gamma+\eta_i)\right]^{(1-c_{it})d_{it}} \cdot \left[\Phi_\upsilon(-z_{it}\gamma-\eta_i)\right]^{(1-d_{it})}\right]} \tag{12}$$

and q_{kit}^{η} denotes the parameters of the individual and time specific probability of η_i

$$q_{kit}^{\eta} = \frac{\sum_{j=1}^{2} p_{kj}\Phi_\upsilon(z_{it}\gamma+\eta_k)}{\sum_{j=1}^{2}\left[(p_{1j}\Phi_\upsilon(z_{it}\gamma+\eta_1))+p_{2j}\Phi_\upsilon(z_{it}\gamma+\eta_2)\right]} \tag{13}$$

THE RISE AND FALL OF SELECTIVITY À LA GRÈCQUE

11

Manos Matsaganis [1]

1. Introduction

Income testing is a relatively novel concept in Greece. In fact, it would be fair to say that, until recently, few people beyond an extremely restricted circle of specialists knew what it meant. References to means testing (or targeting or selectivity, as these terms are used interchangeably) in policy discourse began to appear only in 1996. Indeed, key figures in, or close to, the new "modernising" Government that took office in that year presented selectivity as the *leitmotiv* of the new social policy paradigm.

This paper will show that, after a brief flutter of activity, all this came to very little. The failure of selectivity as a strategy to reform the welfare state (from a centre-left perspective) was inevitable. The reasons are to be found partly in the particular version of selectivity pursued, but mostly in the nature of social protection arrangements in Greece.

The next section contains a brief summary of the story so far, with details of attempts to introduce targeted benefits and means-test existing ones. This is followed by an analysis of the structural limits to selectivity in a welfare state of the conservative-corporatist model (Esping-Andersen, 1990) and, in particular, of its southern variant (Ferrera, 1996). The last section brings together the main insights of the preceding analysis in a comparative perspective.

[1] Department of Economics, University of Crete, Rethymno, Greece.

2.   Selectivity *à la Grécque*

2.1 *The rise of selectivity*

The year 1996 marked a turning point in Greek politics. In January, Costas Simitis was elected prime minister after a closely contested ballot of socialist MPs. A mild-mannered European-minded Social Democrat, he could not have differed more from his charismatic nationalist-populist predecessor and party founder, Andreas Papandreou. The new Prime Minister quickly consolidated his position by becoming party leader in June, then by calling and winning an early general election in September. On presenting his cabinet and programme to parliament in October, Simitis declared European Monetary Union membership to be an overriding aim, while pledging his commitment to a "cohesive society" (Parliament Proceedings, 1996).

The concept of selectivity was chosen as an obvious way to square the circle. Already in June, introduction of the means-tested pension supplement *EKAΣ* had enabled the Government to escape an earlier pledge to restore the link between minimum pensions and minimum wage. Before the year was out, the "Introductory Report" on the 1997 Budget (the first of the new Government) included a resounding endorsement of the welfare state, while announcing a significant shift in policy (Ministry of National Economy, 1996, pp. 22-23):

> A modern and effective welfare state is a key aim of this Budget. (…) Our policy rejects the notion that social protection cannot be expanded because resources are unavailable. Resources will never be adequate when allocated across the board, with no planning, no evaluation of their effectiveness. We adopt the policy of targeted intervention, of efficiency savings and of reinforcement of social protection. (…) Emphasis will be given to initiatives supporting the weakest groups through policies based on identifying real need, not by wasting resources on negligible benefits to all directions.

The new policy was promoted in the daily press. In the words of its most enthusiastic theorist:

> Austerity can go hand-in-hand with social justice when we finally realise that in a society where two thirds prosper and one third is

marginalized, social benefits for all do not reduce but intensify the gap between rich and poor (Mouzelis, 1996).[2]

The ingenuous manner with which targeting was being propounded seemed to spring from a profound lack of awareness of the various fundamental difficulties involved. Or, to quote Sen:

> If the so-called targets were all identifiable and unreacting, that would be the end of the matter – we could converge on a fine strategy whose merit we would all accept. Some of the resonant appeals to the case for more targeting give one the haunting feeling that this is indeed the way the problem of poverty removal is seen by some advocates of no-nonsense targeting (Sen, 1995, p. 12).

Nonetheless, the Government's reforming zeal had some mileage left. In February 1997, it passed a law changing eligibility conditions for the three so-called "many-children benefits" (lifetime pension for many-children mothers, large family benefit and third child benefit). The benefits, introduced in 1990 by an all-party coalition Government in reaction to declining birth rates, had been intended as a "reward" to large families. The new criteria for access to the three benefits, as well as to the pension supplement $EKA\Sigma$ introduced a few months earlier, included a test of incomes based on tax returns. That was hailed by the Government as a milestone in social policy. These benefits, new or newly means-tested, expanded the modest space reserved for benefits within the social security system.

As seen in Table 11.1, the four benefits accounted for 80% of all expenditure on means-tested benefits in 2001. But rather than setting a precedent, they remained an exception. Though eligibility for a disabled person's travel card was later restricted to those below a certain income threshold that was about it for the moment.

---

[2] Since this is a common fallacy, it ought to be pointed out that this is incorrect: increasing everybody's income by a fixed transfer reduces inequality, unless the transfer is financed by a poll tax.

Table 11.1   Means-tested benefits in Greece, 2001

	Beneficiaries		Expenditure		Average benefit	
	Thousand	% population	€ million	% of GDP	€ per month	% minimum wage
Pensioners' social solidarity benefit *EKAΣ*	373.0	3.4	350	0.27	75	14.2
Social pension for non-insured elderly	43.5	0.4	107	0.08	144	27.4
Lifetime pension for many-children mothers	183.6	1.7	179	0.14	78	14.9
Large family benefit	82.0	0.7	103	0.05	140	26.7
Third child benefit	38.3	0.4	64	0.08	136	25.9
Unprotected child benefit	34.4	0.3	18	0.01	44	8.4
OEK rent subsidy	31.0	0.3	31	0.02	85	16.1
Repatriation benefit for low-income elderly	25.0	0.2	11	0.01	35	6.7
Miscellaneous benefits	16.5	0.2	12	0.01	n.a.	n.a.
Total	827.4	7.6	877	0.67	87	16.5

Notes:(i) The monthly minimum wage in 2001 was €526. (ii) The total in average monthly benefit excludes miscellaneous benefits, some of which are paid as a lump sum. *EKAΣ* and the social pension are paid 14 times a year. (iii) Monthly benefit values are rounded to the nearest euro.

Source: Own estimates on the basis of data collected from benefit agencies and other sources

2.2 The fall of selectivity

Subsequent attempts to introduce new-targeted benefits ran into serious trouble or simply came to nothing. At the same time, unexpected policy reversals took place, three characteristic episodes.

Selectivity in trouble

Selectivity was dormant for the rest of the modernising Government's first full term in office, but was revived in the run-up to the April 2000 general election. Indeed, the introduction of a new scheme to boost take-home pay of low earners was presented as a key social policy pledge of the ruling Socialist Party – so much so that the Prime Minister in a speech to announce it a party rally in Athens on the last day of the electoral campaign.

After the Government's re-election, the new scheme was introduced in August 2000. Workers on (or just over) the minimum wage were entitled to a full refund of that part of their social insurance contributions earmarked for pensions (6.67% of gross wage). On a monthly basis, the scheme was worth about €29, a modest but welcome addition to low earnings.

Nevertheless, reports emerged that participation in the scheme was lower than expected. In February 2001, the Prime Minister asked the Ministry of Labour and Social Insurance to conduct an internal inquiry. This revealed that, six months after the scheme's launch, out of the 470,000 workers expected to benefit only 40,000 actually did (i.e. a non-take-up rate of 91.5%). In view of the design flaws and administrative problems identified, it was decided that the refund would thereafter be administered as a tax credit.[3] Yet, recent figures revealed that participation to the scheme declined further (NAP, 2003, p. 30).

Equally disappointing was the case of unemployment assistance for older workers, the showpiece of the 2001 National Action Plan for Social Inclusion (NAP). The scheme, introduced in January 2002, was targeted to long-term unemployed workers aged 45-65 with annual income below €4,100 for a family of four. Official estimates put the number of potential beneficiaries at 35,000 and its annual cost at €59 million. Instead, quite incredibly for a policy personally announced by the Prime Minister, the Ministry of Economy and Economics at first failed to make the necessary provision in the 2002 budget and then finally agreed to earmark a mere €15 million. As it turned out, one-tenth of that amount would have been sufficient: ten months after it was made available, the new benefit was being paid to exactly 711 individuals (2% of those originally expected to claim).

Selectivity reversed

The rise of selectivity was not linear. As Table 11.2 implies, income testing was introduced, revised and then abolished on various occasions in the past. An early example of policy reversal was the ill-fated attempt to standardise rules on means-testing of disability benefits. In 1987, a ministerial decree established income thresholds that varied with family status, household size and age of beneficiary, but were otherwise identical across type of disability. A new procedure was introduced for self-reporting of income with a signed statement, supported by the previous year's income tax return. However, 14 months later, the decree was revoked after protests by officials at the impracticalities and disproportionate costs of control. A ministerial decree, issued in February 1989, abolished all income testing of disability benefits.

---

[3] Benefit rules required that employers pay eligible employees a net wage plus the rebate and pay the social insurance agency IKA the usual contributions minus the rebate. So, the scheme depended on the ability and willingness of employers to carry out the necessary procedure and pass on the benefit to eligible employees. Experience showed that many employers were unable or unwilling to do so.

Table 11.2   Policy changes with respect to means-testing of selected benefits

	Introduced	Revised	Abolished
Disability allowances	1951	1987	1989
OAEΔ family allowances	1959		1999
Unprotected child benefit	1960	1983	
Social pension for non-insured elderly	1982	1992	
Pensioners' social solidarity benefit EKAΣ	1996		
Lifetime pension for many children mothers	1997		2002
Large family benefit	1997		2002
Third child benefit	1997		2002
Unemployment assistance (aged 45-65)	2002		

(i) The oldest disability scheme (for the blind) was introduced in 1951.

(ii) Before 1999 OAEΔ family allowances were not withdrawn from higher-income families but simply paid at lower rate. From 1999, there is a single rate for a given number of children irrespective of income.

Another example was the case of family allowances provided by the tripartite Manpower Employment Organisation (*OAEΔ*) to private sector workers, irrespective of social insurance affiliation (though conditional on contribution record).[4] Previously, the allowances were means-tested: there were four income bands, with higher rates of benefit corresponding to lower incomes. The income band system was abandoned in October 1999 with retrospective effect from January 1999. Since then, allowances are no longer related to income, though they still rise with number of children. The change was not widely noticed because the value of *OAEΔ* allowances is so low (€6 a month for a family with one child, €18 a month for a two-child family in 2001) that it mattered little whether they varied with income or not.

As regards the three "many children" benefits, income tests had been presented as evidence of a paradigm shift in social policy towards "providing benefits to those who really need them". Despite rhetoric, these income tests were unceremoniously dropped in December 2001. There was little public explanation of this curious policy reversal. It can only be assumed that the original pro-family objectives triumphed over selectivity.

Selectivity repudiated

The absence of a national scheme of last resort, acting as the ultimate social safety net, was only a few years ago correctly identified as a defining feature of

---

[4] Note that a separate, more generous and better-run scheme operates for civil servants.

the "rudimentary social assistance regime of south Europe" (Gough, 1996). Nevertheless, policy developments over recent years have been spectacular. In Portugal, *rendimento mínimo garantido* was launched in 1996 as a pilot scheme and extended nationwide in 1997. In Italy, the experiment with *reddito minimo di inserimento* began in 1998 in 39 municipalities and was extended to another 260 in 2000. Although Spain has no national minimum income programme, various schemes – such as the Catalan *renda mínima d'inserció* – have been operated by "autonomous communities" for over a decade. Given that every other European Union country had long before adopted a minimum income scheme or equivalent (CEC, 1998), Greece risked remaining an exception even within the family of south European nations.

The largely successful experience with guaranteed minimum income programmes in Italy and Portugal raised the question whether Greece should follow suit. The three countries shared features (extended families, informal employment etc.) that had earlier been considered unfavourable to the introduction of minimum income.[5] Moreover, all three were at that time ruled by centre-left majorities. What better opportunity for a Government committed to Europe to bring the country's patchy social safety net up to European standards! What was more natural for a Government committed to targeting than to prepare the ground for the introduction of the targeted programme *par excellence*!

A proposal to introduce a guaranteed minimum income programme in Greece was in fact presented to the Prime Minister in January 2000. A shorter version was submitted to the committee responsible for the preparation of the National Action Plan for Social Inclusion (NAP) in March 2001.[6] After brief consideration, the proposal was rejected. As usual, the reasons were not made public, but the NAP hinted that the decisive factor was that income tax returns were not reliable enough for income-testing purposes (NAP, 2001, p. 7).

Despite this targeted benefit programmes were announced: an unemployment assistance scheme plus two less significant tax credit schemes, whose beneficiaries were to be selected on the basis of the same income tax returns. Concerns about their reliability were quietly put aside.

---

[5] For an up-to-date analysis of minimum income schemes in southern Europe see Matsaganis et al. (2003).

[6] The proposal had been drawn up by this author, as an adviser to the Prime Minister. The proposed scheme, in line with standard policy, would combine financial support in case of extreme hardship with individual social reintegration plans. It was estimated that the cost of cash transfers would be the equivalent of 0.23% of GDP. A full account of the methodology used can be found in Matsaganis et al. (2001).

3. Limits to selectivity

The literature on the limits to selectivity is extensive.[7] No attempt is made to rehearse the standard arguments here, other than to reiterate that:

> The scope of governments to target benefits effectively is limited not just by the budgetary cost (…), but also by administrative factors, by the impact on economic incentives and by considerations of political economy (Atkinson, 1998, pp. 130-131).

The reflections that follow address that literature only indirectly, focusing instead on factors that are either additional or qualitatively different from the ones usually cited. These relate to the implications for selectivity of the fact that Greece is a continental European welfare state, a south European welfare state, and a welfare state with a low degree of "stateness".

Bear in mind that in the late 1990s, discussion on selectivity in Greece was mostly conducted out of context. It looked as if the country had suddenly moved from the south-east to the north-west of Europe, with the merits of selectivity being based on British experience alone. In the words of a powerful figure in the Simitis government:

> The income tests and targeted interventions in social policy started by the Simitis Government are similar to those adopted by the Labour Government in Britain.[8]

The modernisers' infatuation with targeting went far beyond the narrow confines of social policy. Selectivity became the key to the revival of the centre-left, invested with wider significance and assigned almost mystical qualities

> If the centre-left forces manage to break the taboo of universal benefits, it will be possible to restructure the welfare state in a much more positive manner for the social classes that really need it (Mouzelis, 1998a).

Soon, selectivity itself became a taboo: questioning its wisdom implied a departure from the faith. More problematically, selectivity was presented as the

---

[7] For a concise review of the main issues, see Atkinson (1995, pp. 223-304 and 1998, pp. 119-149). Sen's paper quoted earlier (1995) introduced a lengthy volume dedicated to targeting, sponsored by the World Bank, whose findings are summarized by van de Walle (1995).

[8] Interview with Nicos Christodoulakis, then finance under-minister, now minister of the economy and finance. The interview was published in the Sunday newspaper *To Βήμα* on 12 April 1998 under the title "We apply the Blair recipe".

answer to the all-important question of welfare reform. But the question itself was poorly understood. There was no serious doubt about the need for welfare reform. But the faults of the Greek welfare state did not lie in an excess of universality.

3.1 Selectivity in a Bismarckian welfare state

The label "conservative-corporatist" (Esping-Andersen, 1990) fits Greece quite well. Social security is dominated by the Bismarckian principle of contributory earnings-related benefits, provided by a large number of social insurance agencies or "funds". By contrast, as Table 11.3 indicates, mean-tested benefits account for no more than 4.7% of total spending on social security.

Non-contributory benefits that are not already means-tested represent a further 11.8% of the social security budget. These may be regarded as a natural candidate for income-testing. However, the largest programme of that category (the farmers' basic pension) is being phased out. As from 1998 the Agricultural Insurance Organization (*ОГА*) has been gradually introducing a contributory pension. In terms of Table 11.3, this marks a move from the bottom-right to the upper-right part of the matrix, not from bottom-right to bottom-left as proponents of selectivity might have wished.

The eventual disappearance of the farmers' basic pension will complete the Bismarckian imprint of Greek social security. The remaining non-contributory non-means-tested benefits amount to a mere 2.5% of total expenditure. That will leave only one possibility: income-testing of social insurance. But restricting access to contributory benefits on the grounds of high income usually proves to be politically risky and legally ambiguous, given that contributors regard such benefits as theirs "by right" through paying contributions.

The predominance of social insurance evidently has serious implications for the prospects of selectivity, which allows limited room for manoeuvre. As one observer noted, "Even if the insurance logic has in large part become a façade, nonetheless it is a façade that considerably constrains selectivity." (Ferrera, 1998, p. 90).

Table 11.3   Share of total expenditure on social security benefits, 2001 (%)

	Means-tested	Not means-tested	Total
Contributory	0.2	83.5	83.7
Non-contributory	4.5	11.8	16.3
Total	4.7	95.3	100.0

Note Total expenditure on social security benefits in 2001 was €18,644 or 14.28% of GDP.

Source Matsaganis, 2003

Examples of successful attempts to restrict social insurance benefits on the basis of income are very rare. The oft-cited case of high earners in Germany and the Netherlands being exempted from compulsory health insurance (Ferrera, 1998, p. 86) points to a counter-productive outcome: exclusion of high earners not only weakens the contribution base, but since they tend to pay more into the social insurance fund than they receiveredistributes resources in their favour.

Nor is the strategy of targeting contributory benefits supported by the French experience (Levy, 1999, pp. 246-52). In the 1998 budget, the first of his Government, Prime Minister Lionel Jospin announced the introduction of income tests to exclude "the rich" from gaining access to contributory family allowances. Nevertheless, the new policy came under criticism "from Left and Right". In line with the recommendations of policy reviews commissioned by it, the Government, restored of universal family allowances in the 1999 Budget. The additional costs were financed by restructuring the highly regressive "family quotient" system of child tax credits –a more plausible target for a progressive government all along.

That selectivity was the wrong answer to a wrongly formulated question also became evident in Greece. Universal benefits, as seen earlier, have been so weak that it seems incredible that they could offend anybody's sense of justice. On the other hand, a reformist government wishing to promote equity and efficiency needed to look no further than pensions. This is a vast and separate subject, more extensively treated elsewhere (Matsaganis, 2003). Nonetheless, it might be useful to list the main conclusions here.

Spending on pensions in Greece accounts for more than 90% of all benefits and is among the highest in Europe as a share of GDP; it also is rising fast. Moreover, the design of pension programmes favours early retirement and contribution evasion, leading to the paradoxical effect that many pensions are at once too low (compared to earnings) and too high (compared to contributions paid).

In terms of equity, fragmentation by category often results in variations in pension levels that are not only positively related to income but also negatively related to prior contributions. More specifically, between identical workers in terms of age and income, current arrangements systematically favour those in "noble" funds over those in "popular" ones, civil servants over private sector workers, the middle-aged over the young, men over women, unionised over precarious workers, and so on.

It could be argued that the survival of the existing pension system constitutes a gross violation of any principle of justice, and is a serious obstacle to the growth of the smallest (relative to population) national economy in Europe.

Pension reform remains the litmus test for reform-minded progressives, in Greece as everywhere else in continental Europe. Here, the "modernising" Government's record (by the standards it set on taking office) can only be described as disappointing. Faced with unrealistic expectations it fanned when in opposition, the Government stumbled from one policy failure to another, found itself repeatedly obliged to deny what it had announced shortly before, and settled for a limited face-saving exercise of tinkering at the margin.

In this context, the preoccupation with selectivity proved a distraction from the main task. Once more, the problem was redefined in order to fit the solution. In the words of the Government figure cited earlier:

> There exist pensioners with high pensions and particularly privileged treatment, while there also exist pensioners with incomes around the poverty line. The greatest unfairness would be a policy of across-the-board rises that would not benefit the privileged, nor would they help the poor substantially. The correct and fair solution in this case would be greater support for the weaker, as with $EKA\Sigma$.[9]

Whether that was indeed "the correct and fair solution" has become clearer. Six years after the Government came to office announcing pension reform as a key priority, the perennial "privileges" remain largely intact. And despite its expansion, $EKA\Sigma$ (the celebrated income-tested supplement to low pensions) only accounts for about 2% of total pension expenditure.

3.2 Selectivity in a south European welfare state

As seen above, fragmentation by category is often at the root of what is wrong with social security in Greece. Unlike elsewhere in continental Europe, the traditional division of schemes along occupational lines has not been offset by measures aimed at universal social rights.

As a result, the parameters defining pension rights (contribution rates, minimum length of contributory period, reference earnings, replacement rates, standard retirement age) are subject to a bewildering array of rules that differ systematically between categories. Obviously, distribution of privileged treatment is anything but random, and can usually be explained by a group's ability to bend rules in its favour. This may be due to political influence, as in

---

[9] Interview with finance under-minister Christodoulakis (*To Βήμα*, 12 April 1998).

the case of the "liberal professions", or simply a matter of proximity to power, as in the case of civil servants (Sotiropoulos, 2001).

The "particularist-clientelist" (Ferrera, 1996) aspect of social protection arrangements in Greece was noted in the late 1980s by a backbench MP who was later to become Prime Minister: "The welfare state in Greece has been built haphazardly. (...) It is the product of repeated compromises with pressure groups or of short-term crisis management" (Simitis, 1989).

The outcome might be termed "fragmented selectivity". Besides the breakdown of the pension system into a plethora of social insurance funds, each with its own rules, other examples of the same phenomenon might also be added.

Disability allowances vary widely by type of disability and by category of recipient. There are 10 categories and 22 sub-categories of disability allowances. These include a special benefit for blind practising lawyers (claimed by 26 persons in 1999), worth 2.3 times as much as the standard benefit for blind workers and pensioners.

The main form of housing assistance to tenants is a rent subsidy provided by the tripartite Workers' Housing Organisation, covering private sector workers irrespective of social insurance affiliation. The benefit is means-tested and yet dependent on contributions. Single applicants need a contributory record of at least 10 years, although lower eligibility criteria apply to categories of claimants (such as families with many children, single mothers, the disabled, young couples, temporary workers, residents of remote areas and returned migrants). By implication, no housing assistance is available for those with insufficient contributions, such as workers in the large informal economy.

In the area of unemployment protection, the main scheme is ordinary unemployment benefit. This is available on a contributory basis, for a maximum period of 12 months. Because of strict contributory conditions, coverage is limited (44% of registered unemployed in 1999). By way of compensation, there also exist various extraordinary unemployment benefits with less stringent rules. These include a five-month benefit for first-time job seekers aged 20-29 who can prove they have been out of work for over a year, lump-sum support for former recipients who remain unemployed after eligibility expired, and special schemes for seasonal workers, returned migrants, former prisoners and so on.

Income transfers to families with children also come in many forms. Their common characteristic is that the amount of benefit increases almost exponentially with number of children. Occupational family allowances introduce a further division between civil servants and private sector workers, as the former receive much more substantial and timely assistance than the latter. Since most children live in families not headed by a civil servant and with fewer than three children, the structure of family benefits exposes many to the risk of poverty.

The list could be expanded. The fragmented selectivity, apart from offending basic notions of equity, leaves in place a typically south European social protection system that combines welfare privileges and coverage gaps:

> This dualistic system of income maintenance tends to generate a peculiar polarization within the social clientele of the southern welfare states. On the one hand we find in these countries a group of hyper-protected beneficiaries: typically public employees, white collar workers and private wage-earners of medium and large enterprises working on a full contract, with job security (...). On the other hand we find large numbers of under-protected workers and citizens, who only (occasionally) draw meagre benefits and may thus find themselves in conditions of extreme hardship: typically irregular workers in weak sectors without job security, workers of the informal economy, young and long-term unemployed people etc. (Ferrera, 1996, p. 20).

The corollary of that dualism (aggravated by the absence of a minimum income benefit of last resort) is that the social safety net is full of holes, through which a large number of individuals and their families fall into poverty.[10]

Recent policy has left untouched this perverse form of selectivity, and has even intensified it. The National Action Plan for Social Inclusion (NAP) even tried to justify fragmented selectivity: "Precisely because the causes of poverty are complex and often vary among different vulnerable groups, our policy focuses on specific target groups" (NAP, 2001, p. 7).

In line with this assessment, three new schemes were introduced in 2002. The first, unemployment assistance for older workers, is a significant step in the direction of strengthening the social safety net. Still, the maximum duration of benefit (12 months) is too short by unemployment assistance standards, while there seems to be little reason to impose the over-45 age requirement, given that there is also an income test. The other two, even more in keeping with the tradition of fragmented selectivity, are tax credits aimed at households in mountainous and less favoured areas, and at families with children aged 6-16. This choice of target groups was not explained. Households in more favoured

---

[10] Relative poverty in Greece is higher than in most European Union countries, while the impact of social transfers in terms of poverty reduction is considerably lower than is the European norm (CEC, 2001, pp. 169-76). For analysis of poverty and social assistance in Greece, see Matsaganis, 2002.

areas and families with younger children remain ineligible for assistance, even if poor.

The "danger that some groups experiencing poverty may not be eligible for income support" (CEC, 2001, p. 34) remains largely undiminished. And the concept of selectivity, promoted as the quintessence of progressive politics for the 21st century, has mutated into an embrace of the most antiquated traits of welfare *à la grècque*.

3.3 Selectivity in a "soft" state

"Targeting welfare in a 'soft' state" is the title of a paper on Italy, which introduces its subject with the following remark:

> Effective targeting requires some institutional preconditions that are often taken for granted in much of the comparative debate: an efficient state administration, a reliable tax system and, more generally, a civic culture capable of circumscribing fraudulent and corrupt behaviours on the part of both users and bureaucrats" (Ferrera, 2001, p. 160).

This is certainly true, although there has been considerable interest in imperfect targeting, mainly though not exclusively on the part of economists. [11] For instance, Atkinson analysed this as a case of imperfect information:

> In the operation of a transfer programme, there is often an asymmetry of information in that the needs of the individual are known to him or her but not to the administering agency. (…) It is possible to imagine circumstances in which there is no problem of information. *If* the government operates a personal income tax, *if* everyone files a tax return, and *if* this information is deemed sufficient to determine the payment, then in theory it would be possible for the agency to identify from the income tax records those people with low incomes, calculate the necessary benefit amount, and *if* the administrative machinery exists, to mail a payment to the beneficiary. (…) In this situation, one could operate an "automatic'" income-related programme. However, these conditions are highly unlikely to be satisfied (Atkinson, 1998, pp. 131-132).

---

[11] Atkinson (1998, pp. 130-140 and 1995, pp. 247-255). On the determinants of low take-up of benefits and its implications for equity, see Duclos (1995a and (1995b). For an extensive study of take-up of *Sozialhilfe* in Germany, see Rihpahn (2001). Van Oorschot's survey (1991) is an early review of empirical research on low take-up by a non-economist.

Benefit delivery and administration

In the absence of an automatic system of targeted transfers, the availability of information about benefits to potential claimants becomes an elementary requirement. On this count, the performance of Greek benefit agencies leaves much to be desired:

> The Office of the Ombudsman on a daily basis receives citizens' requests concerning inadequate or non-existent information on the part of the administration. In this sense, inadequate information emerges as one of the greatest problems of administrative practice. On many occasions, citizens are constrained to look for information from unofficial sources, with the result of being referred from desk to desk; unable to obtain authoritative information on the issue that concerns them. Yet, in an area such as social security, characterised by the technical nature and complexity of the relevant legislation, authoritative information is a decisive factor for access to benefits, while conversely lack of information translates to *de facto* negation of citizen rights (Ombudsman, 2002, p. 108).

Benefits are often administered by agencies that were not established for the purpose; for instance, the "many children" benefits are provided through the Agricultural Insurance Organisation *ΟΓΑ*. The requirement of timely provision is not satisfied: benefits are often delivered with great delay, arrears are common and some schemes pay benefits once a year or every two months. Instead of an open system of applications to ensure that urgent needs are met when they arise, such periods are usually short and with strict deadlines. If missed, beneficiaries must wait for another year. Until recently, no effective procedure for addressing grievances was available. Since October 1998, when the Office of Ombudsman was created, it has become the main depository of complaints about the benefit agencies' alleged failures (30% of all cases taken up in 2001). Finally, benefit agencies do not normally take the view that ensuring a decent level of take up is their responsibility, with the result that the issue does not receive the attention it deserves. Such failures might be blamed on under-staffing were it not for the fact that the various agencies employ over 1% of the Greek workforce.

To assess the incomes of potential claimants, all agencies rely on signed statements supported by evidence from the previous year's tax return. But poor tax compliance is known to constitute a serious obstacle. An OECD report attributed this to the high share of the informal economy in GDP (estimated at between 24% and 40%), the large number of self-employed in the workforce; inefficient tax administration, lack of a land register, the complexity and continuous revisions and amendments of tax laws, loopholes due to numerous tax allowances and exemptions, and the so-called "third-party" taxes extensively used to fund various institutions, such as the pension funds of lawyers, engineers and media workers (OECD, 2001, p. 93).

It was seen earlier that, while concern over "leakages" to illegitimate beneficiaries (due to unreliable tax data) lay behind much official opposition to the idea of a minimum guaranteed income scheme, this did not stop the Government from introducing two tax credit schemes aimed at low-income families. In any case, a legal exemption from filing an income tax return operates below a certain threshold, affecting 1.4 million individuals (about 13% of the population). As a result, income tax data are of little use for identifying the poor. The proposed guaranteed minimum income scheme would have combined cash assistance with participation in reintegration programmes, the latter acting both as an "activation" mechanism and as a screening device.[12]

Benefit design

The design of decent targeting needs to conform to some minimum standards. For example, the amount of benefit must be inversely related to claimants' income, either linearly or at least in a "graduated" form, with higher rates corresponding to lower income bands. To avoid the "poverty trap", the rate of benefit reduction as income rises must be less than 100%. Income disregards (exceptions from income as assessed by the benefit agency) play a similar role. Income must be defined in a uniform fashion. Care must be taken to calculate incomes net of the benefit itself, if received.

The above conditions may seem obvious, but more often than not they are violated. As Table 11.4 shows, most means-tested benefits are paid as a lump sum to all those who meet the eligibility criteria. That means that individual A with an original income just below the threshold is better off than individual B with one just above the threshold. A will receive the full benefit while B will get nothing.[13] This contradicts common sense (not to mention optimal taxation theory), and constitutes an obvious incentive to manipulate income tax returns.

---

[12] Although this smacks of workfare and the Poor Law, that is not necessary. The French *revenu minimum d'insertion* includes a participation requirement that does not extend to a work availability condition. For a benevolent view of such requirements as self-selection mechanisms, see Sen (1995, pp. 18-19).

[13] The pension supplement *EKAΣ* was originally better designed, with four benefit rates interacting with an equal number of income bands. Successive revaluations of both benefit rate and income thresholds distorted the original design. As a result, in 2001 a recipient of lower-rate *EKAΣ* risked ending up worse off than a full-rate recipient: for annual pension income up to €5,263 full benefit was awarded (€1,146 a year), while for higher pension income (up to €5,469 annually) benefit was reduced to €859 a year. In other words, total pension income including *EKAΣ* was lower for the pensioner with higher original pension (€6,328 versus €6,409). Incentives are complicated further

Furthermore, the income concept varies between benefits and agencies, for no apparent reason but with implications for eligibility. Income disregards are rare and non-standardised. Some benefits are taxed as income (a feature usually associated with universal benefits), while others are not. Finally, on three cases, the benefit itself is included in the definition of income used when assessing claims. This gives rise to a rather bizarre situation in which year one beneficiaries, whose income from other sources remains fixed, risk losing the benefit in year two, qualifying again in year three, losing it again in year four and so on.[14]

Table 11.4 Programme design features of Greek mean-tested benefits

	Graduated benefit	Income concept	Benefit itself included	Income disregards	Benefit taxed
Pensioners' social solidarity benefit *EKAΣ*	yes	taxable	no	none	yes
Social pension for non-insured elderly	no	declared	no	social assistance	no
Lifetime pension for many-children mothers	no	presumptive	yes	none	yes
Large family benefit	no	presumptive	yes	none	yes
Third child benefit	no	presumptive	yes	none	yes
Unprotected child benefit	no	total	no	expenditure on rent	no
OEK rent subsidy	yes	declared	no	interest on savings, benefits	yes

(i) *EKAΣ* has a full rate and three reduced rates that correspond to four pension income bands (personal and family incomes are also taken into account but there is a single income threshold for each). *OEK* rent subsidy is reduced euro for euro as income rises within a certain band. All other benefits are paid at a single rate and withdrawn in full as soon as income crosses the threshold.

(ii) Declared income is higher than taxable income because various exemptions operate. The income concept used to assess applications for many-children benefits included "presumptive income" if greater than declared income (means-testing of these benefits was abolished in 2002). In the case of unprotected child benefit, the income concept includes private transfers and social benefits. The income concept used to assess applications for *OEK* rent subsidy excludes income from interest on savings, family benefits, unemployment compensation (both ordinary benefit and severance pay), disability allowances, as well as pension payments in arrears.

by the fact that the other incomes taken into consideration (total personal income and total family income) are not "graduated" but have only a single cut-off point.

[14] The possibility of this seesaw pattern was drawn to my attention by Spyros Yannopoulos (personal correspondence dated 6 May 1998), then director of the Agricultural Insurance Organisation *OΓA*.

Indexation of benefits (and of the relevant income thresholds) provides a similar example. Although the minimum requirement is consistency, as Table 11.5 shows, indexation is usually *ad hoc* and sometimes skipped altogether. Revaluation policy is erratic, with some benefits receiving higher increases than others and no explanation given. Even more so than benefit rates, income thresholds fail to keep pace with inflation or are left unchanged in nominal terms, so that beneficiaries with fixed real income risk crossing the threshold and being disqualified.

On a final note, it has been rightly pointed out (Ferrera, 1998, pp. 87-93) that there are different types of selectivity. For instance, stringent means tests aimed to identify the poor are qualitatively different from "affluence tests" to exclude the rich. It would therefore be interesting to see where across that spectrum the Greek case lies. After all, the argument in favour of targeting was described in terms of "generous selectivity" versus "miserly universality" (e.g. Mouzelis, 1998b). It is not clear that this is the case.

Table 11.5   Indexation and revaluation of selected benefits (1996-2001)

	Indexation		Real change in:	
	Method applied	No. of times skipped	Benefit amount	Income threshold
Pensioners' social solidarity benefit *EKAΣ*	Inflation	1 / 1	108.1	9.0
Social pension for non-insured elderly	Ad hoc	0 / 0	63.8	63.8
Lifetime pension for many-children mothers	Inflation	1 / 3	-1.3	-12.5
Large family benefit	Inflation	0 / 3	14.5	-6.3
Third child benefit	Inflation	0 / 3	16.2	-2.8
Unprotected child benefit	Ad hoc	4 / 4	6.4	49.9
OEK rent subsidy	Ad hoc	2 / 1	11.3	-0.1
IKA minimum pension	Ad hoc	0 / n.a.	11.6	n.a.
Unemployment insurance	Minimum wage	3 / n.a.	3.0	n.a.
Disability allowances	Ad hoc	0 / n.a.	37.0	n.a.

(i) *EKAΣ* and (on one occasion) third child and large family benefits have been raised above inflation. The inflation rate applied is that of the year prior to revaluation.

(ii) Unemployment insurance benefit was originally set at two thirds of minimum wage "if resources permit". In 2001 the relevant ratio had fallen to 48%.

(iii) The figures in the "number of times skipped" column refer to benefit amount and income threshold respectively. The length of the period examined is five years (1996-2001) except for lifetime pension for many-children mothers, large family benefit and third child benefit, which became income-tested in March 1997. *EKAΣ* was introduced in mid-1996 and was not revalued until 1998.

(iv) The income threshold in the case of the social pension (for a two-person household) is the farmers' basic pension (if received by the claimant's partner). The value of these two pensions is fixed at the same rate.

(v) *IKA* minimum pensions, unemployment insurance benefit and disability allowances are not income tested. Disability allowances are proxied by severe disability allowance, claimed by over 55% of all disability allowance recipients.

Table 11.6 gives the income thresholds for access to various benefits in relation to a survey-based poverty line, set at 60% of median equivalent income. While a pattern is difficult to discern, most benefits except for "many children" are below or just over the poverty line. The example of the social pension, the only benefit in Greece coming close to the definition of a last resort safety net, is illustrative and sobering, given the generosity of the rest of the pension system. If an elderly couple's resources are below the equivalent of 24% of the poverty line, then the social pension may be awarded to one of the two. This is surely not the finest example of "generous selectivity".

Table 11.6   Income thresholds as percentage of the poverty line (2001)

	Single	Couple plus (no. of children)					
		0	1	2	3	4	5
Pensioners' social solidarity benefit *EKAΣ*	124	129	107	92			
Social pension for non-insured elderly	36	24	20	17			
Lifetime pension for many-children mothers	189	126					
Large family benefit			300	257	225	200	198
Third child benefit					180		
Unprotected child benefit			29	27	25		
OEK rent subsidy	151	101	97	94	91	90	88
Unemployment assistance (aged 45-65)	52	38	35	32			

(i) The poverty line was assumed to be 60% of median equivalent income, adjusted for family size with the OECD modified equivalence scale also used by Eurostat (which assigns a value of 1.0 to the household head, 0.5 to other adults and 0.3 to each child). The poverty line for a family of four in January 2001 was €951 (€992 in January 2002). Poverty estimates were drawn from Tsakloglou andand Mitrakos (forthcoming).

(ii) The figures for *EKAΣ* were derived by taking the personal income threshold for claimants living alone and the family income threshold for all others

(iii) Unemployment assistance for those aged 45-65 (and out of work for more than 12 months) was only introduced in 2002. The figures given in the last row were calculated with respect to the poverty line of that year.

4.   Conclusion

The most serious challenges facing Greece's welfare state have little to do with targeting. The priorities are the same as in 1996 - reforming pensions to restore equal treatment, reversing fragmentation by unifying conditions of access across programmes, rebalancing the welfare mix to cater for new risks, and strengthening the social safety net by introducing a benefit of last resort.

The insistence on targeting was based on lack of understanding of the institutional context, which ignored the structural limits to selectivity in a

Bismarckian, southern European "soft" state. It is hardly surprising that, six years after it became the buzzword of Greece's "new social policy" selectivity, has very little to show for it. And it diverted energy and resources from the main task of modernising Greece's welfare state, to which it scarcely contributed. As a recipe for welfare reform, the strategy of selectivity was seriously flawed.

The search for positive-sum solutions goes well beyond the simplistic assumption that targeted benefits are always superior, and recognizes that universal benefits may be both equitable and efficient. In any case, as long as propping up a fragmented and over-stretched social insurance edifice continues to be official policy, the selectivity versus universality debate will remain largely irrelevant. The separation of contributory from non-contributory benefits (funding the latter out of general taxation and the former through payroll contributions) would provide a more rational framework in which to assess alternative options.[15]

As an illustration, redeploying of state finance from subsidies to social insurance funds to a non-contributory pension programme would allow the incorporation of existing instruments (minimum pensions, social pensions and *EKAΣ*) into a more effective system of old-age income support. The resources freed would cover the provision of a universal basic pension to all residents aged over 65, worth nearly 60% of the poverty threshold to an elderly couple on a fiscally neutral basis.[16] Whether first-pillar pensions ought to be means-tested or universal can be more usefully debated only after that point.

The preceding analysis emphasises institutional features of social protection that are not unique to Greece but are common elsewhere, especially in southern Europe. However, the failure of selectivity in Greece seems to contradict more encouraging evidence from Italy (Ferrera, 2001; Baldini et al., 2002).

---

[15] Neatly separating contributory from non-contributory benefits is a promising policy path taken in other southern European countries. In Spain, the principle was enshrined in the Toledo Pact and confirmed in the tripartite "Accord to improve and develop the social protection system", signed in 2001 (Blanco Angel, 2002). In Italy, it was a key recommendation of the *Commissione per l'analisi delle compatibilità macroeconomiche della spesa sociale* (1997).

[16] Own calculations, from unpublished work on a pension reform proposal submitted in summer 2001 to the Government by the small left-of-centre organisation *AEKA*. The proposal involved a three-tier pension structure with a "notional defined contribution" main tier, as in the Swedish and Italian systems. For a wider discussion of the issues involved, see Schokkaert and van Parijs (2003). For a compatible ILO view, see Gillion, 2000.

A closer look at that evidence shows that the contradiction is only apparent. For a start, pension reform in Italy was tackled earlier and more successfully, removing some inequities and inefficiencies. Targeting was part of a wider reform aimed at overcoming the corporate fragmentation and rudimentary nature of social assistance, mainly through the unifying influence of the *indicatore di situazione economica*. Last but not least, the experimental introduction of *reddito minimo di inserimento* marks progress towards establishing a national scheme of last resort. On the whole, social assistance in Italy has been made more targeted but yet more universal in scope: a case of "selective universalism" (Baldini et al., 2002, p. 72).

The critique of selectivity *à la grecque* is not motivated by outright rejection of selectivity. The choice between selectivity and universality can be more sensibly tackled by striking the right balance. Or as the World Bank survey concluded:

> The key question is what *degree* of targeting is optimal. (...) In general, what is needed is a combination of universalism in certain categories of spending and finer targeting in others, such as in providing safety nets. Such a two-pronged approach is a sound starting point for policy design. In implementing it, one should, however, never confuse the ends and the means of policy. Targeting should be seen as a potential instrument, never as an objective in its own right (van de Walle, 1995, p. 616).

References

Atkinson, A. 1995. "On targeting and social benefits", in *Incomes and the Welfare State: Essays on Britain and Europe* (Cambridge, Cambridge University Press).

———. 1998. *Poverty in Europe* (Oxford, Basil Blackwell).

Baldini, M., Bosi, P. and Toso, S. 2002. "Targeting welfare in Italy: Old problems and perspectives on reform", in *Fiscal Studies*, Vol. 23(1), pp. 51-75.

Blanco Angel, F. 2002. "The Spanish public retirement pensions system: principal challenges and recent developments", in *International Social Security Review*, Vol. 55(3), pp. 57-72.

Commission of the European Communities. 1998. *Report from the Commission on the Implementation of the Recommendation 92/441/EEC of 24 June 1992 on common criteria concerning sufficient resources and social assistance in social protection systems*, COM (98) 774 (Brussels, European Commission), (http://www.europa.eu.int).

_____. 2001. *Draft Joint Report on Social Inclusion. Communication from the Commission,* COM (2001) 565 final (Brussels, European Commission), (http://www.europa.eu.int).

Duclos, J.-Y. 1995a. "Modelling the take-up of state support", in *Journal of Public Economics*, Vol. 58, pp. 391-415.

_____. 1995b. "On equity aspects of imperfect income redistribution", in *Review of Income and Wealth*, Vol. 41(2), pp. 177-190.

Esping-Andersen, G. 1990. *The Three Worlds of Welfare Capitalism* (Cambridge, Polity Press).

_____. 1996. "Welfare states without work: the impasse of labour shedding and familialism in continental European social policy", in *Welfare states in transition: National adaptations in national economies* (London, Sage Publications).

Ferrera, M. 1996. "The 'southern model' of welfare in social Europe", in *Journal of European Social Policy*, Vol. 6(1), pp. 17-37.

_____. 1998. "The four "social Europes": Between universalism and selectivity", in M. Rhodes and Y. Mény (eds.) *A new social contract? Charting the future of European welfare* (Houndmills, Basingstoke, Macmillan).

_____. 2001. "Targeting welfare in a "soft" state: Italy's winding road to selectivity", in N. Gilbert (ed.) *Targeting social benefits: International perspectives and trends* (London, Transaction Publishers).

Gillion, C. 2000. "The development and reform of social security pensions: The approach of the International Labour Office", in *International Social Security Review*, Vol. 53(1), pp. 35-63.

Gough, I. 1996. "Social assistance in Southern Europe", in *South European Society and Politics*, Vol. 1(1), pp. 1-23.

Levy, J. D. 1999. "Vice into virtue? Progressive politics and welfare reform in continental Europe", in *Politics and Society*, Vol. 27(2), pp. 239-273.

Matsaganis, M. 2002. *Fighting poverty and social exclusion in southern Europe: Report on Greece,* Paper presented at the FIPOSC (Fighting Poverty and Social Exclusion in Southern Europe) seminar, Milan, 23-24 May.

_____. 2003. *Muddling through: Trials and tribulations of social security in Greece*, European University Institute Working Paper SPS03.

_____, Papadopoulos, F. and Tsakloglou, P. 2001. "Eliminating extreme poverty in Greece", in *Journal of Income Distribution*, Vol. 10 (1), pp. 1-30.

_____ et al. 2003. "Mending nets in the South: Anti-poverty policies in Greece, Italy, Portugal and Spain", in *Social Policy and Administration*, Vol. 37(6), pp. 639–655.

Ministry of National Economy. 1996. *Introductory report on the State budget for the year 1997 by the Minister of National Economy and Finance Mr. Yannos Papantoniou* (Athens {in Greek}).

Mouzelis, N. 1996. "Austerity with social justice", in *To Βήμα*, 23 June (in Greek).

_____. 1998a. "Blairism the answer to neoliberalism", in *To Βήμα*, 5 April (in Greek).

_____. 1998b. "Is there a third way?", in *To Βήμα*, 11 October (in Greek).

NAP/incl. 2001. *National action plan for social inclusion 2001–2003* (Athens), (http://www.europa.eu.int).

_____. 2003. *National action plan for social inclusion 2003–2005* (Athens), (http://www.europa.eu.int).

Organization for Economic Cooperation and Development (OECD). 2001. *Economic surveys: Greece* (Paris, OECD).

Ombudsman. 2002. *Annual Report 2001. Athens* (Paris, Office of the Ombudsman), (http://www.synigoros.gr) (in Greek).

Parliament Proceedings. 1996. *Presentation of the Government's Programme by Prime Minister Mr. Costas Simitis and Debate* (10-11 October) (Athens, House of Parliament {in Greek}).

Riphahn, R. T. 2001. "Rational poverty or poor rationality? The take-up of social assistance benefits", in *Review of Income and Wealth*, Vol. 47(3), pp. 379–398.

Schokkaert, E. and Van Parijs, P. 2003. "Social justice and the reform of Europe's pensions", in *Journal of European Social Policy*, Vol. 13(3), pp. 245–263.

Sen, A. 1995. "The political economy of targeting", in D. van de Walle and K. Nead (eds.) *Public spending and the poor: Theory and evidence* (Baltimore, Johns Hopkins University Press).

Simitis, C. 1989. *Development and modernization of Greek society* (Athens, Gnosis Publications {in Greek}).

Sotiropoulos, D. 2001. *Interpretations of the post-war development of the welfare state in Greece: Working hypotheses and empirical data*, Paper presented at the 1st Conference of the Hellenic Social Policy Society, Komotini, 10–13 May (in Greek).

Tsakloglou, P. and Mitrakos, T. (forthcoming). "Poverty and inequality in Greece", in M. Petmesidou and E. Mossialos (eds.) *Social policy in Greece* (Aldershot, Ashgate Press).

van de Walle, D. 1995. "Incidence and targeting: an overview of implications for research and policy", in D. van de Walle and K. Nead (eds.) *Public spending and the poor: Theory and evidence* (Baltimore, John Hopkins University Press).

van Oorschot, W. 1991."Non-take up of social security benefits in Europe", in *Journal of European Social Policy*, Vol. 1(1), pp. 15–30.